# FOREWORD.

30-plus years of listening to punk rock has taught me this:

You don't have to be Eddie Van Halen if you want to play guitar.

Me, I like comics.

Thanks for reading.

**xoxo,**

**Ferris**

ps. Yeah, I know, I know....

Apologies for my sloppy lettering. If it were gonna get any better, it woulda happened by now.

And, yes, I tried typing the dialogue. It looks like shit. If you know so much, go make your own fuckin' comic. It's not hard. It's not easy, either. But it's not hard.

# Surburban Metal Dad FAQ [frequently asked questions] and FMC [frequently made comments].

**Q: What's the premise if this comic? What is Suburban Metal Dad about?**
**A:** Technically, it's "Suburban [Heavy] Metal Dad." Even though I draw like a 2nd grader, the guy with a square head is not a metal robot. He is (a) Suburban Metal Dad.

You grew up listening to Megadeth. You thought authority figures were full of shit. You didn't know the half of it. Now you have to deal with middle management. And you can't punch motherfuckers in the head who are just begging for it—because you have a mortgage, wife, and kids, so you need to be a responsible role model. You are a Metal Dad.

*The saga continues...*

**Suburban Metal Dad appears every Monday and Friday at Popdose, a rad pop culture sight music news with** tons of info-tainment and downloads and reading related to books, movies, TV, comics, all that good stuff.

**Q: What's kind of strip is Suburban Metal Dad?**
**A:** Technically, it's a gag-a-day strip. There are some characters and story arcs. But I try to give you a potential giggle in ever strip. It is NSFW. Rated M for (im)Mature. Parental Advisory: Explicit ish, yo.

**Q: Who's your audience?**
**A:** If you have kids, you should get most of it. If you're married or have been, you should get most of it. If you dig heavy metal, own a firearm, can quote Caddyshack, and are at war with moles, it was written with you in mind.

**Q: Why would you make this kind of bullshit?**
**A:** Essentially, Suburban Metal Dad is me warming up for couple unrelated projects I'm developing: a comic book and some picture books. Also, I have some manuscripts lying around, and I need to maintain a little bit more web presence if it's gonna sell better than my previous books (which are now available for your Kindle machine, by the way).

When I started the strip, it had been some time since I had done any creative writing. And I had never written anything for a visual medium before. So by banging out these sketches, I'm building up my chops for some bigger & better stuff. Essentially, you're reading my demos. And I appreciate it.

No, I don't think I'll draw the next projects. Yes, I know I have the spatial skills of a 5 year old.

**Q: No origin story?**
**A:** There is one, but I'm saving it for the TV show.

**Q: I don't get this strip.**
**A:** Sometimes I think things that aren't funny are funny. Or maybe I wrote it poorly. I'm workin' on it.

**Q: What are your favorite superhero movies?**
**A:** In order: Winter Soldier, Civil War, Scott Pilgrim, Unbreakable, Deadpool, then a bunch of Marvel joints. Sure as shit not Batman '89. Last time I was in NYC, I could have seen Tutankhamun's sarcophagus, but I went to Iron Man 2 instead. And I feel like that was the right move. We live in an age of glorious miracles.

# SUBURBAN METAL DAD

# COMPENDIUM ONE:
# RAGING BULLSHIT
## (YEARS III AND IV)

## A TERRIBLE ~~WEB~~COMIC BY

# D.X. FERRIS

ASPECTS OF THIS PRESENTATION MAY REFLECT LIMITATIONS OF THE SOURCE MATERIAL, TECHNICAL COMPLICATIONS FROM THE GREAT HARD DRIVE CRASH, OR THE WRITER-ILLUSTRATOR'S COMPLETE LACK OF TALENT. NOT KIDDING, DUDE. YOU'VE BEEN WARNED.

6623 PRESS COMICS

AKRON • BEAVER FALLS

**$1 from every copy of this book sold goes to a charity Ferris is into. Contact him for details if you're curious. He's sympathetic to education and people who, literally or figuratively, are on the bottom of the world & don't get much help or attention. Thank you for your support.**

## Also from 6623 Press

The 66 & 2/3 Series...

*Slayer, The Jeff and Dave Years: A Metal Band Biography...*
by D.X. Ferris

*For Whom the Cowbell Tolls:*
*25 Years of the Beastie Boys'* Paul's Boutique
by Dan LeRoy and Peter Relic

6623 Motivational...

*The Successful Lodge: Best Practices in Freemasonry*
by Ohio Past Grand Master James F. Easterling Jr. and Ferris

*The Martial Arts Parent's Frequently Asked Questions:*
*How to Unlock Your Child's Potential*
by Grandmaster Ryan Andrachik and Ferris

6623 Press is an independent outfit. We make creator-owned, useful, unconventional, reasonably priced books about popular culture, success, and other cool stuff.

People seem to like 'em.
Available from Amazon and your local independent retailer.

Twitter: @6623Press
Online: 6623Press.com
The Facebook: Facebook.com/6623Press

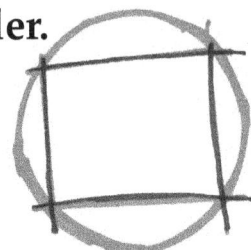

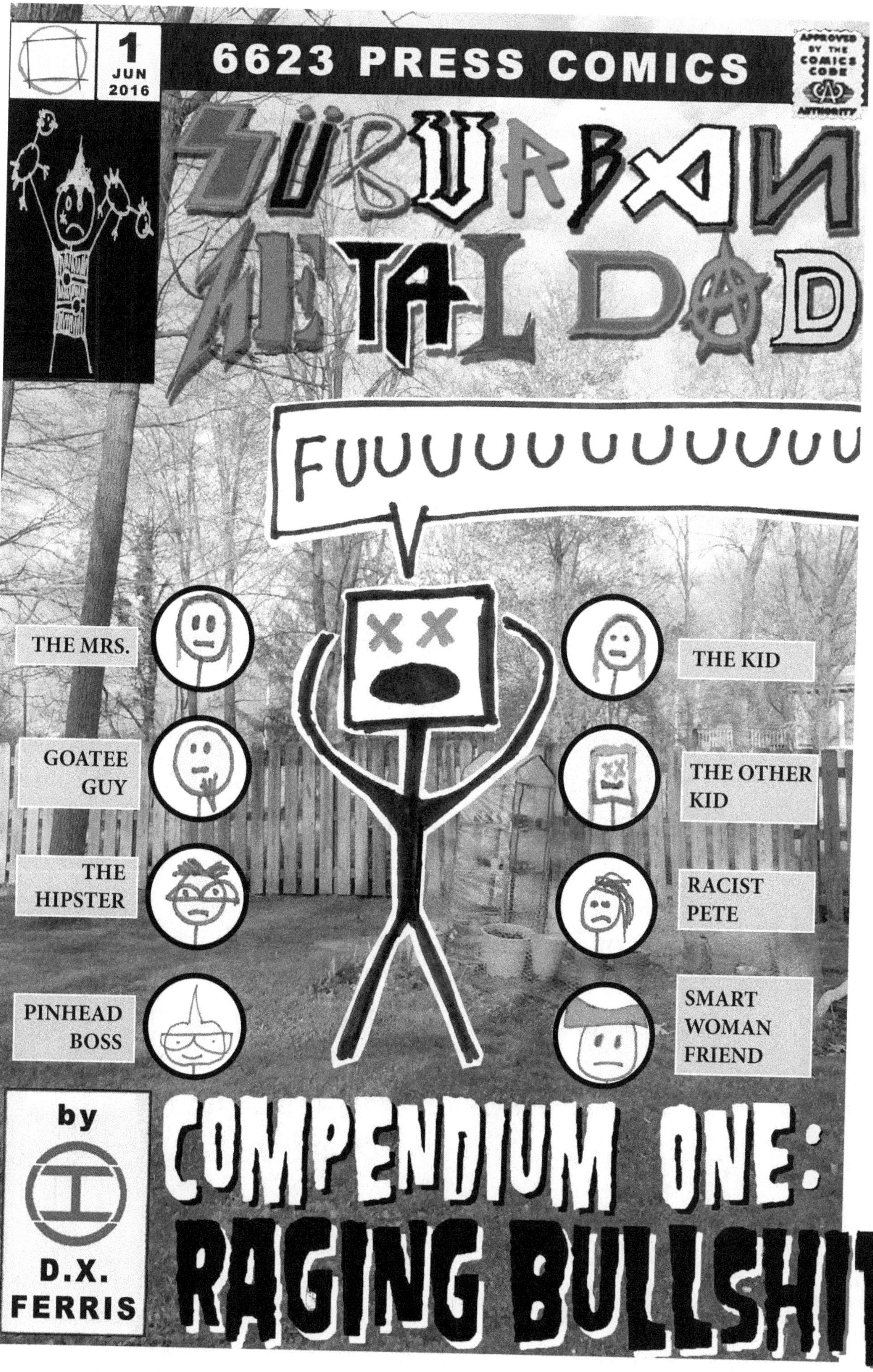
1
JUN
2016
6623 PRESS COMICS
APPROVED BY THE COMICS CODE AUTHORITY
SUBURBAN METAL DAD
FUUUUUUUUUUUU
THE MRS.
THE KID
GOATEE GUY
THE OTHER KID
THE HIPSTER
RACIST PETE
PINHEAD BOSS
SMART WOMAN FRIEND
by
D.X. FERRIS
COMPENDIUM ONE:
RAGING BULLSHIT

Originally published June 2016 (v1.0)

**6623 Press**
www.6623Press.com

Library of Congress Cataloging-in-Publication Data
Ferris, D.X.
Suburban Metal Dad: Compendium One / D.X. Ferris. p. cm.

ISBN-13: 978-0997597905  (pbk..: alk. Paper)
ISBN-10: 0997597909

I. Ferris, D.X.  II. Title

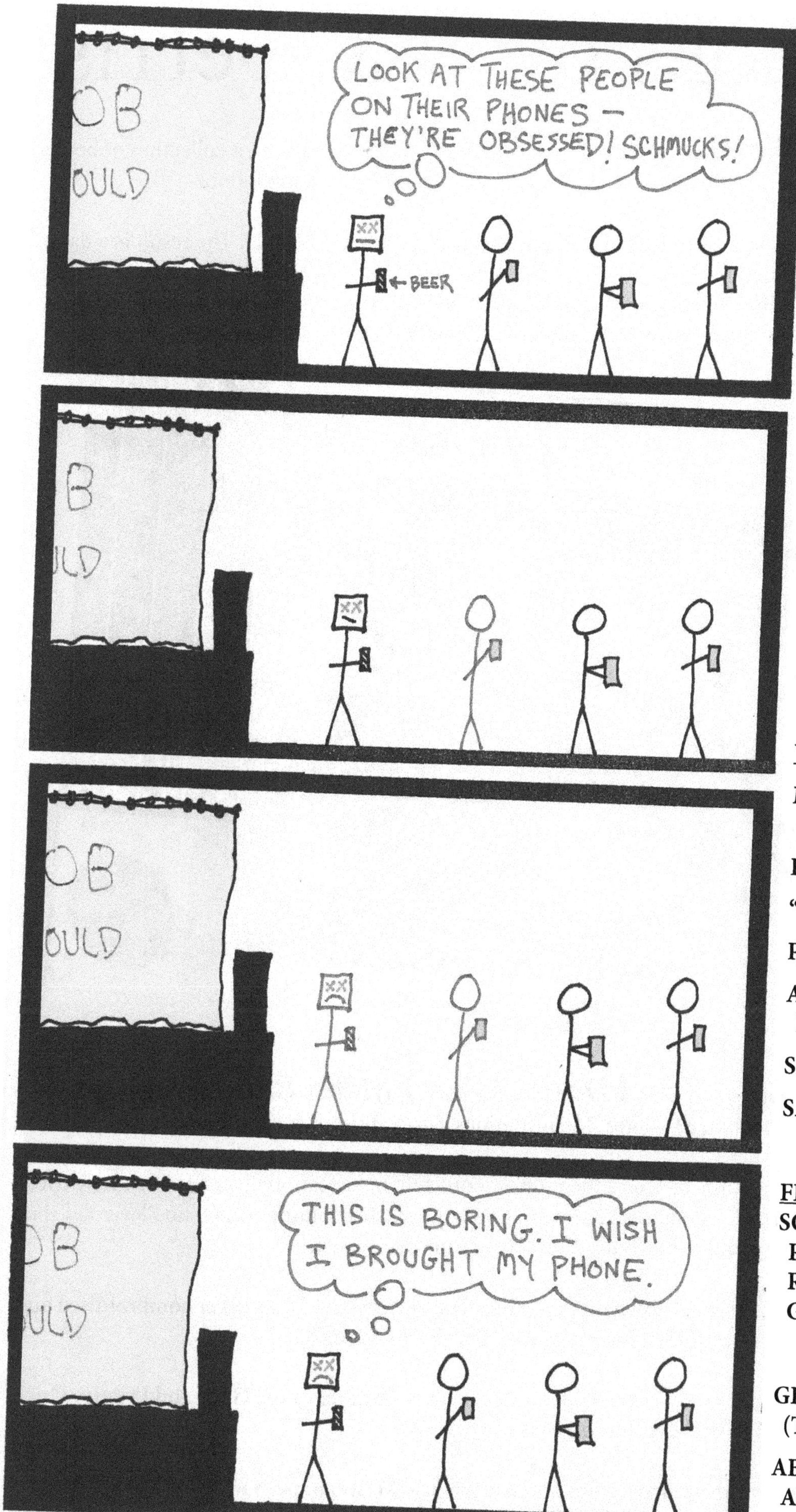
LOOK AT THESE PEOPLE ON THEIR PHONES — THEY'RE OBSESSED! SCHMUCKS!
← BEER
THIS IS BORING. I WISH I BROUGHT MY PHONE.

# TABLE O' CöNTENTS

# Real books by D.X. Ferris...

***Slayer's Reign in Blood***, part of Bloomsbury's prestigious 33 1/3 series, a collection of books about & inspired by classic albums. 160 pages, also available as Kindle, iBook, and audiobook.

"A short, intense, meticulous history of Reign In Blood and really, the whole band... The result is a damn perfect look at this one album."

— **Martin Popoff, ex-editor in chief of *Brave Words & Bloody Knuckles*, author of *Rush: The Illustrated History* and *The Collector's Guide to Heavy Metal* series**

**AND...**

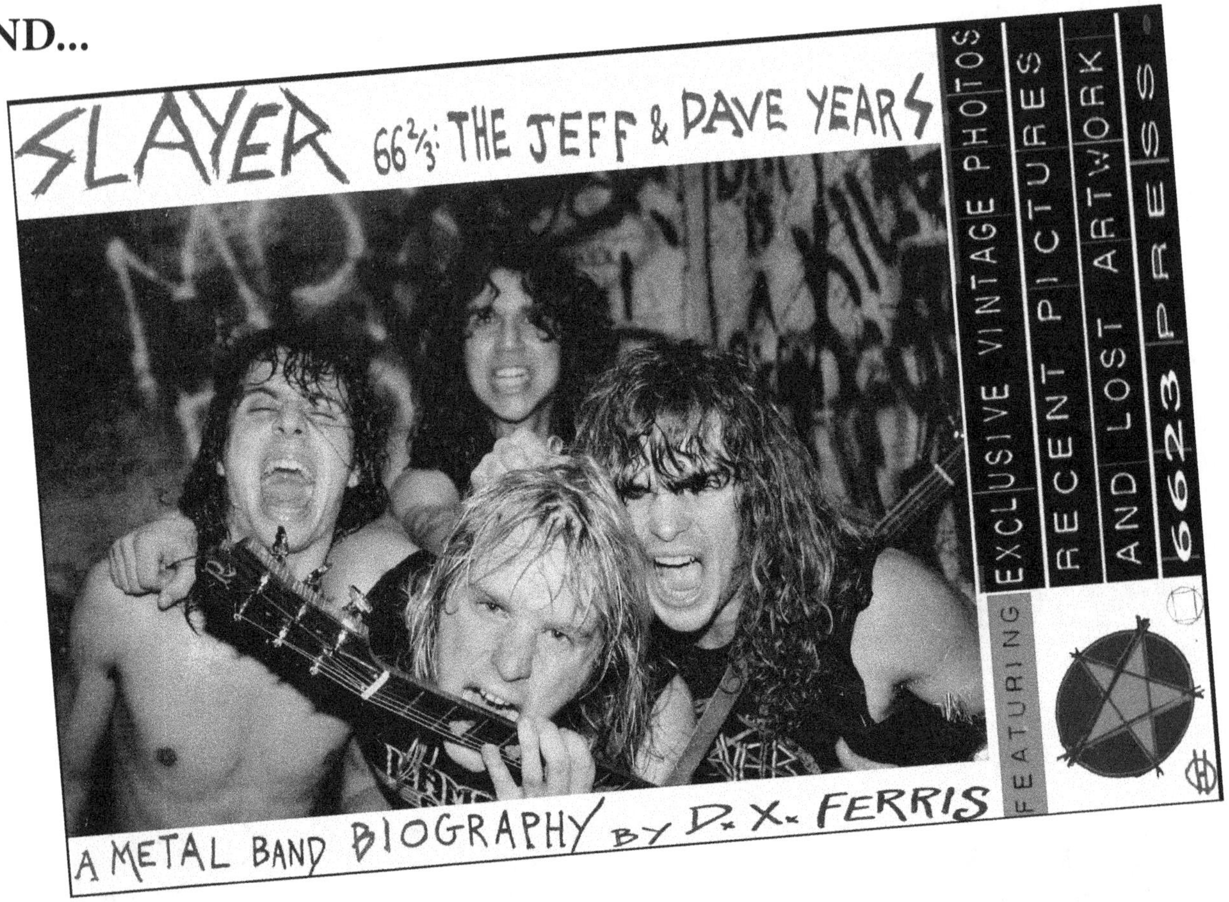
SLAYER 66⅔: THE JEFF & DAVE YEARS
EXCLUSIVE VINTAGE PHOTOS
RECENT PICTURES
AND LOST ARTWORK
6623 PRESS
FEATURING
A METAL BAND BIOGRAPHY BY D. X. FERRIS

***Slayer 66 & 2/3, The Jeff and Dave Years: A Metal Band Biography...***

Featuring 400 footnotes, 59 chapters, 33 photos, 11 illustrations, and 3 appendices (in e-book, two in paperback).

"A book documenting the good, the bad, and the ugly without spin or sensationalism has been long overdue, and hats off to D.X. Ferris for getting it all down in this remarkable volume, which no Slayer fan should be without." — **David Konow, author of Bang Your Head and Reel Terror**

"Finally someone like D.X. Ferris puts down on paper how Slayer never sold out, never compromised and never, ever turned it down." — **Jay Mohr, Jay Mohr Sports & Mohr Stories**

"This book should sit on your shelf alongside Led Zeppelin tome Hammer of the Gods and [Mötley Crüe tell-all] The Dirt." — **Michael Nirenberg, Huffington Post**

**Online at Amazon.com: $6.66 e-book • $16.66 paperback**
**Learn more at www.SlayerBio.com • @SlayerBook**

**Q: You know this is shite, right?**
A: Again, I have the spatial skills of a five-year-old.

**Q: How fucking hard is it to make a proper G?**
A: Hard. I'm workin' on it. I work on an uneven desk.

**Q: Hey wiseass: Managers make the tough decisions that enable the rest of you peons to make a living and provide for your family.**
A: Yeah; when they're not making bad decisions based on a lack of imagination and experience — not to mention their fear of shaking up the status quo and contributing to progress that might ultimately eliminate their useless ass. There are good managers out there, but... You keep kissing up to the man an "doing what you have to do." Let me know how that works out for you when shit gets real, you numbnut.

Any moron or sociopath can be in charge; real leadership means you take care of your people, serve others, and make a difference. I've worked in industries where the bosses talked a big game — then when things went south, they were powerless to make anything good happen that could change — or slow — their reversing fortunes. People lost jobs, usually the wrong people. There are more bad managers than good. Fact.

**Q: Dude, this isn't very metal.**
A: Yeah. I know. I'm working on that, too. A lack of hardcore shit is endemic in the life of an aging metal dude.

**Q: You know you're supposed to [insert comics strip convention here], right?**
A: Yeah, yeah, yeah. I know the narrative element could be stronger, but the twice-a-week frequency kinda hamstrings that. I'd like to do it as a daily (Mon-Fri), but there's not enough time. Trust me: Rough as this shit is, it could be worse.

**Q: "You think your funny but your not."**
A: You are correct. You are always correct. Your friends know this already.

**Q: Can I buy some original artwork or such?**
A: Yes. See the back of the book for official T-shirts. I also draw original customized strips of a figure who is similar to your boss but legally distinct. I'm serious. Get in touch, and we'll set it up.

**Q: Would you still throw it all away to make out with anyone from Fuzzbox?**
A: Probably.

**Q: Should I buy the Metallia reissue/remaster boxed sets?**
A: Greg Van Krol says it's a sweet package. The sound levels are loud, but the remastering sounds good to me, and I'm picky about that shit. I heard the DCC Gold remasters are really good too, if you can find them.

**Q: You watch a lot of TV, huh?**
A: It's a golden age. The entire music industry is fucking up. Serialized TV storytelling is the new music.

**Q: What about [certain people I think you know]?**
A: I'm all about live-and-let-live, but fuck those dudes.

Thanks again for reading.

      – **Ferris**

# YEAR

# III

(2013)

fuckin'
shit
sunuvabitch
christmas lights
© 219 • FERRIS

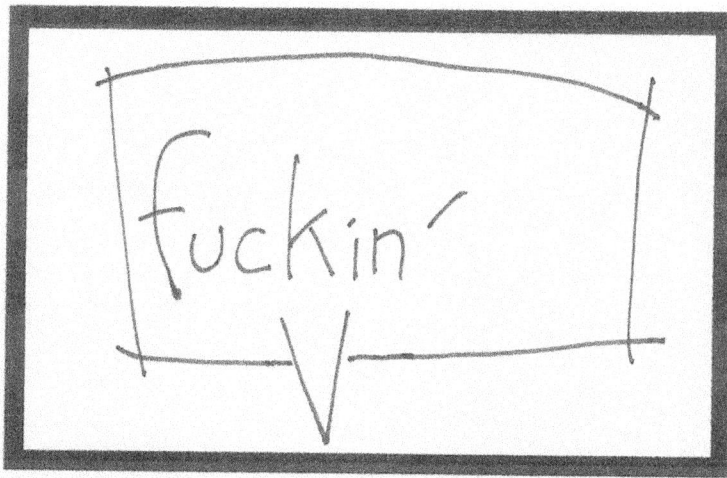

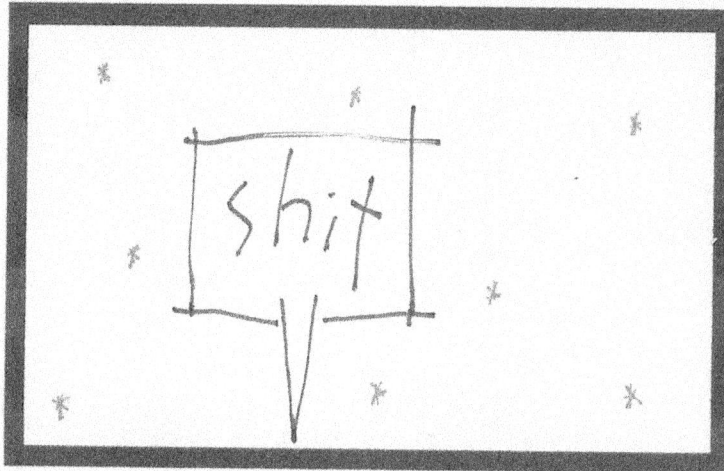

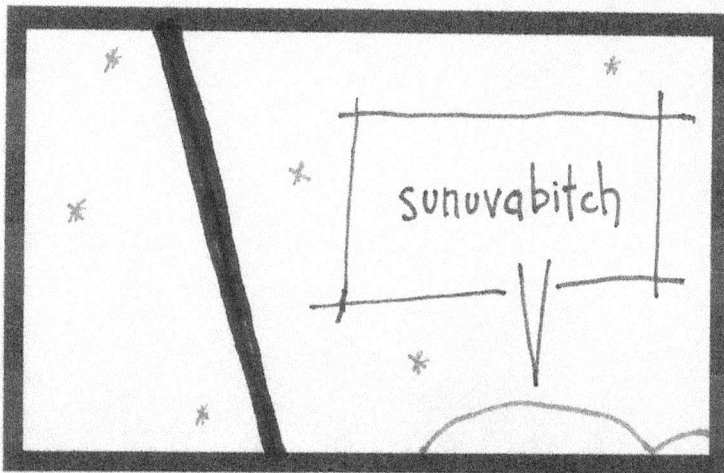

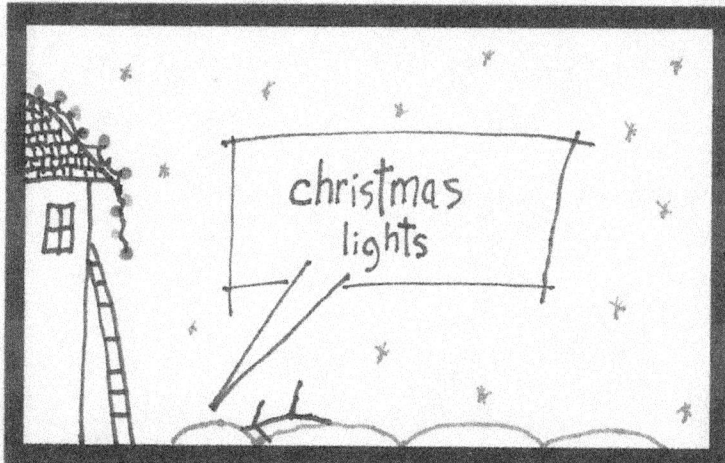

OUCH
WELL, I CAN FEEL SHARP PAINS IN MY BACK, AND I CAN MOVE MY TOES.
LET'S TRY TO GET UP. ARGH MAYBE I'LL LIE HERE AWHILE.
DADDY'S BEEN OUT THERE TWO HOURS, AND HE DIDN'T SHOUT ANY SWEAR WORDS.
IT'S A CHRISTMAS MIRACLE.
·220·FERRIS

YOU WERE OUT THERE THREE HOURS, AND YOU ONLY HUNG ONE STRING OF LIGHTS?
YUP.
WELL, WHY— WAIT, ARE YOU ALL WET? AND LIMPING?
YEP. I'M DONE.
SO YOU'RE NOT GOING TO PUT UP ANY MORE LIGHTS?
NOPE.
THE KIDS WILL BE DISAPPOINTED.
NO THEY WON'T. I HAVE A PLAN.
•221•FERRIS

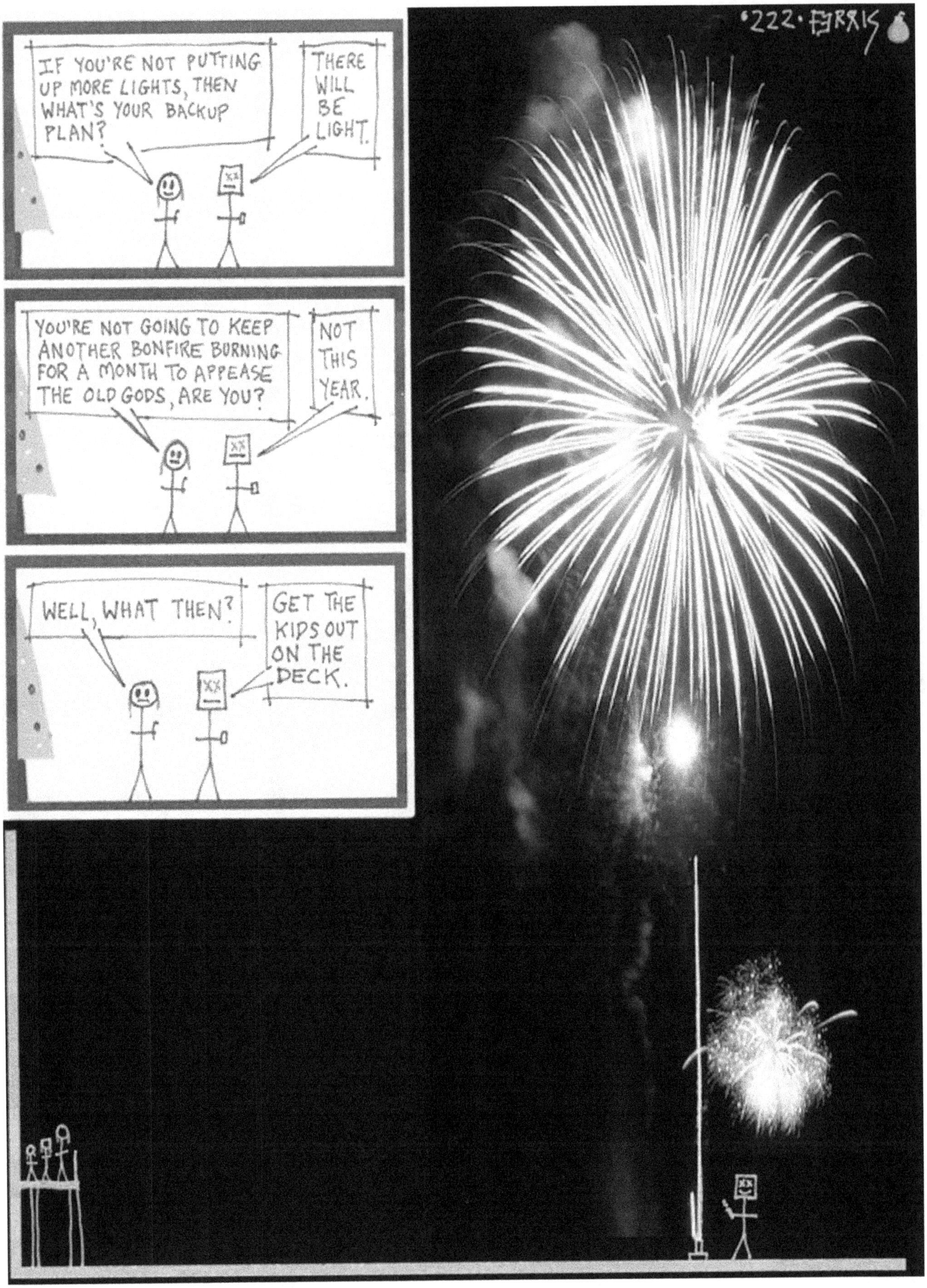
•222• FERRIS
IF YOU'RE NOT PUTTING UP MORE LIGHTS, THEN WHAT'S YOUR BACKUP PLAN?
THERE WILL BE LIGHT.
YOU'RE NOT GOING TO KEEP ANOTHER BONFIRE BURNING FOR A MONTH TO APPEASE THE OLD GODS, ARE YOU?
NOT THIS YEAR.
WELL, WHAT THEN?
GET THE KIDS OUT ON THE DECK.

HI NEIGHBOR. THOSE NIGHTLY FIREWORKS ARE NICE, BUT HOW LONG ARE YOU GOING TO DO IT?
UNTIL THE NEW YEAR.
WELL, IT'S JUST...
WHICH DON'T YOU FEEL DESERVES COMMEMORATION —AMERICAN FREEDOM OR THE BIRTH OF CHRIST?
I, UH, DIDN'T MEAN...
SEE? I KNEW YOU WERE A GOOD AMERICAN, A REAL AMERICAN. HELL YEAH. FIRE IN THE HOLE!
IS THERE ANY CHANCE YOU COULD MAYBE CUT THE LOUD EXPLOSIONS FROM THE MIDNIGHT DISPLAY?
I WOULD, BUT THE SECOND SHIFT GUYS TWO TOWNS OVER REALLY LIKE IT.
·223· FERRIS

THAT WAS ANOTHER COMPLAINT ABOUT YOUR NIGHTLY XMAS FIREWORKS.
-CLICK-
WHO? THE NEIGHBORS?
THE AIRPORT.
FUCK 'EM. HOMELAND SECURITY DROPPED THEIR INVESTIGATION. THAT SHOULD BE GOOD ENOUGH FOR THE FAA.
CAN'T YOU JUST PUT UP MORE LIGHTS, PLEASE? MAYBE JUST THE BUSHES?
TARGET IS ALL OUT OF LIGHTS. THEY'RE ALSO OUT OF THOSE LIGHT-UP DEER. I COULD GO BACK AND GET THE PINK GLOWING YARD PIG.
HOW ABOUT YOU SET OFF SOME WEEPING WILLOWS AND SKIP THE LOUD ONES?
I POLLED THE CROWD LAST NIGHT, AND THEY PREFERRED THE NOISE OVER TSO.
•224• FERRIS

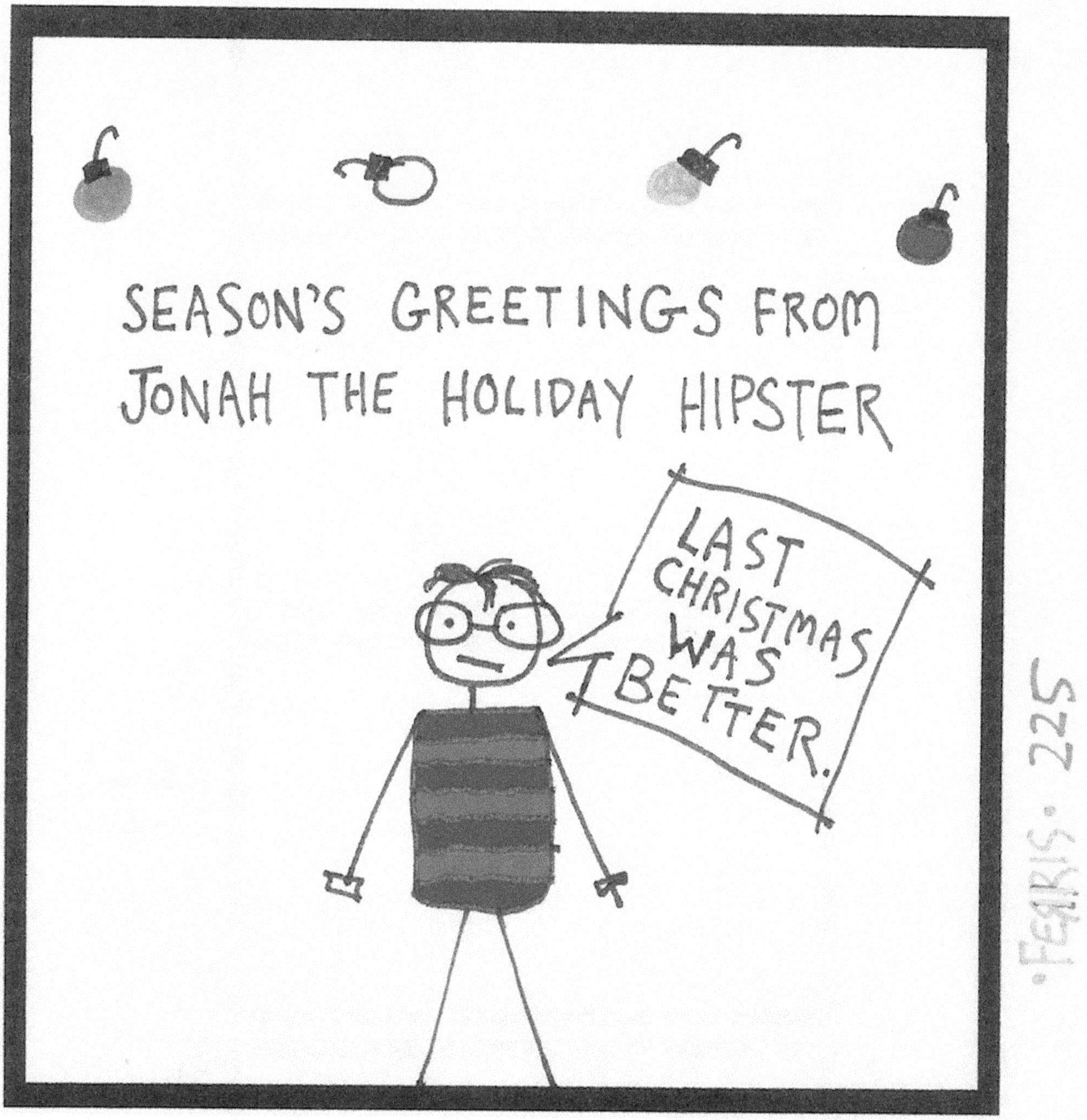
SEASON'S GREETINGS FROM
JONAH THE HOLIDAY HIPSTER
LAST CHRISTMAS WAS BETTER.
•FEARIS• 225

IS IT RUDE TO PUSH PEOPLE AND CALL THEM A FUCKIN' SLOWPOKE?
IN THE MALL OR AT THE LIBRARY?
THE MALL.
AT CHRISTMAS?
YES.
NO.
YOU F
I WAS KIDDING.
•226 • FERRIS

AAAA
AAAAAH
AAAAAHH
NEXT PLEASE
DID THAT MAKE THE LINE GO FASTER?
FOR ME, IT SEEMED TO.
·227· FERRIS ·

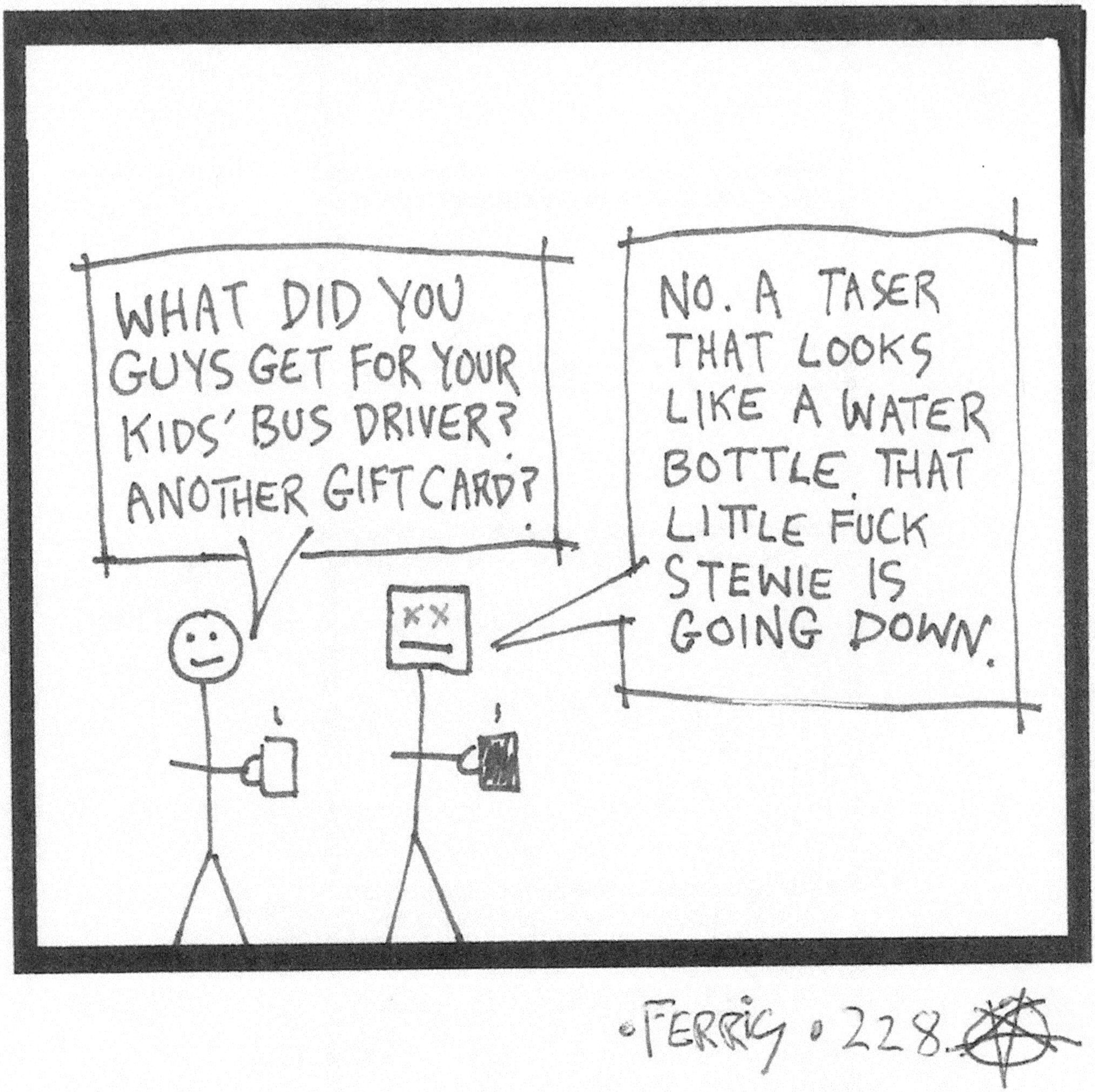
WHAT DID YOU GUYS GET FOR YOUR KIDS' BUS DRIVER? ANOTHER GIFT CARD?
NO. A TASER THAT LOOKS LIKE A WATER BOTTLE. THAT LITTLE FUCK STEWIE IS GOING DOWN.
•FERRIS • 228.

I'M / DREAMING / ON A WHITE CHRISTMAS / WHERE REINDEER GLISTEN / AND CHILDREN LISTEN.
IS THAT IT?
YUP. CHILDREN WHO LISTEN IS THE ONLY CHRISTMAS MIRACLE I NEED.
·229 FERRIS

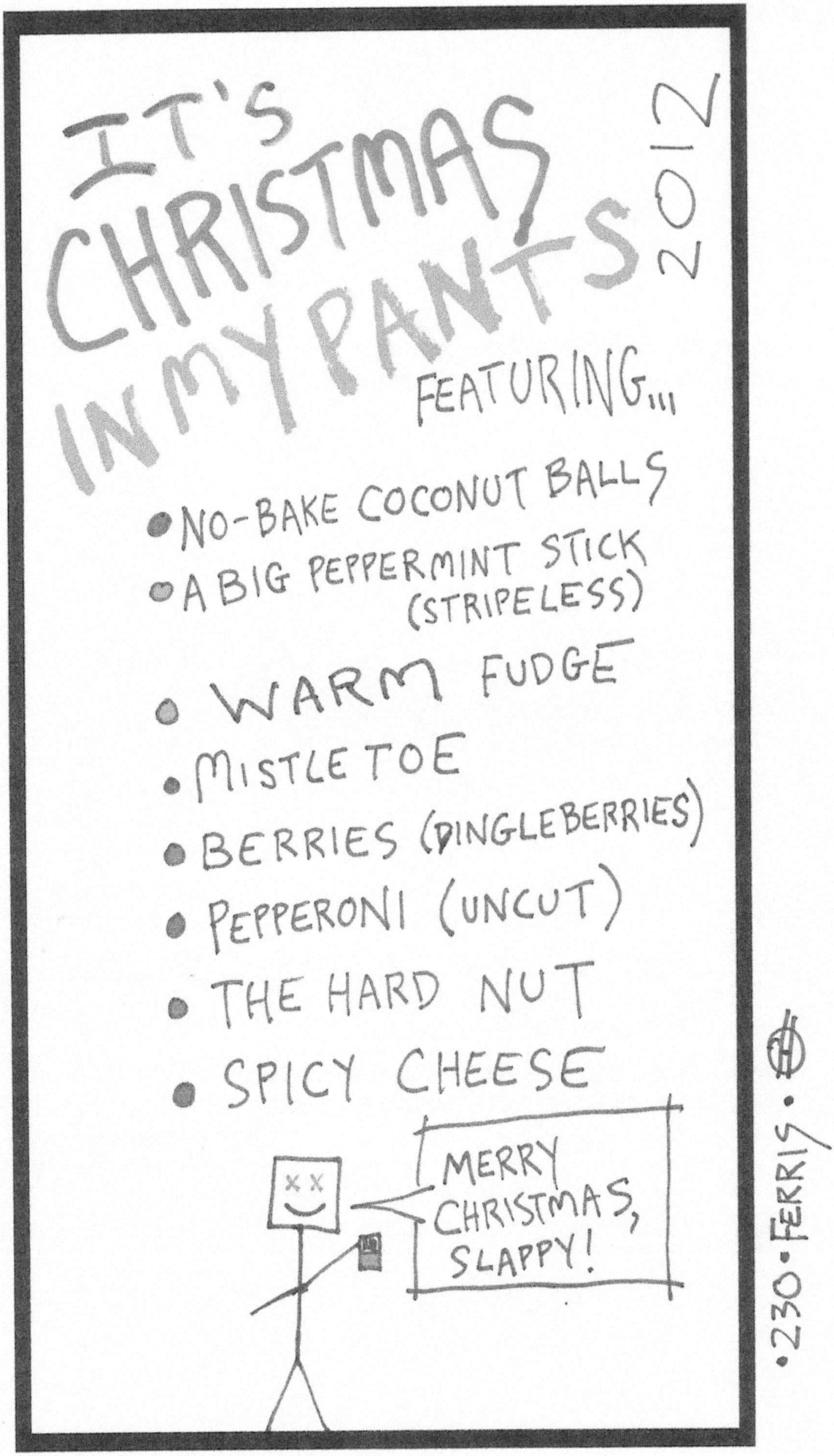
IT'S CHRISTMAS IN MY PANTS 2012
FEATURING...
• NO-BAKE COCONUT BALLS
• A BIG PEPPERMINT STICK (STRIPELESS)
• WARM FUDGE
• MISTLETOE
• BERRIES (DINGLEBERRIES)
• PEPPERONI (UNCUT)
• THE HARD NUT
• SPICY CHEESE
MERRY CHRISTMAS, SLAPPY!
•230•FERRIS•

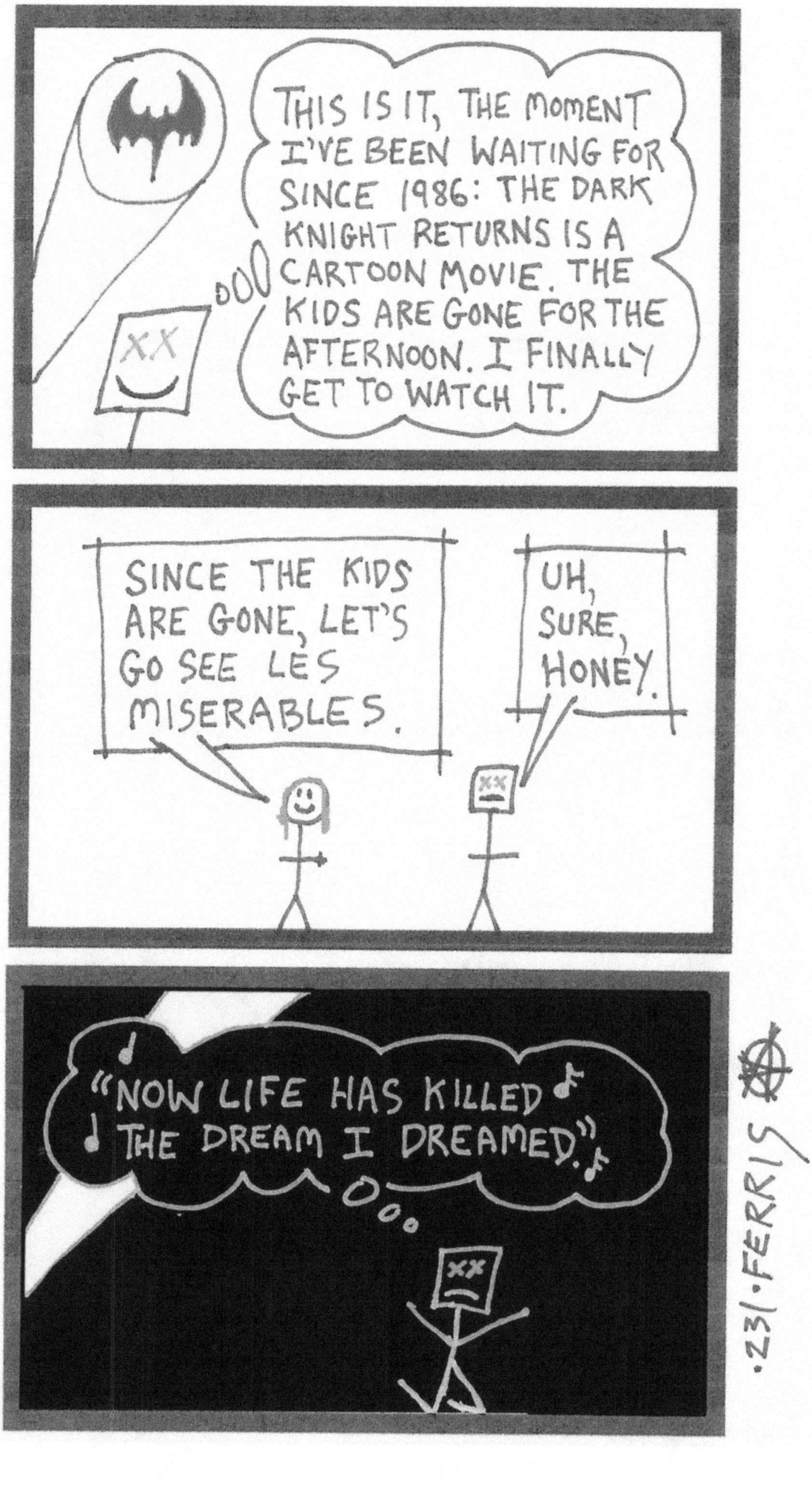
THIS IS IT, THE MOMENT I'VE BEEN WAITING FOR SINCE 1986: THE DARK KNIGHT RETURNS IS A CARTOON MOVIE. THE KIDS ARE GONE FOR THE AFTERNOON. I FINALLY GET TO WATCH IT.
SINCE THE KIDS ARE GONE, LET'S GO SEE LES MISERABLES.
UH, SURE, HONEY.
"NOW LIFE HAS KILLED THE DREAM I DREAMED".
·231·FERRIS

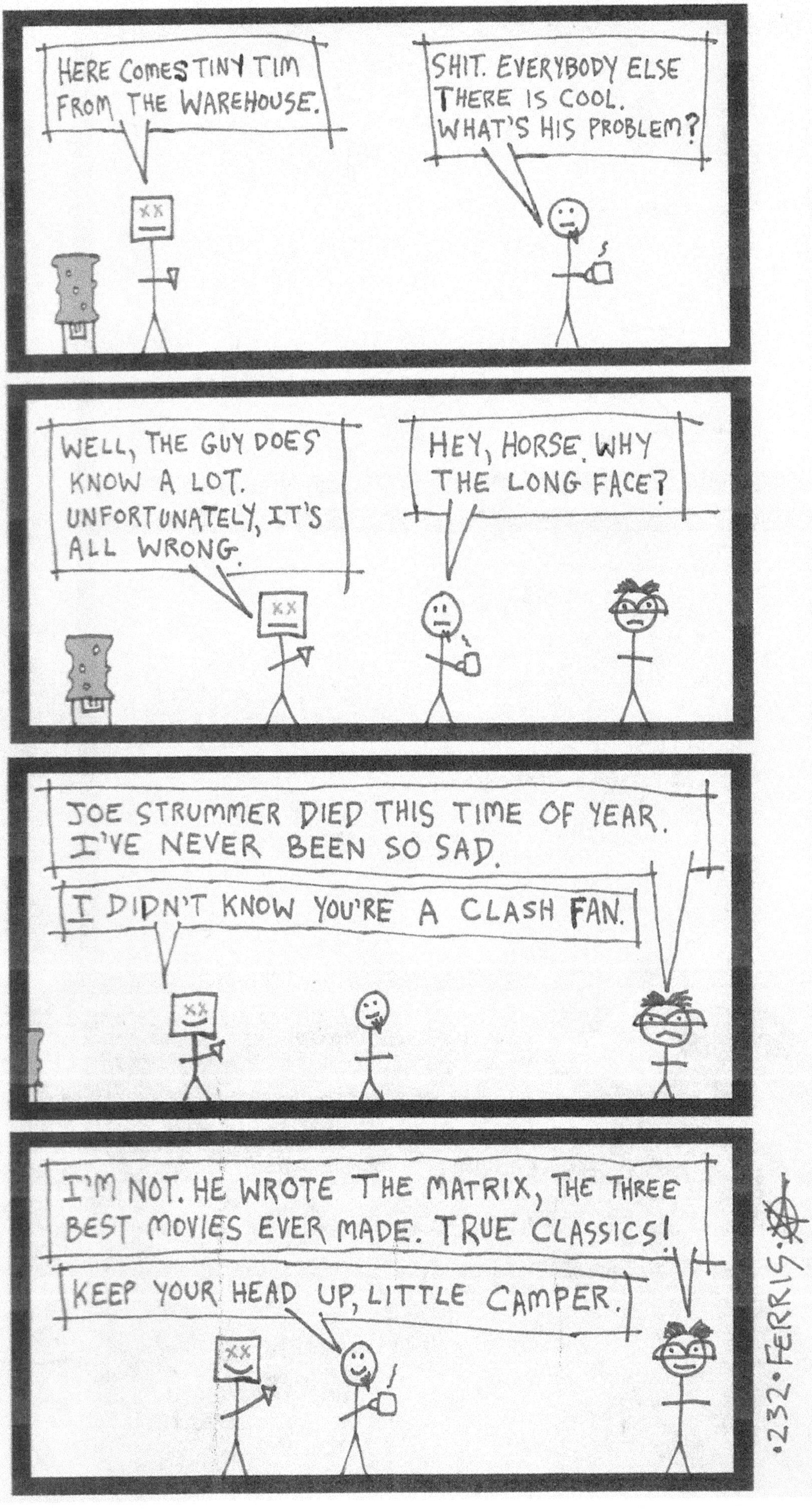
HERE COMES TINY TIM FROM THE WAREHOUSE.
SHIT. EVERYBODY ELSE THERE IS COOL. WHAT'S HIS PROBLEM?
WELL, THE GUY DOES KNOW A LOT. UNFORTUNATELY, IT'S ALL WRONG.
HEY, HORSE. WHY THE LONG FACE?
JOE STRUMMER DIED THIS TIME OF YEAR. I'VE NEVER BEEN SO SAD.
I DIDN'T KNOW YOU'RE A CLASH FAN.
I'M NOT. HE WROTE THE MATRIX, THE THREE BEST MOVIES EVER MADE. TRUE CLASSICS!
KEEP YOUR HEAD UP, LITTLE CAMPER.
•232•FERRIS•

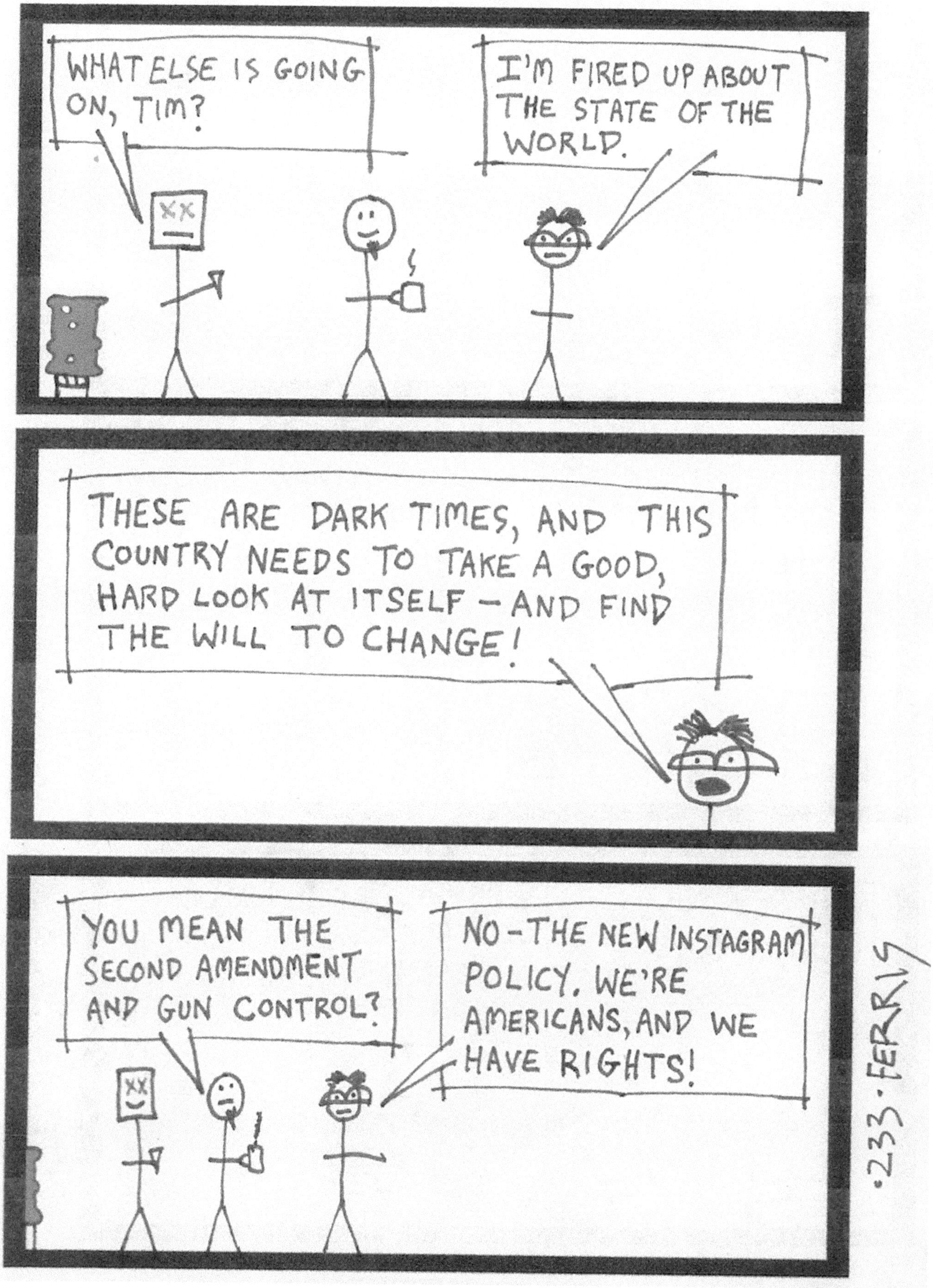
WHAT ELSE IS GOING ON, TIM?
I'M FIRED UP ABOUT THE STATE OF THE WORLD.
THESE ARE DARK TIMES, AND THIS COUNTRY NEEDS TO TAKE A GOOD, HARD LOOK AT ITSELF — AND FIND THE WILL TO CHANGE!
YOU MEAN THE SECOND AMENDMENT AND GUN CONTROL?
NO — THE NEW INSTAGRAM POLICY. WE'RE AMERICANS, AND WE HAVE RIGHTS!
•233•FERRIS

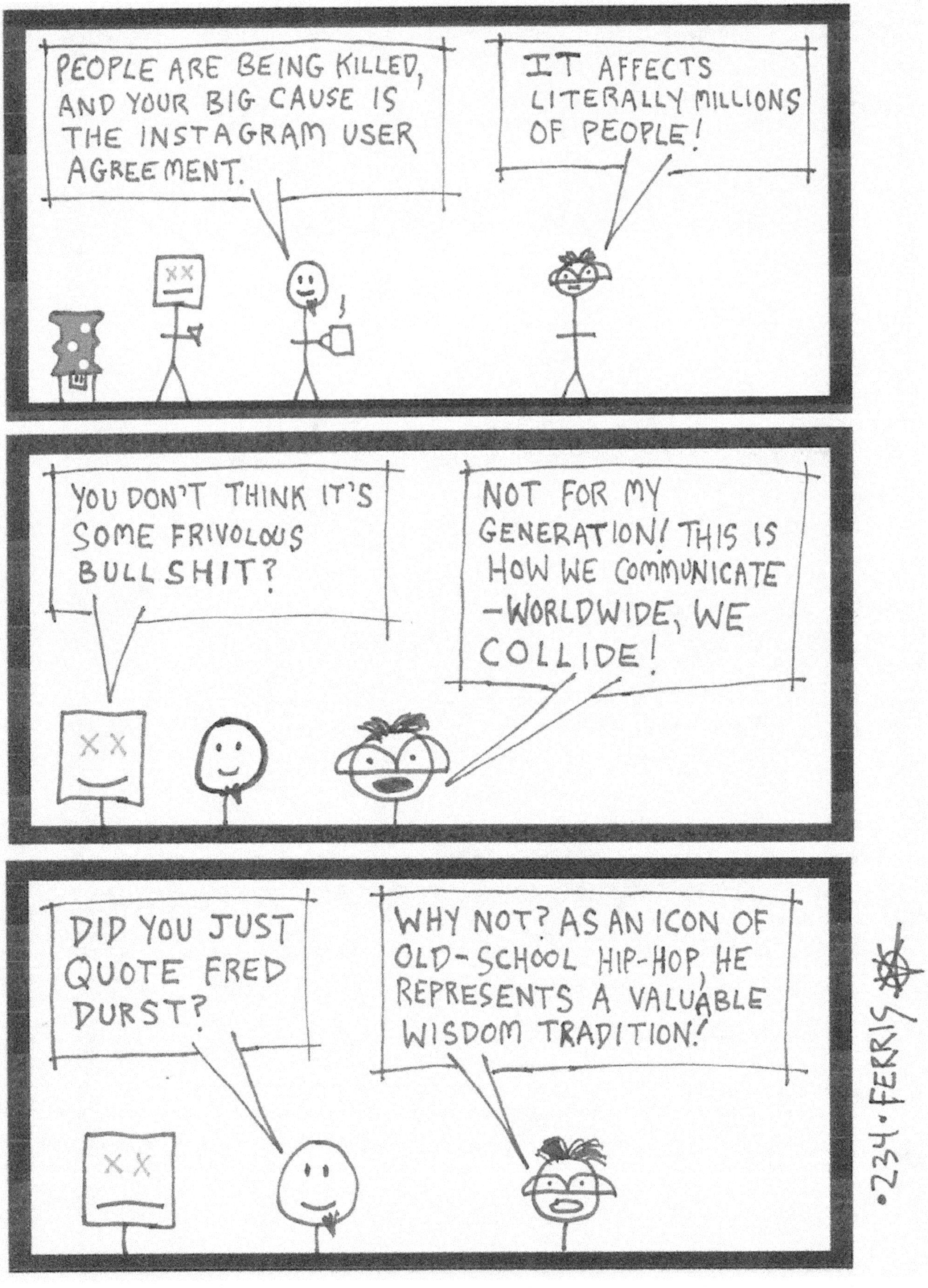
PEOPLE ARE BEING KILLED, AND YOUR BIG CAUSE IS THE INSTAGRAM USER AGREEMENT.
IT AFFECTS LITERALLY MILLIONS OF PEOPLE!
YOU DON'T THINK IT'S SOME FRIVOLOUS BULLSHIT?
NOT FOR MY GENERATION! THIS IS HOW WE COMMUNICATE —WORLDWIDE, WE COLLIDE!
DID YOU JUST QUOTE FRED DURST?
WHY NOT? AS AN ICON OF OLD-SCHOOL HIP-HOP, HE REPRESENTS A VALUABLE WISDOM TRADITION!
•234•FERRIS

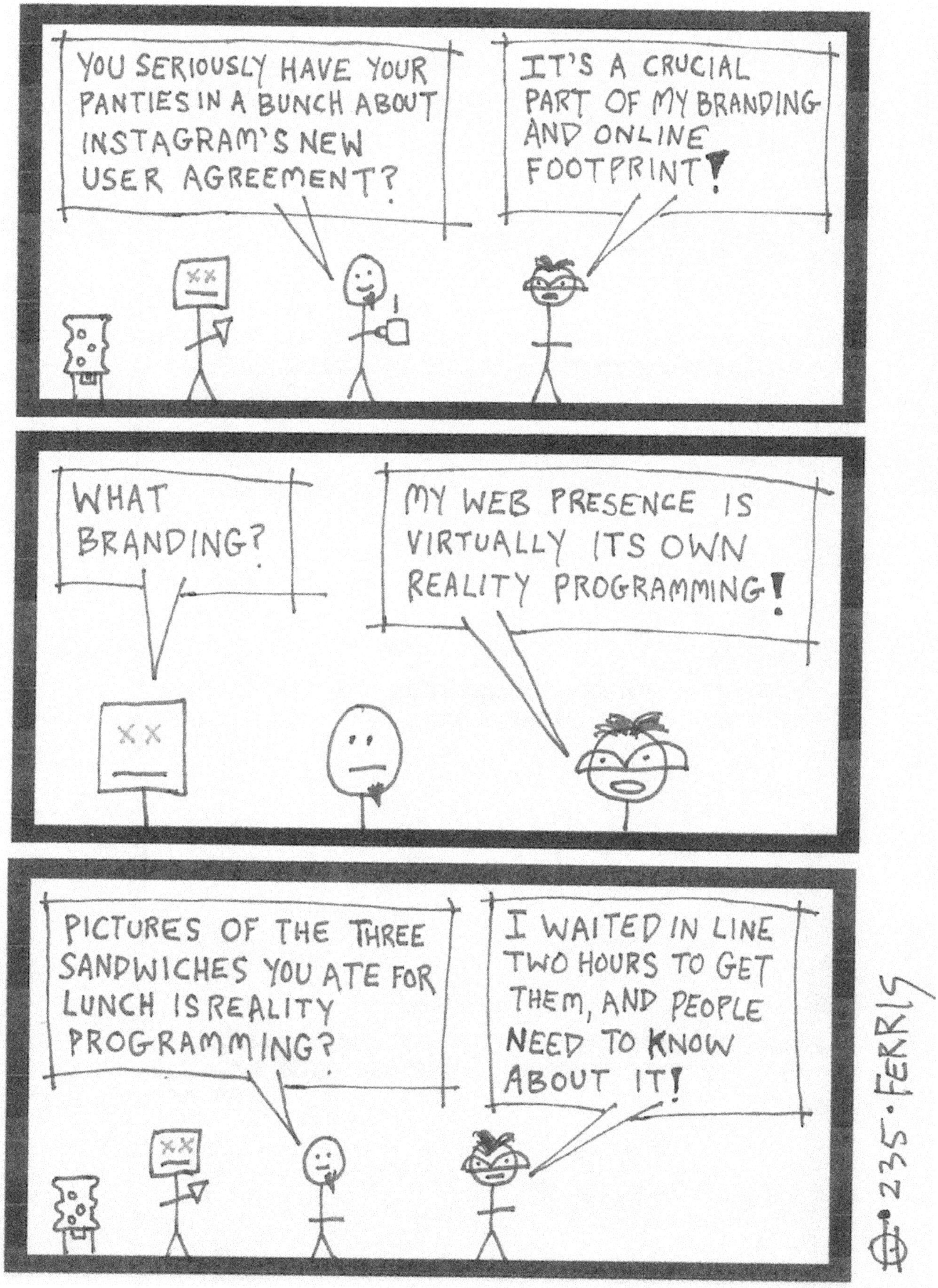
YOU SERIOUSLY HAVE YOUR PANTIES IN A BUNCH ABOUT INSTAGRAM'S NEW USER AGREEMENT?
IT'S A CRUCIAL PART OF MY BRANDING AND ONLINE FOOTPRINT!
WHAT BRANDING?
MY WEB PRESENCE IS VIRTUALLY ITS OWN REALITY PROGRAMMING!
PICTURES OF THE THREE SANDWICHES YOU ATE FOR LUNCH IS REALITY PROGRAMMING?
I WAITED IN LINE TWO HOURS TO GET THEM, AND PEOPLE NEED TO KNOW ABOUT IT!
235 • FERRIS

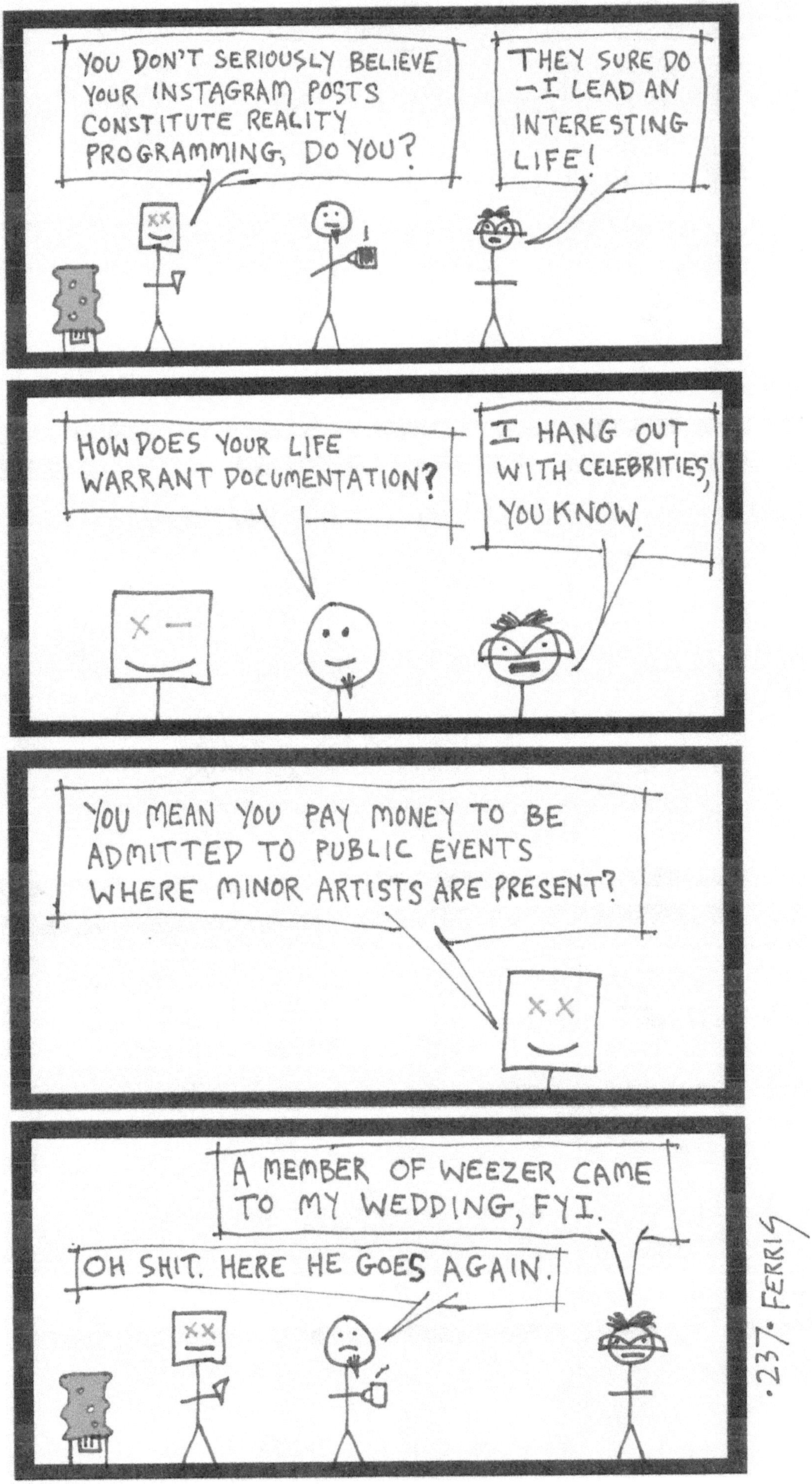
YOU DON'T SERIOUSLY BELIEVE YOUR INSTAGRAM POSTS CONSTITUTE REALITY PROGRAMMING, DO YOU?
THEY SURE DO —I LEAD AN INTERESTING LIFE!
HOW DOES YOUR LIFE WARRANT DOCUMENTATION?
I HANG OUT WITH CELEBRITIES, YOU KNOW.
YOU MEAN YOU PAY MONEY TO BE ADMITTED TO PUBLIC EVENTS WHERE MINOR ARTISTS ARE PRESENT?
A MEMBER OF WEEZER CAME TO MY WEDDING, FYI.
OH SHIT. HERE HE GOES AGAIN.
·237· FERRIS

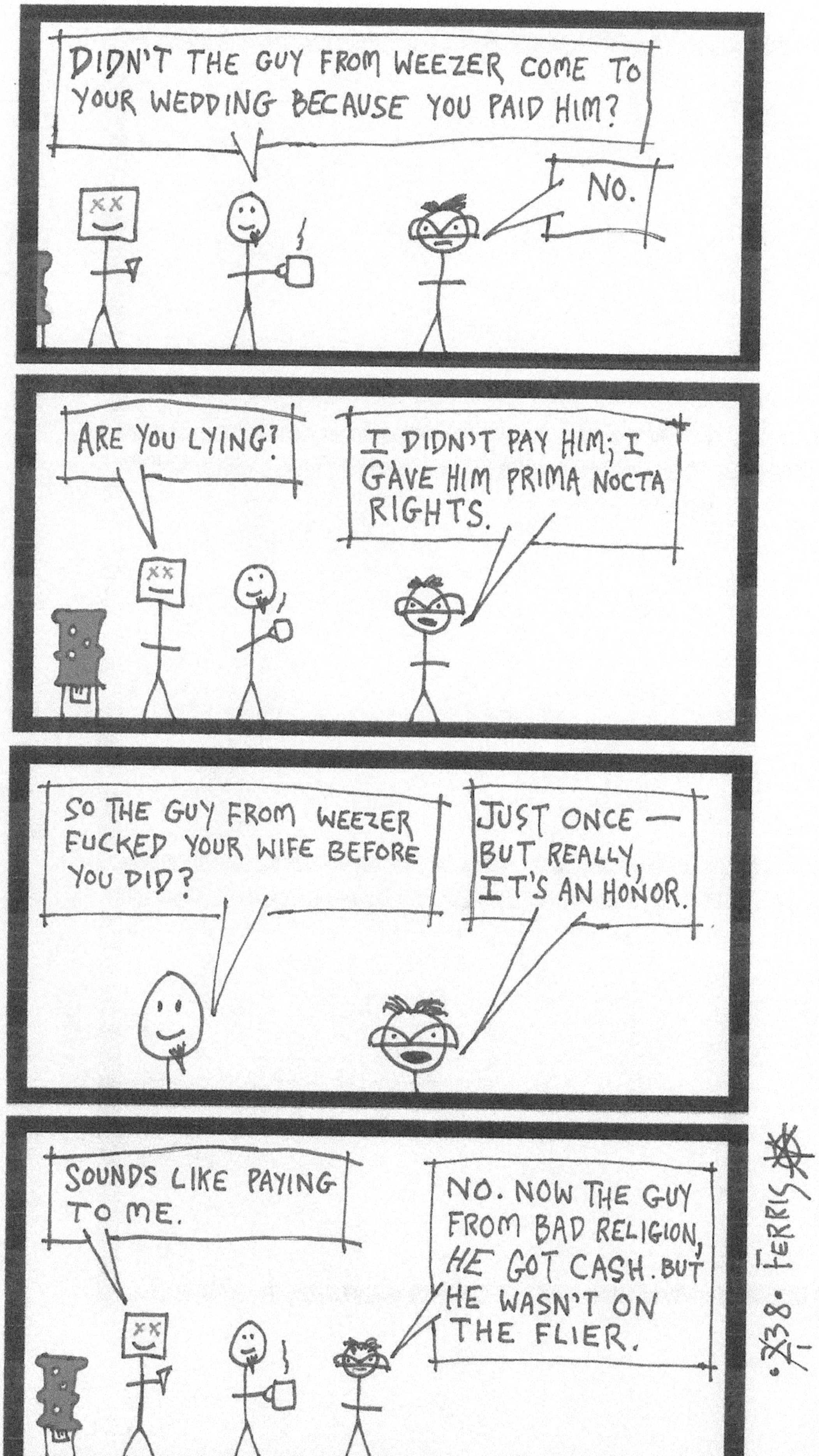
DIDN'T THE GUY FROM WEEZER COME TO YOUR WEDDING BECAUSE YOU PAID HIM?
NO.
ARE YOU LYING?
I DIDN'T PAY HIM; I GAVE HIM PRIMA NOCTA RIGHTS.
SO THE GUY FROM WEEZER FUCKED YOUR WIFE BEFORE YOU DID?
JUST ONCE — BUT REALLY, IT'S AN HONOR.
SOUNDS LIKE PAYING TO ME.
NO. NOW THE GUY FROM BAD RELIGION, HE GOT CASH. BUT HE WASN'T ON THE FLIER.
FERRIS

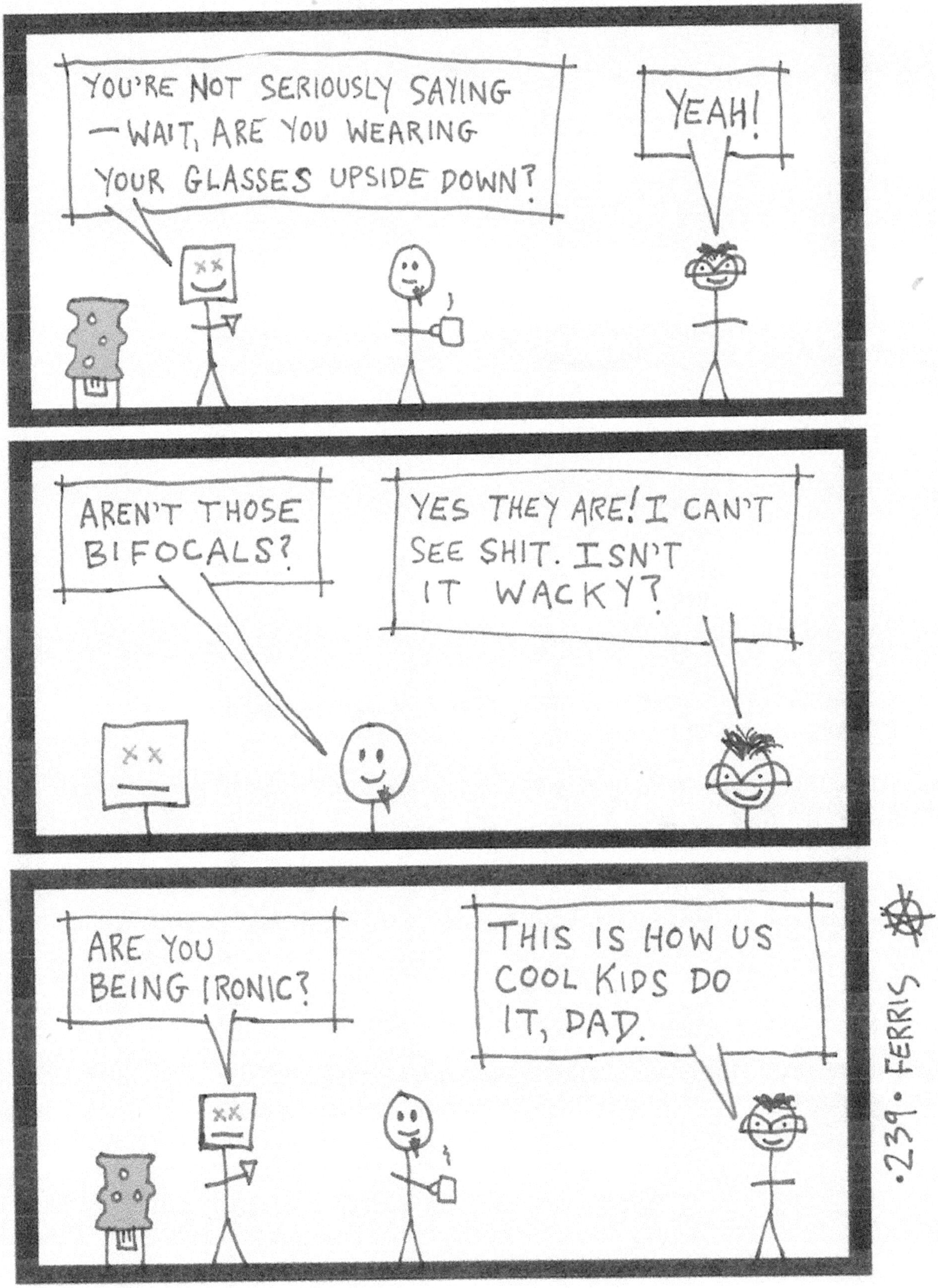
YOU'RE NOT SERIOUSLY SAYING —WAIT, ARE YOU WEARING YOUR GLASSES UPSIDE DOWN?
YEAH!
AREN'T THOSE BIFOCALS?
YES THEY ARE! I CAN'T SEE SHIT. ISN'T IT WACKY?
ARE YOU BEING IRONIC?
THIS IS HOW US COOL KIDS DO IT, DAD.
•239• FERRIS

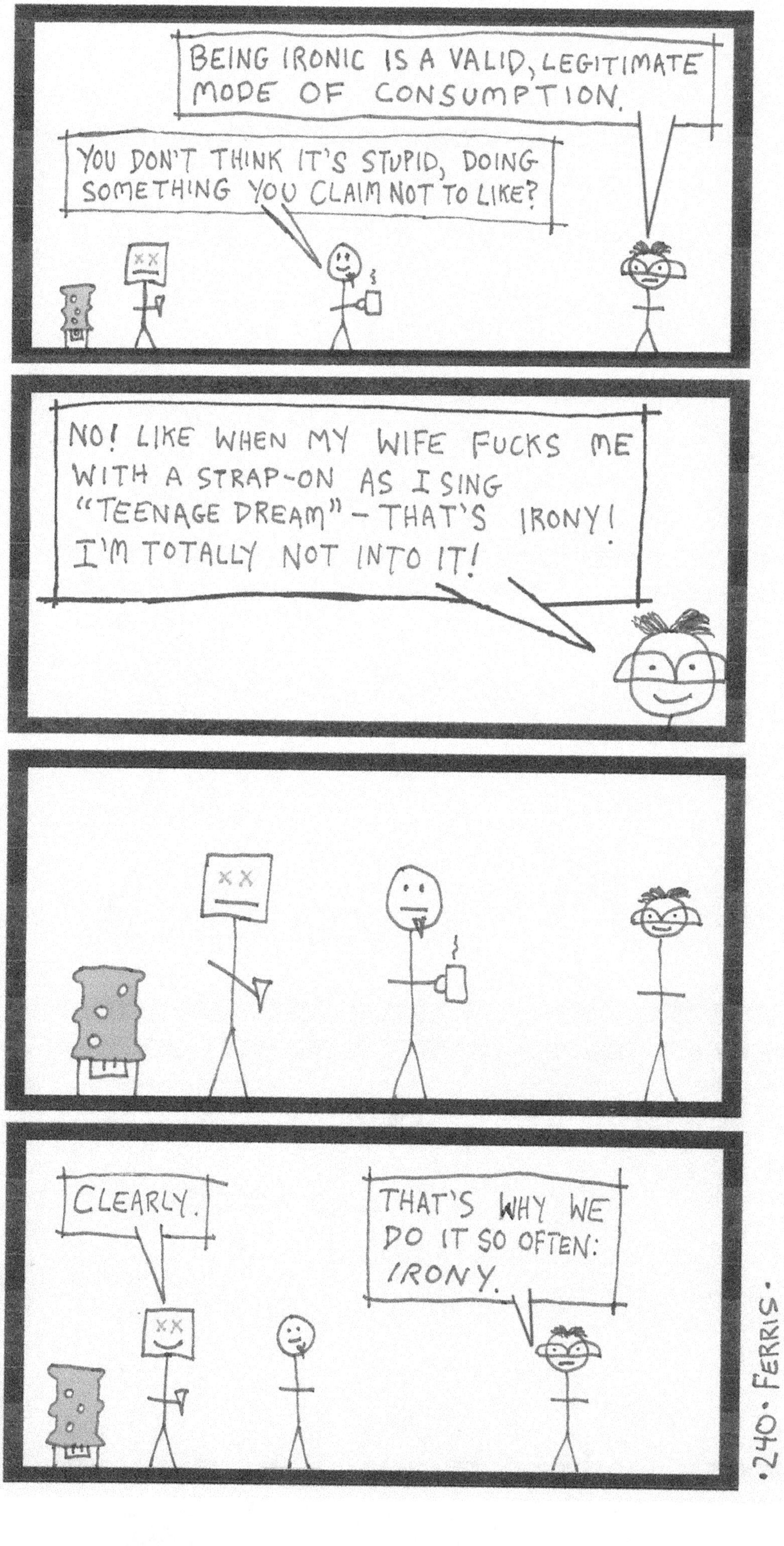
YOU DON'T THINK IT'S STUPID, DOING SOMETHING YOU CLAIM NOT TO LIKE?
BEING IRONIC IS A VALID, LEGITIMATE MODE OF CONSUMPTION.
NO! LIKE WHEN MY WIFE FUCKS ME WITH A STRAP-ON AS I SING "TEENAGE DREAM" – THAT'S IRONY! I'M TOTALLY NOT INTO IT!
CLEARLY.
THAT'S WHY WE DO IT SO OFTEN: IRONY.
•240• FERRIS•

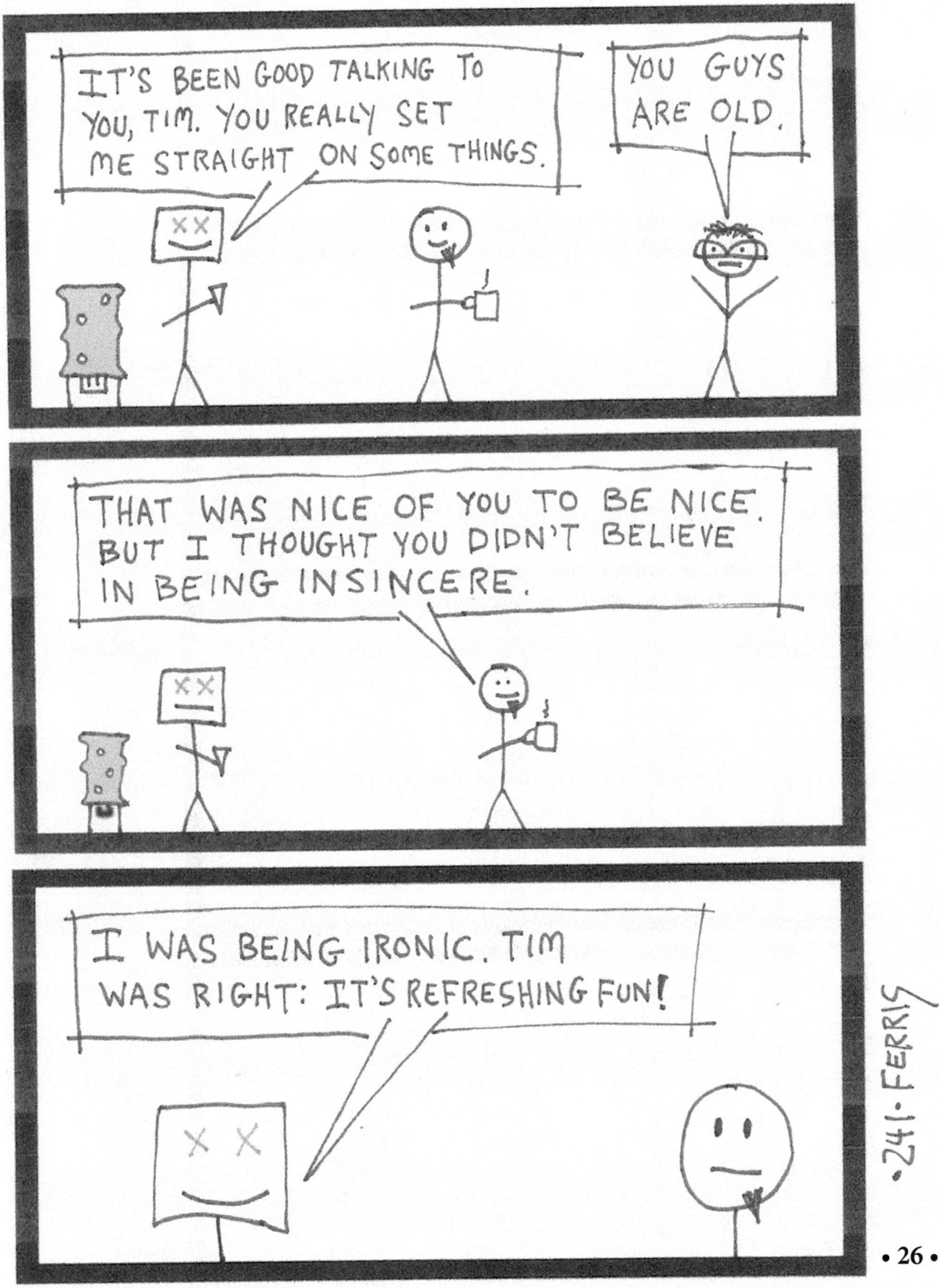
IT'S BEEN GOOD TALKING TO YOU, TIM. YOU REALLY SET ME STRAIGHT ON SOME THINGS.
YOU GUYS ARE OLD.
THAT WAS NICE OF YOU TO BE NICE. BUT I THOUGHT YOU DIDN'T BELIEVE IN BEING INSINCERE.
I WAS BEING IRONIC. TIM WAS RIGHT: IT'S REFRESHING FUN!
•241• FERRIS

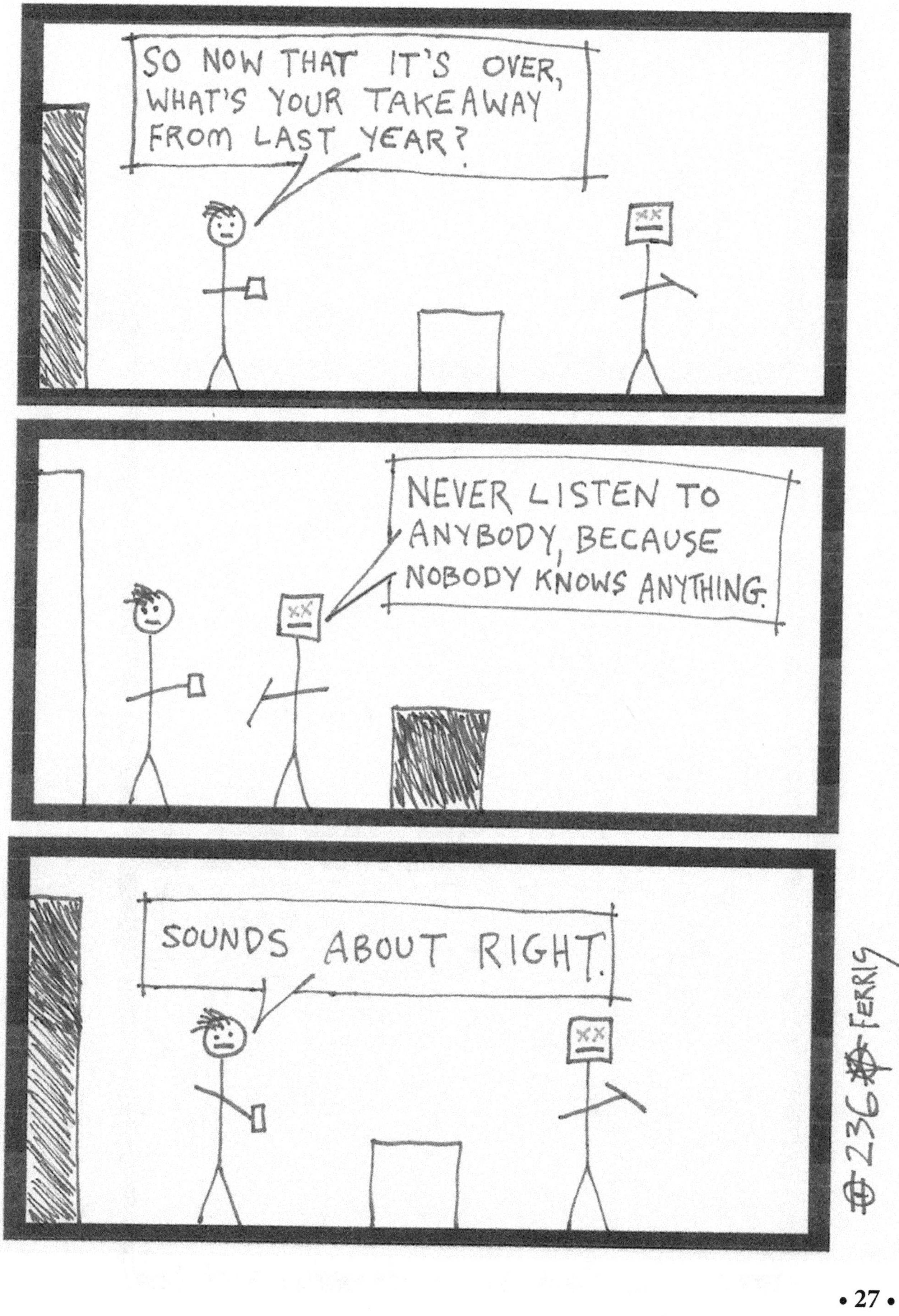
SO NOW THAT IT'S OVER, WHAT'S YOUR TAKEAWAY FROM LAST YEAR?
NEVER LISTEN TO ANYBODY, BECAUSE NOBODY KNOWS ANYTHING.
SOUNDS ABOUT RIGHT.
236 FERRIS

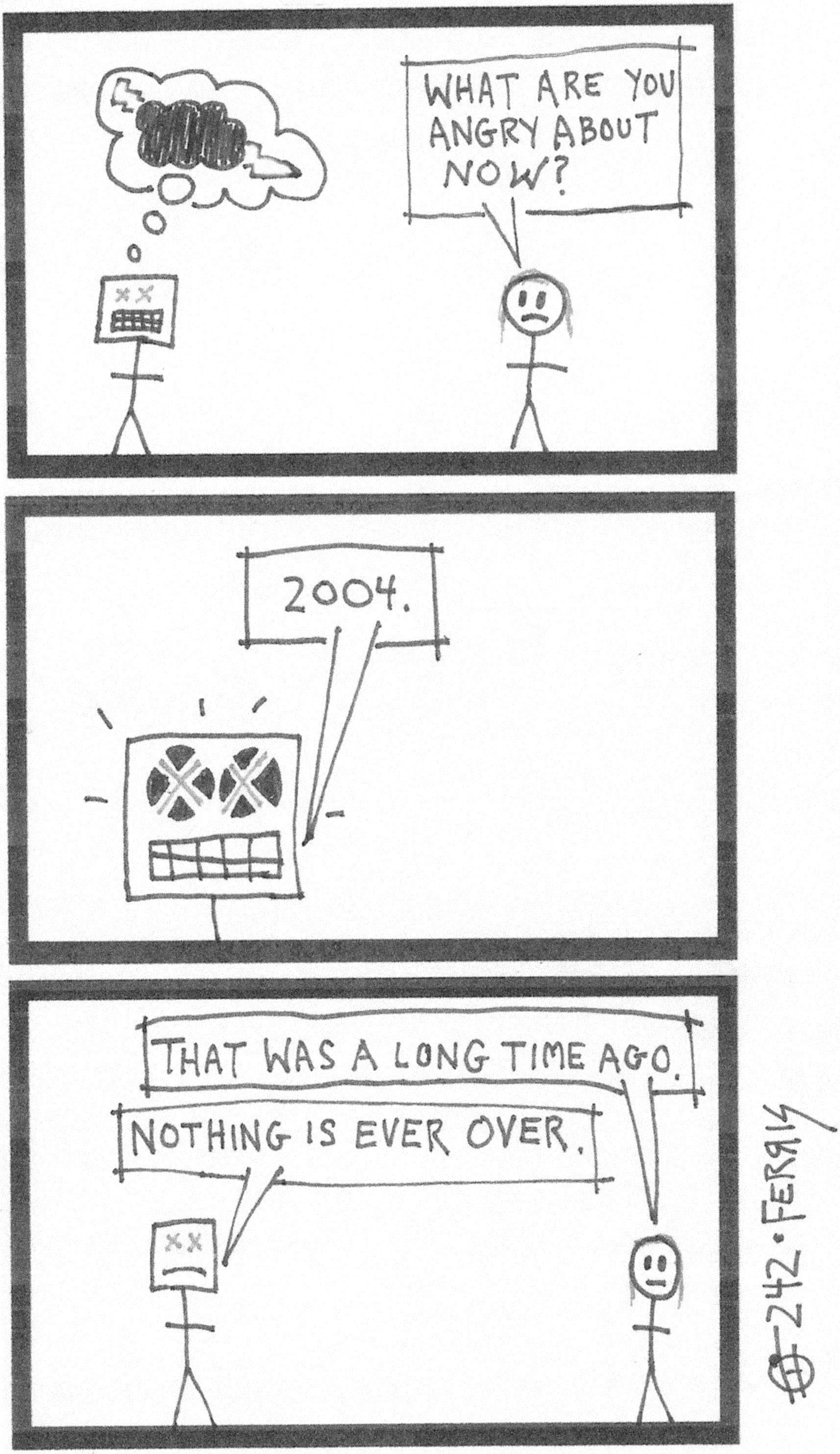
WHAT ARE YOU ANGRY ABOUT NOW?
2004.
THAT WAS A LONG TIME AGO.
NOTHING IS EVER OVER.

sup
dude
dude
dude
·243·FERRIS

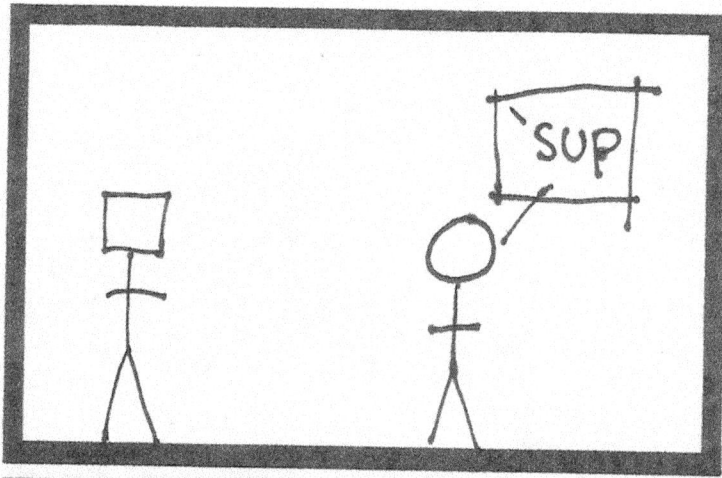

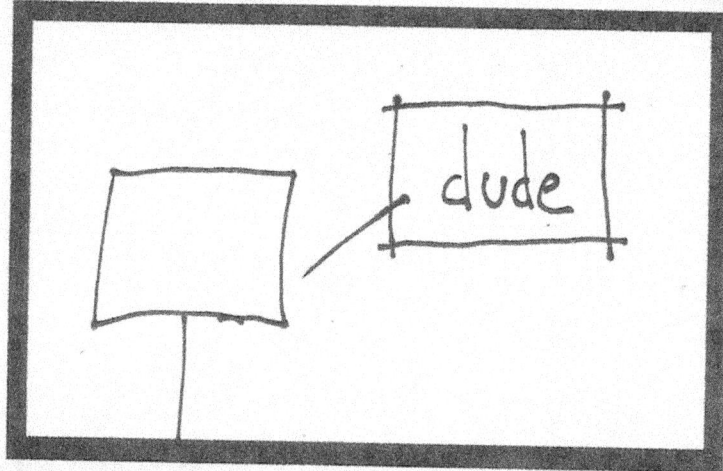

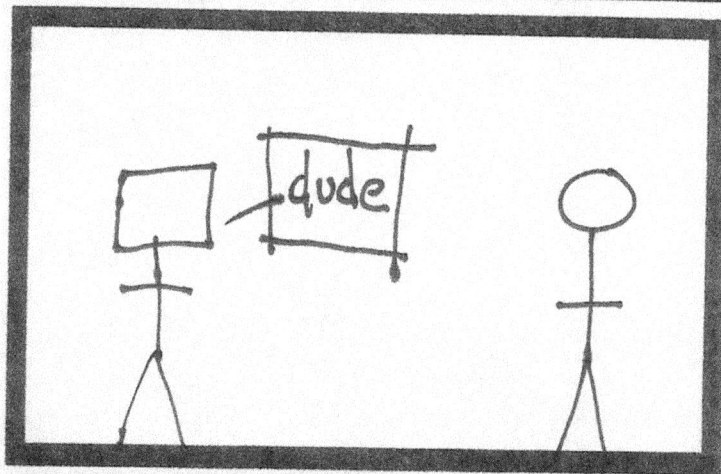

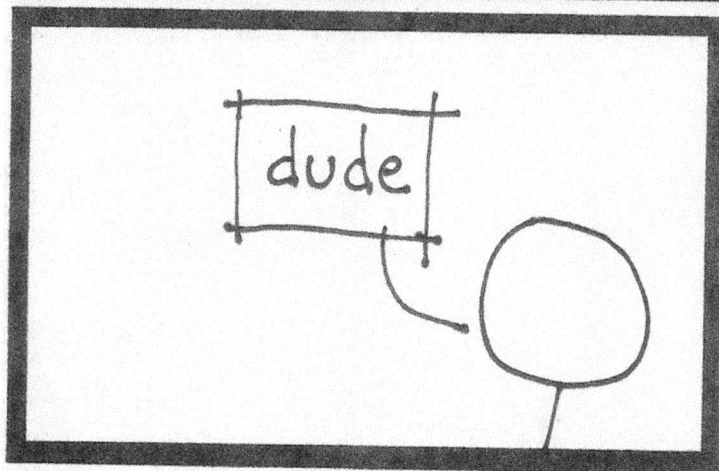

-CLICK-
MOOOO
DAIRY
MOOOO
IT NEVER GETS TIRED.
•244• FERRIS

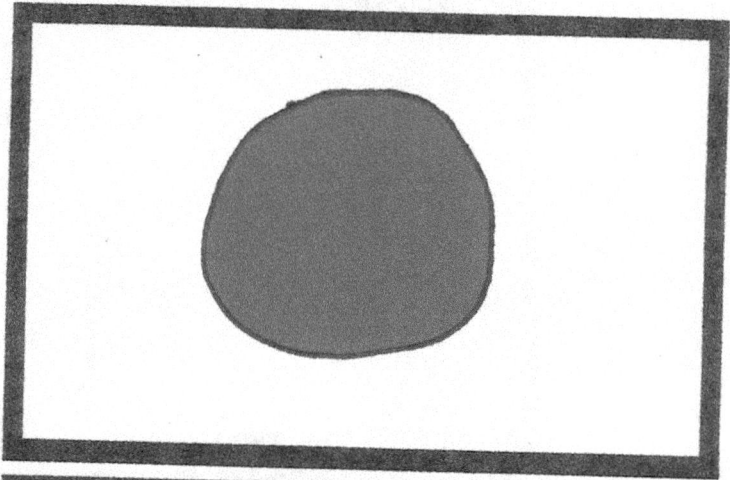

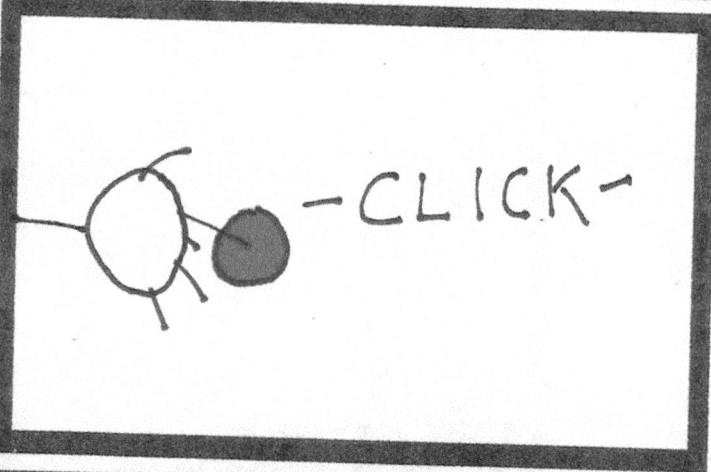

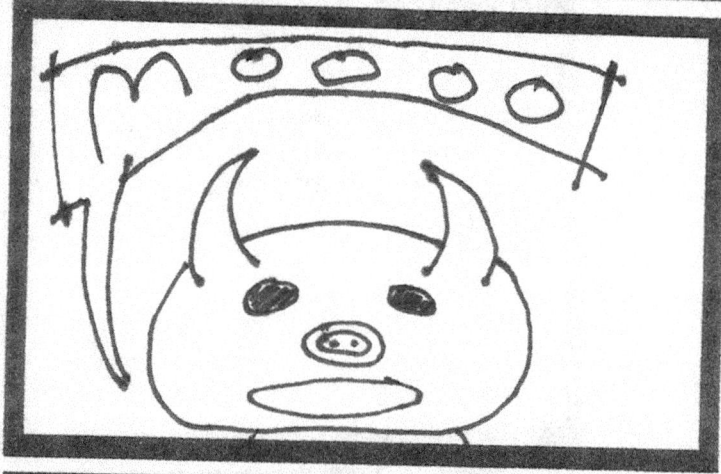

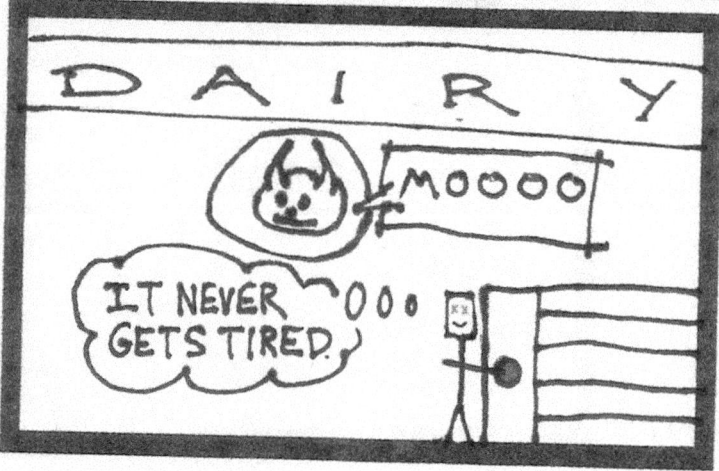

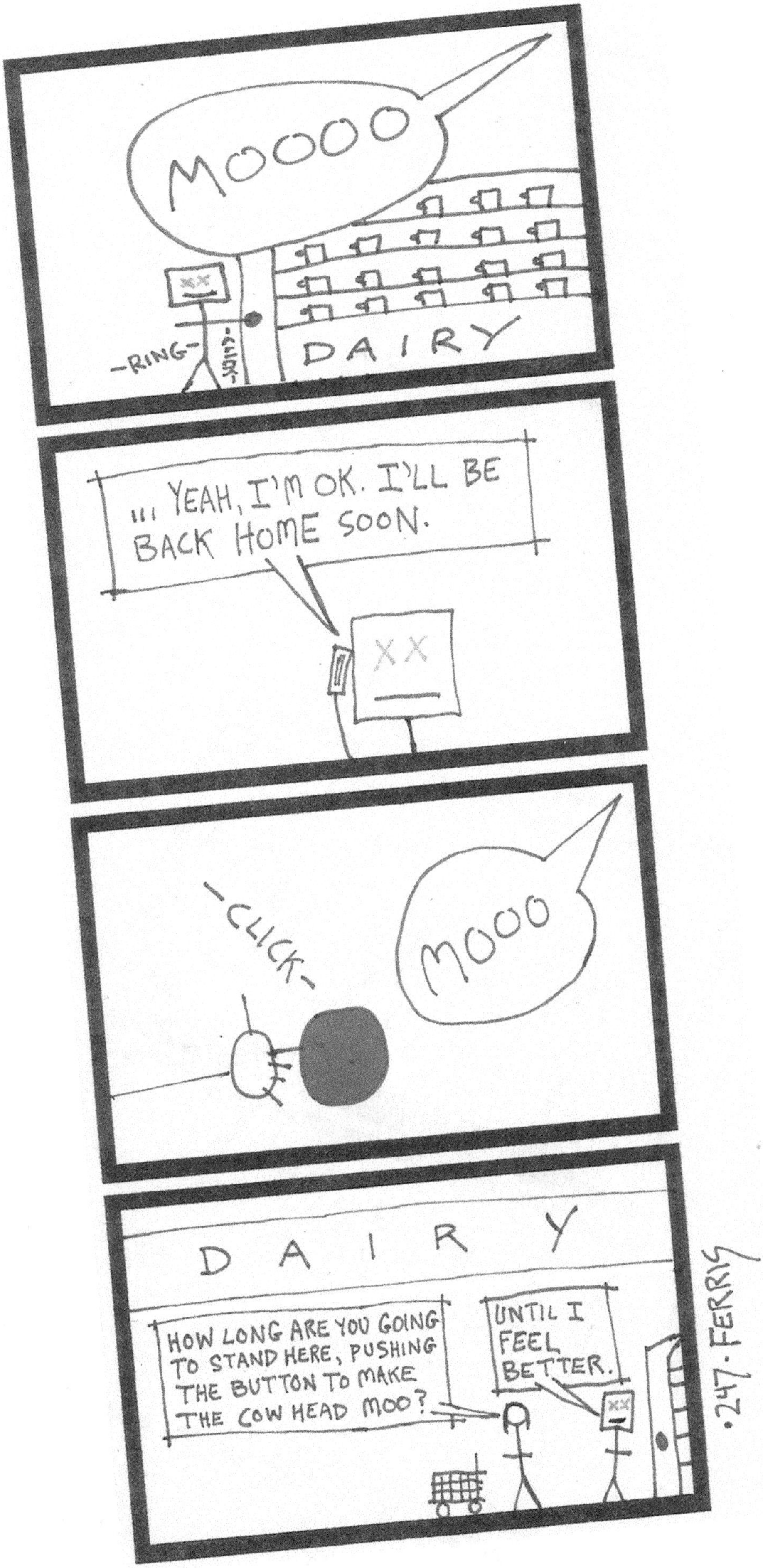
MOOOO
-RING-
DAIRY
... YEAH, I'M OK. I'LL BE BACK HOME SOON.
-CLICK-
MOOO
DAIRY
HOW LONG ARE YOU GOING TO STAND HERE, PUSHING THE BUTTON TO MAKE THE COW HEAD MOO?
UNTIL I FEEL BETTER.
·247· FERRIS

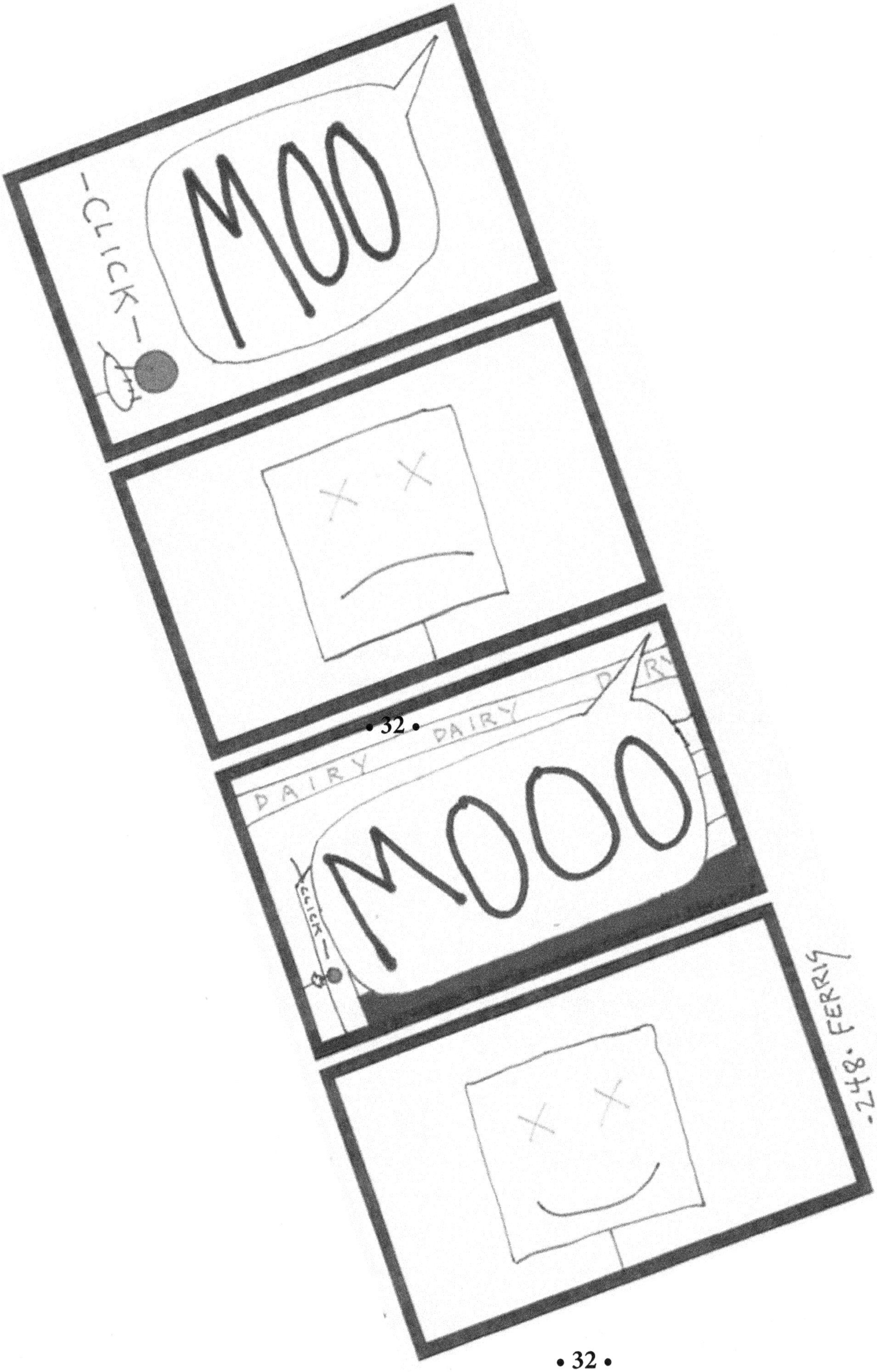
-CLICK-
MOO
DAIRY
DAIRY
DAIRY
DAIRY
-CLICK-
MOOO
-248- FERRIS

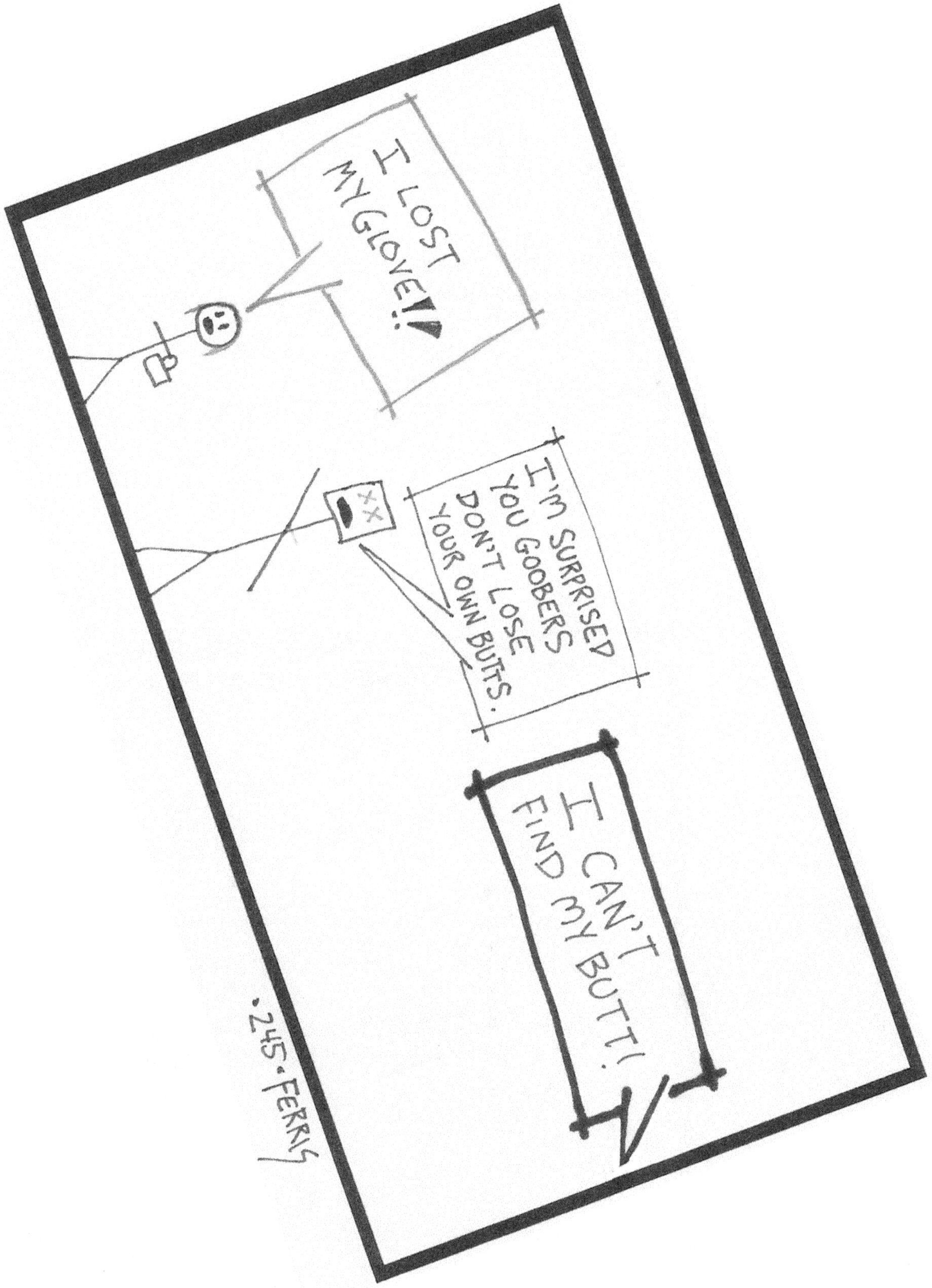
I LOST MY GLOVE!!
I'M SURPRISED YOU GOOBERS DON'T LOSE YOUR OWN BUTTS.
I CAN'T FIND MY BUTT!
•245• FERRIS

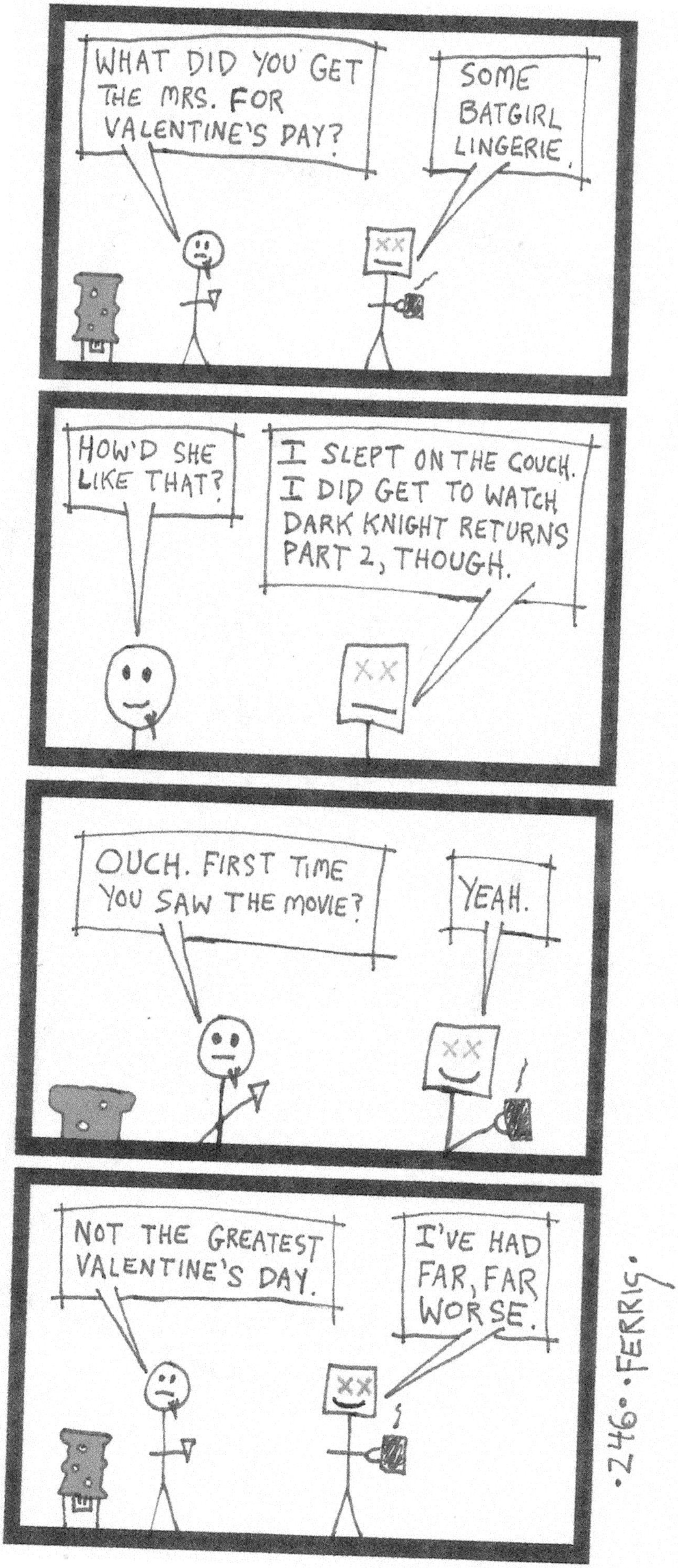
WHAT DID YOU GET THE MRS. FOR VALENTINE'S DAY?
SOME BATGIRL LINGERIE.
HOW'D SHE LIKE THAT?
I SLEPT ON THE COUCH. I DID GET TO WATCH DARK KNIGHT RETURNS PART 2, THOUGH.
OUCH. FIRST TIME YOU SAW THE MOVIE?
YEAH.
NOT THE GREATEST VALENTINE'S DAY.
I'VE HAD FAR, FAR WORSE.
•246• •FERRIS•

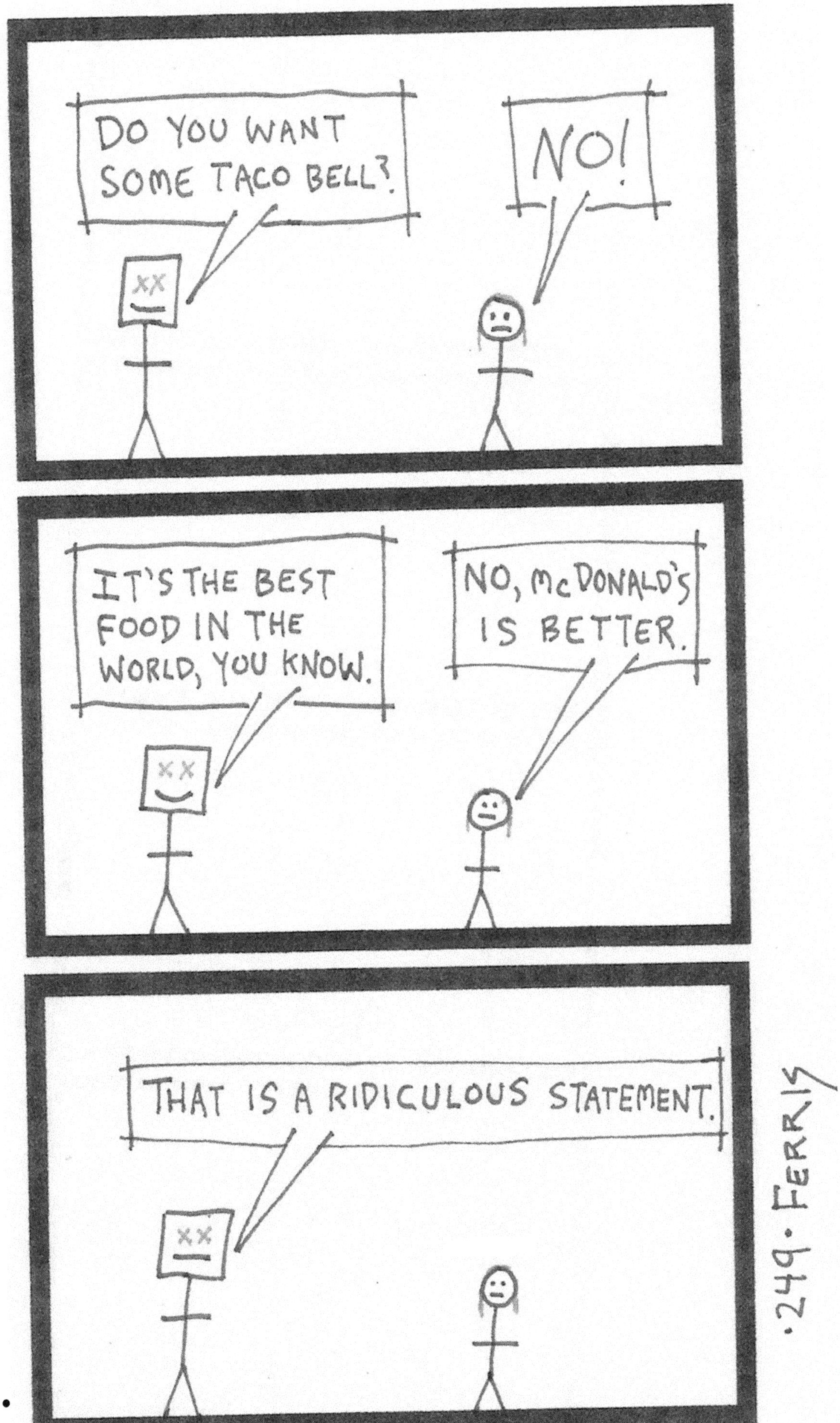
DO YOU WANT SOME TACO BELL?
NO!
IT'S THE BEST FOOD IN THE WORLD, YOU KNOW.
NO, McDONALD'S IS BETTER.
THAT IS A RIDICULOUS STATEMENT.
•249• FERRIS

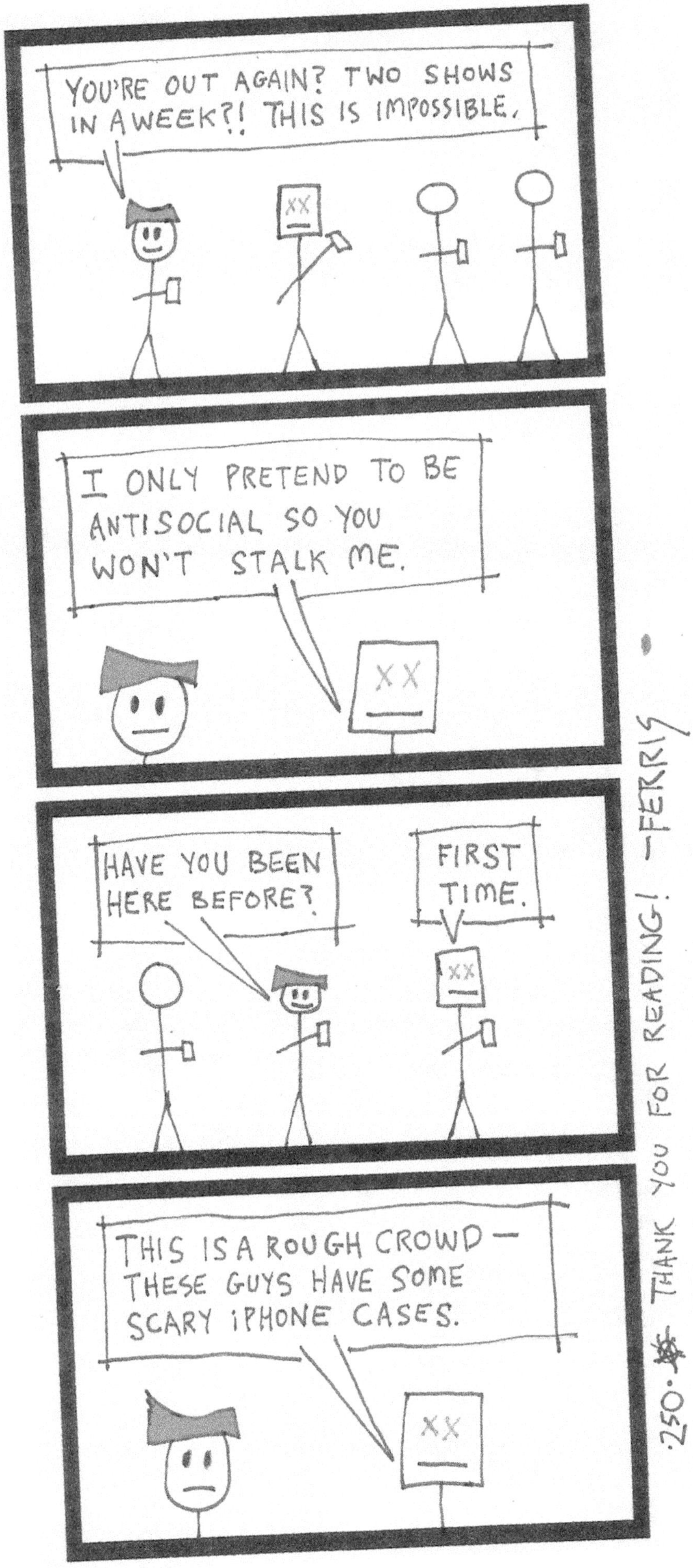
YOU'RE OUT AGAIN? TWO SHOWS IN A WEEK?! THIS IS IMPOSSIBLE.
I ONLY PRETEND TO BE ANTISOCIAL SO YOU WON'T STALK ME.
HAVE YOU BEEN HERE BEFORE?
FIRST TIME.
THIS IS A ROUGH CROWD — THESE GUYS HAVE SOME SCARY iPHONE CASES.
·250· THANK YOU FOR READING! —FERRIS

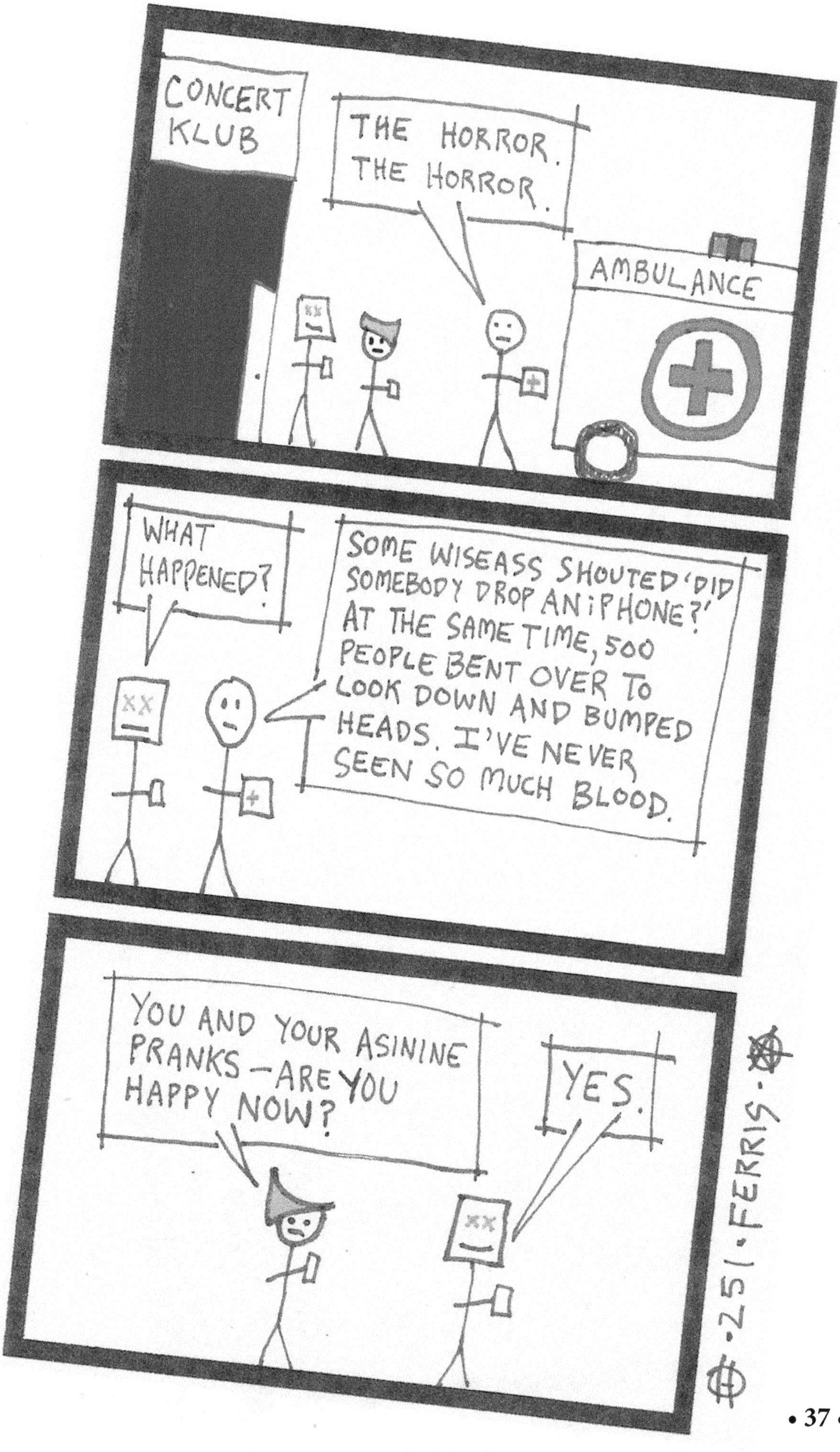
CONCERT KLUB
THE HORROR. THE HORROR.
AMBULANCE
WHAT HAPPENED?
SOME WISEASS SHOUTED 'DID SOMEBODY DROP AN iPHONE?' AT THE SAME TIME, 500 PEOPLE BENT OVER TO LOOK DOWN AND BUMPED HEADS. I'VE NEVER SEEN SO MUCH BLOOD.
YOU AND YOUR ASININE PRANKS—ARE YOU HAPPY NOW?
YES.
251 • FERRIS •

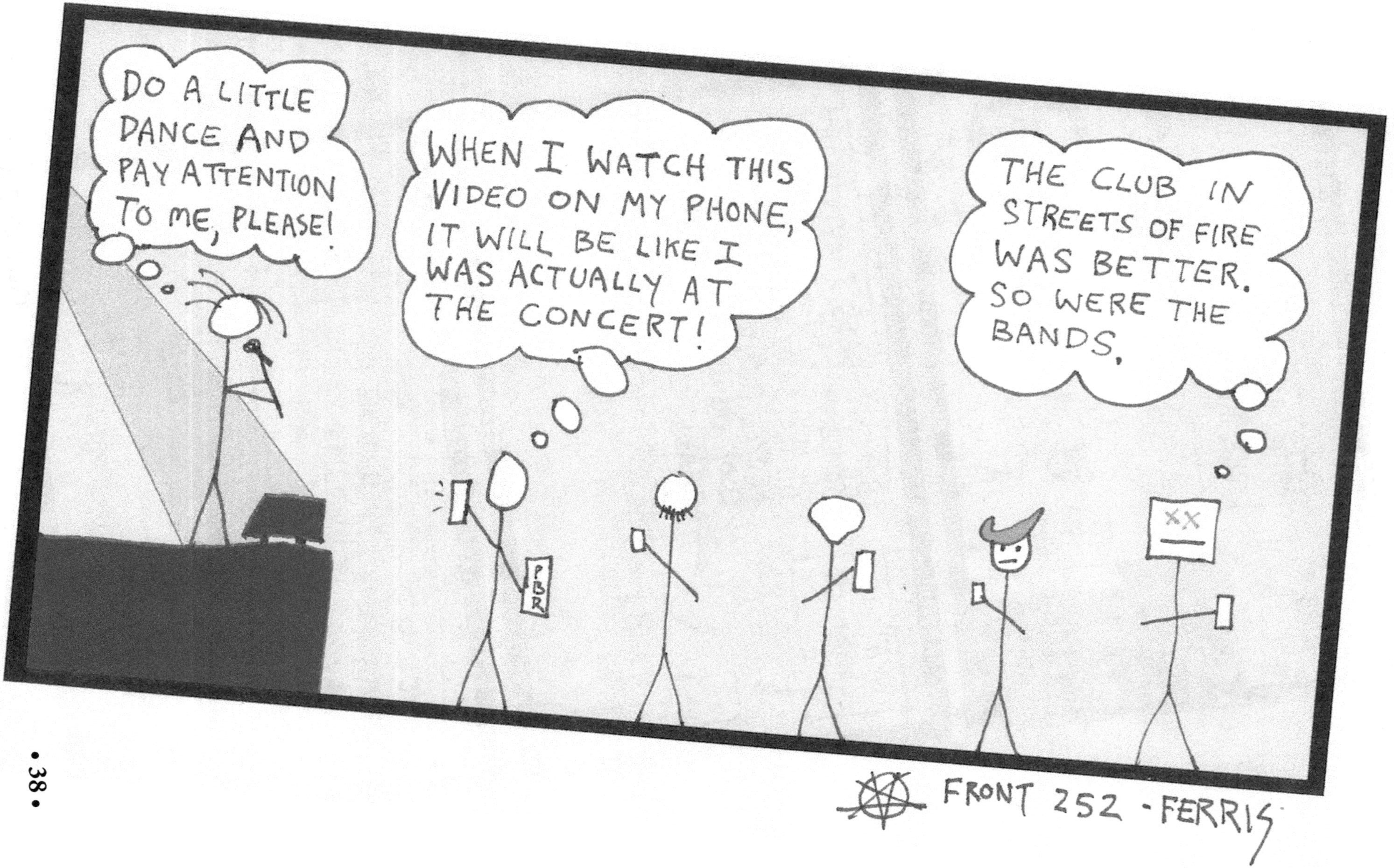
DO A LITTLE DANCE AND PAY ATTENTION TO ME, PLEASE!
WHEN I WATCH THIS VIDEO ON MY PHONE, IT WILL BE LIKE I WAS ACTUALLY AT THE CONCERT!
THE CLUB IN STREETS OF FIRE WAS BETTER. SO WERE THE BANDS.
PBR
FRONT 252 - FERRIS

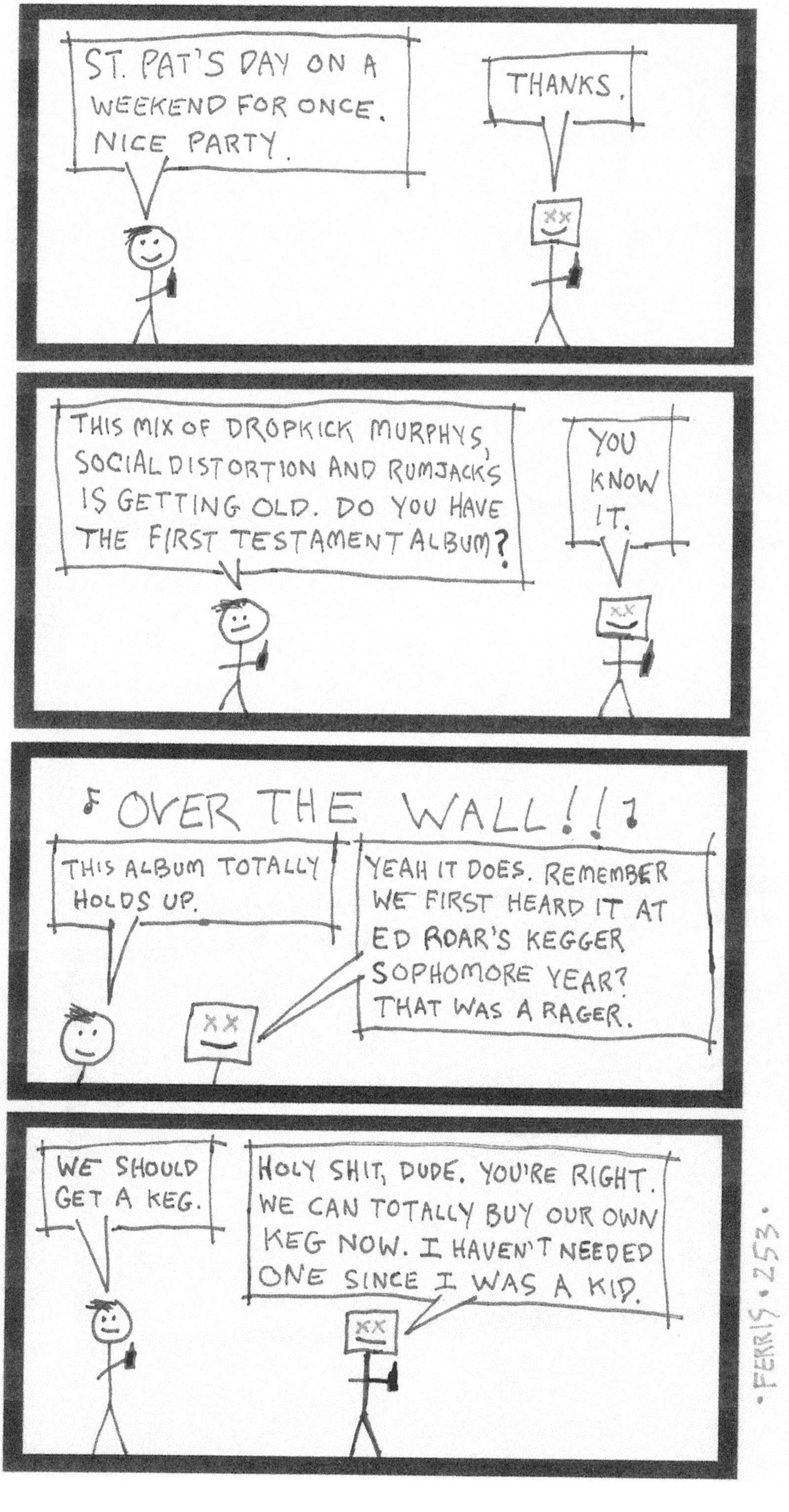
ST. PAT'S DAY ON A WEEKEND FOR ONCE. NICE PARTY.
THANKS.
THIS MIX OF DROPKICK MURPHYS, SOCIAL DISTORTION AND RUMJACKS IS GETTING OLD. DO YOU HAVE THE FIRST TESTAMENT ALBUM?
YOU KNOW IT.
OVER THE WALL!!!
THIS ALBUM TOTALLY HOLDS UP.
YEAH IT DOES. REMEMBER WE FIRST HEARD IT AT ED ROAR'S KEGGER SOPHOMORE YEAR? THAT WAS A RAGER.
WE SHOULD GET A KEG.
HOLY SHIT, DUDE. YOU'RE RIGHT. WE CAN TOTALLY BUY OUR OWN KEG NOW. I HAVEN'T NEEDED ONE SINCE I WAS A KID.
• FERRIS • 253 •

THAT'S A GREAT IDEA, GETTING A KEG.
WE'RE NOT 16 ANY MORE. WE CAN DO WHATEVER THE FUCK WE WANT.
I'M ALREADY BUZZING. WE'D NEED A RIDE.
SOME SHIT NEVER CHANGES, I GUESS.
•254• FERRIS

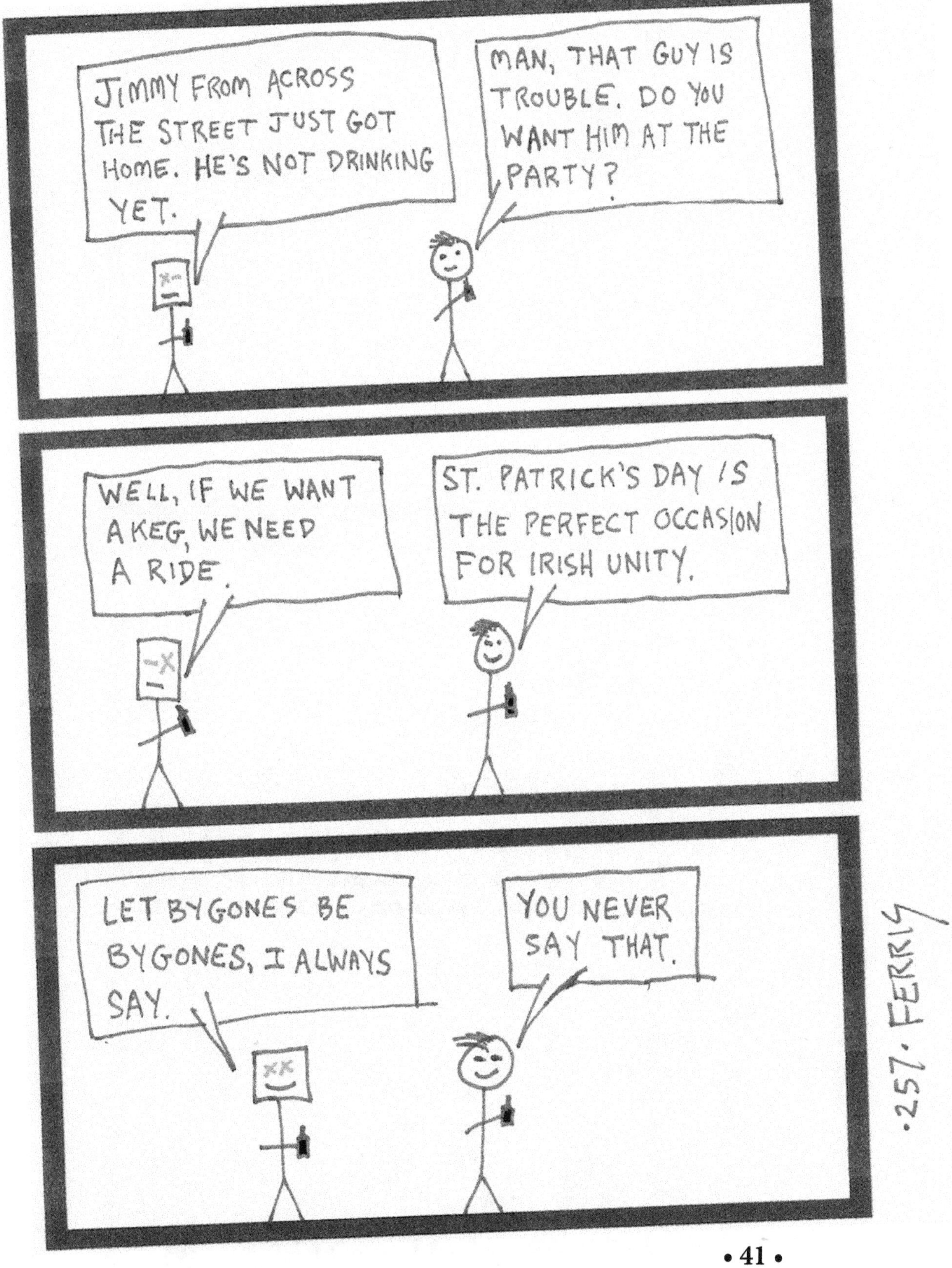
JIMMY FROM ACROSS THE STREET JUST GOT HOME. HE'S NOT DRINKING YET.
MAN, THAT GUY IS TROUBLE. DO YOU WANT HIM AT THE PARTY?
WELL, IF WE WANT A KEG, WE NEED A RIDE.
ST. PATRICK'S DAY IS THE PERFECT OCCASION FOR IRISH UNITY.
LET BYGONES BE BYGONES, I ALWAYS SAY.
YOU NEVER SAY THAT.
·257· FERRIS

DO YOU WANT IN ON THE OFFICE NCAA POOL THIS YEAR?
NO. FUCK BASKETBALL.
THAT'S HARSH.
GO STEELERS.

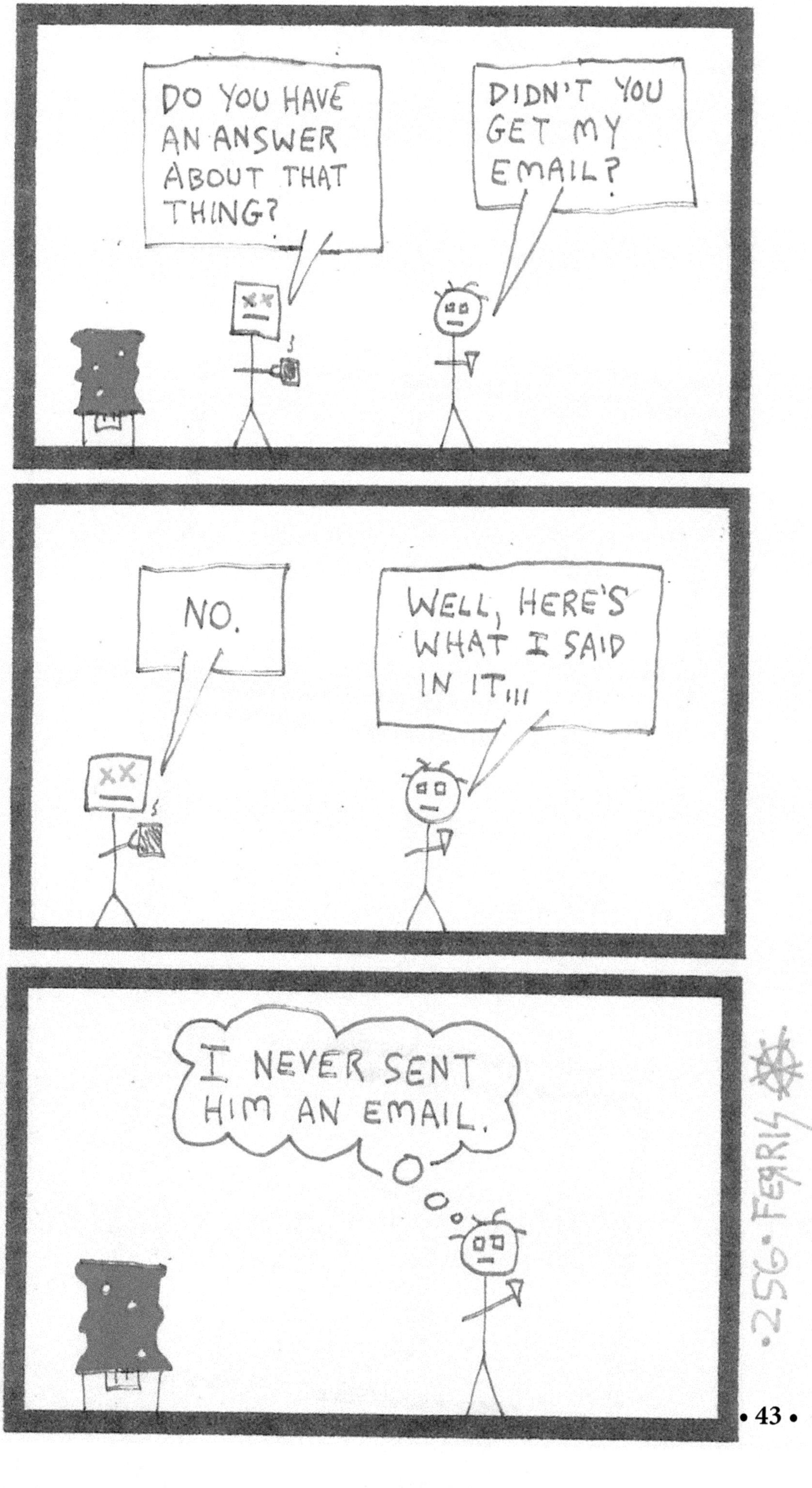
DO YOU HAVE AN ANSWER ABOUT THAT THING?
DIDN'T YOU GET MY EMAIL?
NO.
WELL, HERE'S WHAT I SAID IN IT...
I NEVER SENT HIM AN EMAIL.
•256• FERRIS

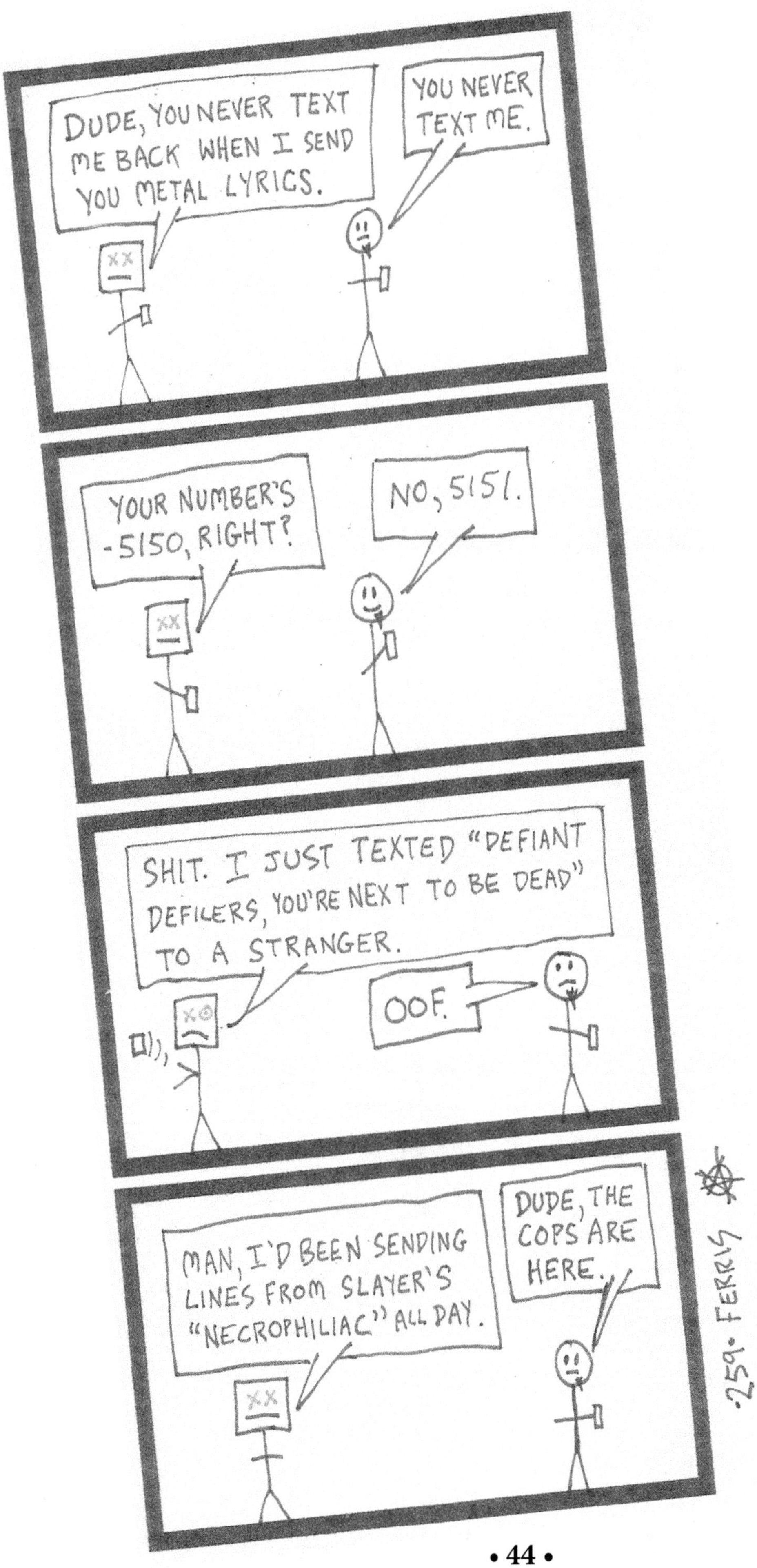
DUDE, YOU NEVER TEXT ME BACK WHEN I SEND YOU METAL LYRICS.
YOU NEVER TEXT ME.
YOUR NUMBER'S -5150, RIGHT?
NO, 5151.
SHIT. I JUST TEXTED "DEFIANT DEFILERS, YOU'RE NEXT TO BE DEAD" TO A STRANGER.
OOF.
MAN, I'D BEEN SENDING LINES FROM SLAYER'S "NECROPHILIAC" ALL DAY.
DUDE, THE COPS ARE HERE.
·259· FERRIS

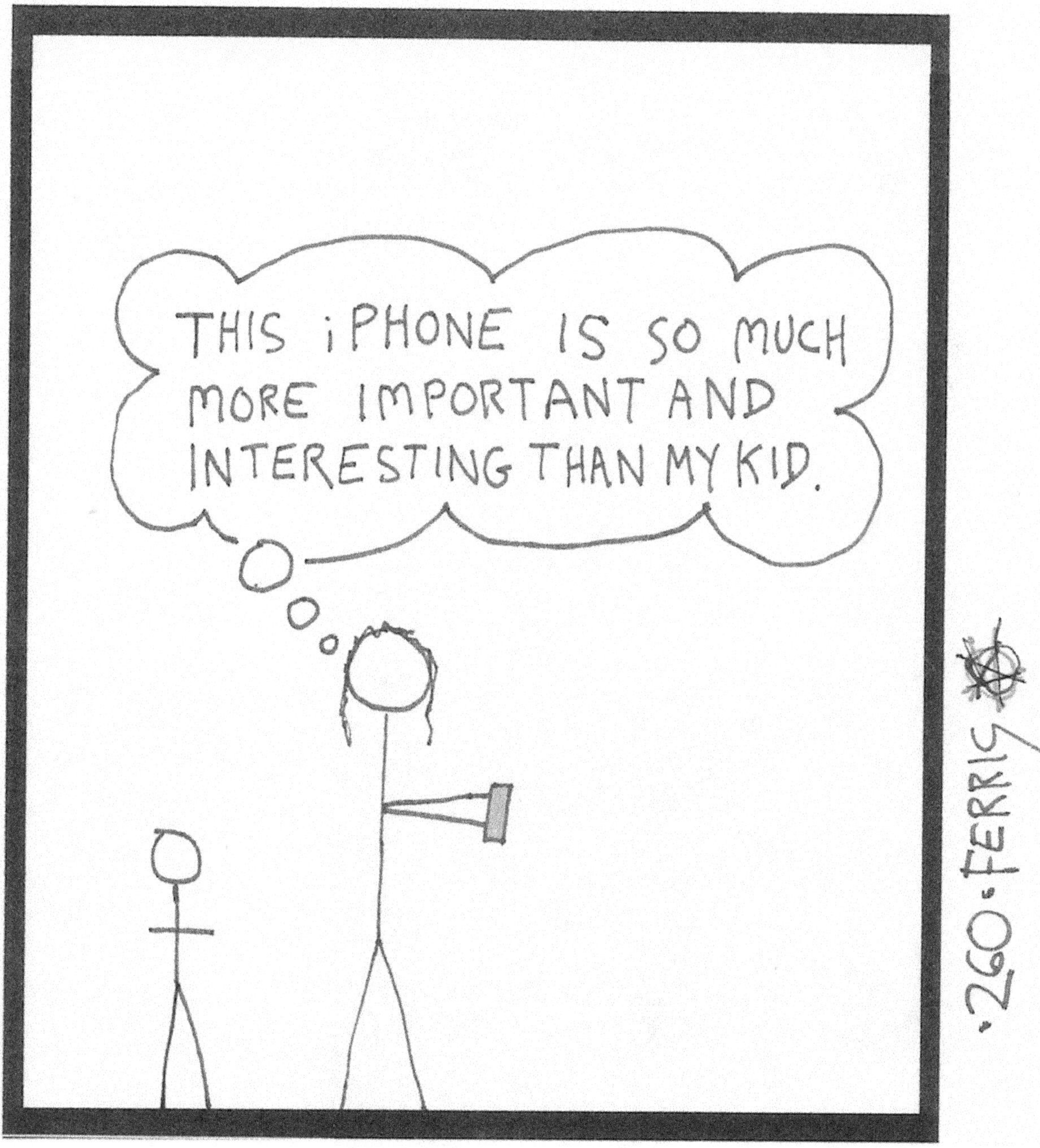
THIS iPHONE IS SO MUCH MORE IMPORTANT AND INTERESTING THAN MY KID.
•260•FERRIS

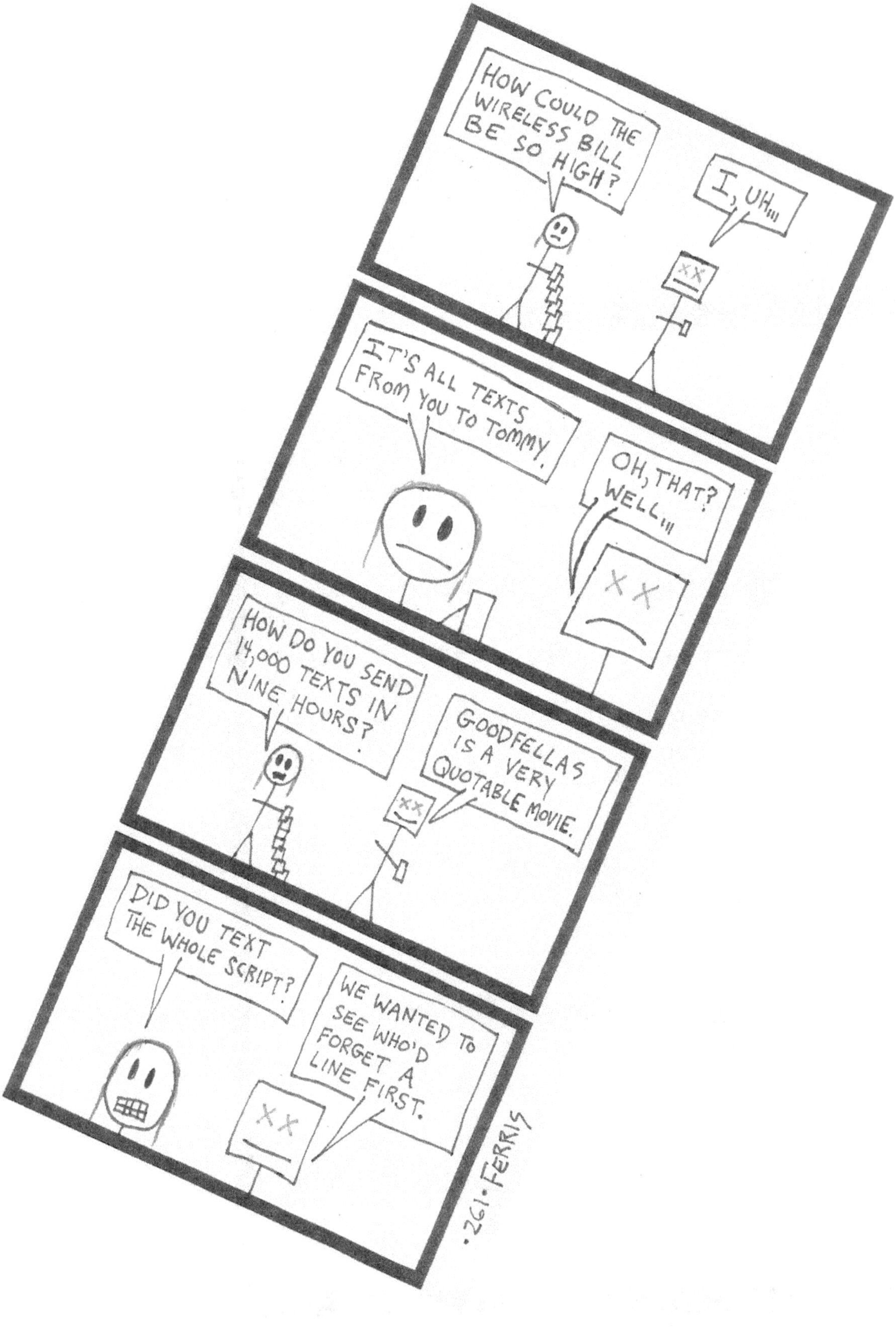

HOW COULD THE WIRELESS BILL BE SO HIGH?
I, UH...
IT'S ALL TEXTS FROM YOU TO TOMMY.
OH, THAT? WELL...
HOW DO YOU SEND 14,000 TEXTS IN NINE HOURS?
GOODFELLAS IS A VERY QUOTABLE MOVIE.
DID YOU TEXT THE WHOLE SCRIPT?
WE WANTED TO SEE WHO'D FORGET A LINE FIRST.
•261• FERRIS

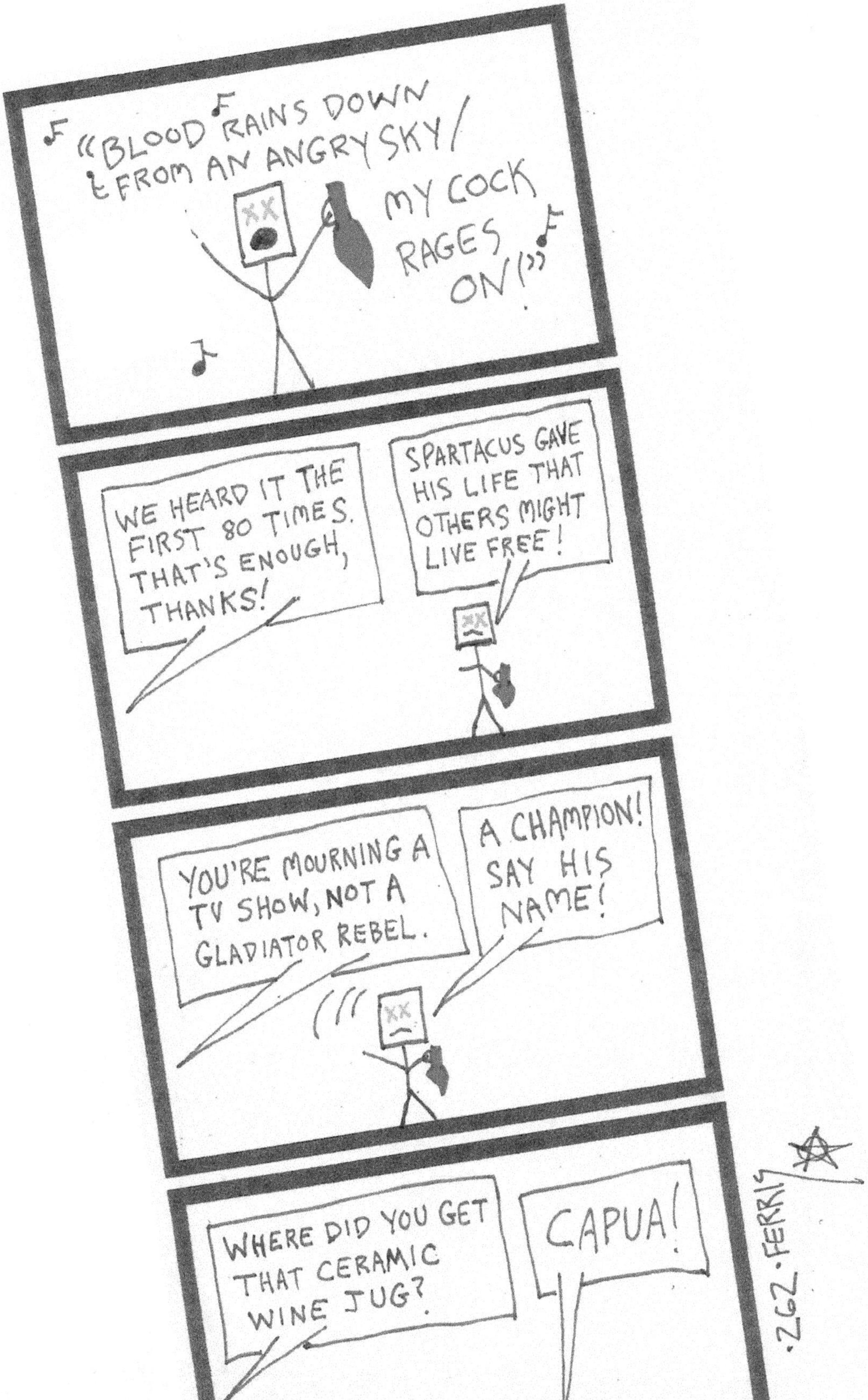
"BLOOD RAINS DOWN FROM AN ANGRY SKY/
MY COCK RAGES ON!"
WE HEARD IT THE FIRST 80 TIMES. THAT'S ENOUGH, THANKS!
SPARTACUS GAVE HIS LIFE THAT OTHERS MIGHT LIVE FREE!
YOU'RE MOURNING A TV SHOW, NOT A GLADIATOR REBEL.
A CHAMPION! SAY HIS NAME!
WHERE DID YOU GET THAT CERAMIC WINE JUG?
CAPUA!
ZGZ·FERRIS

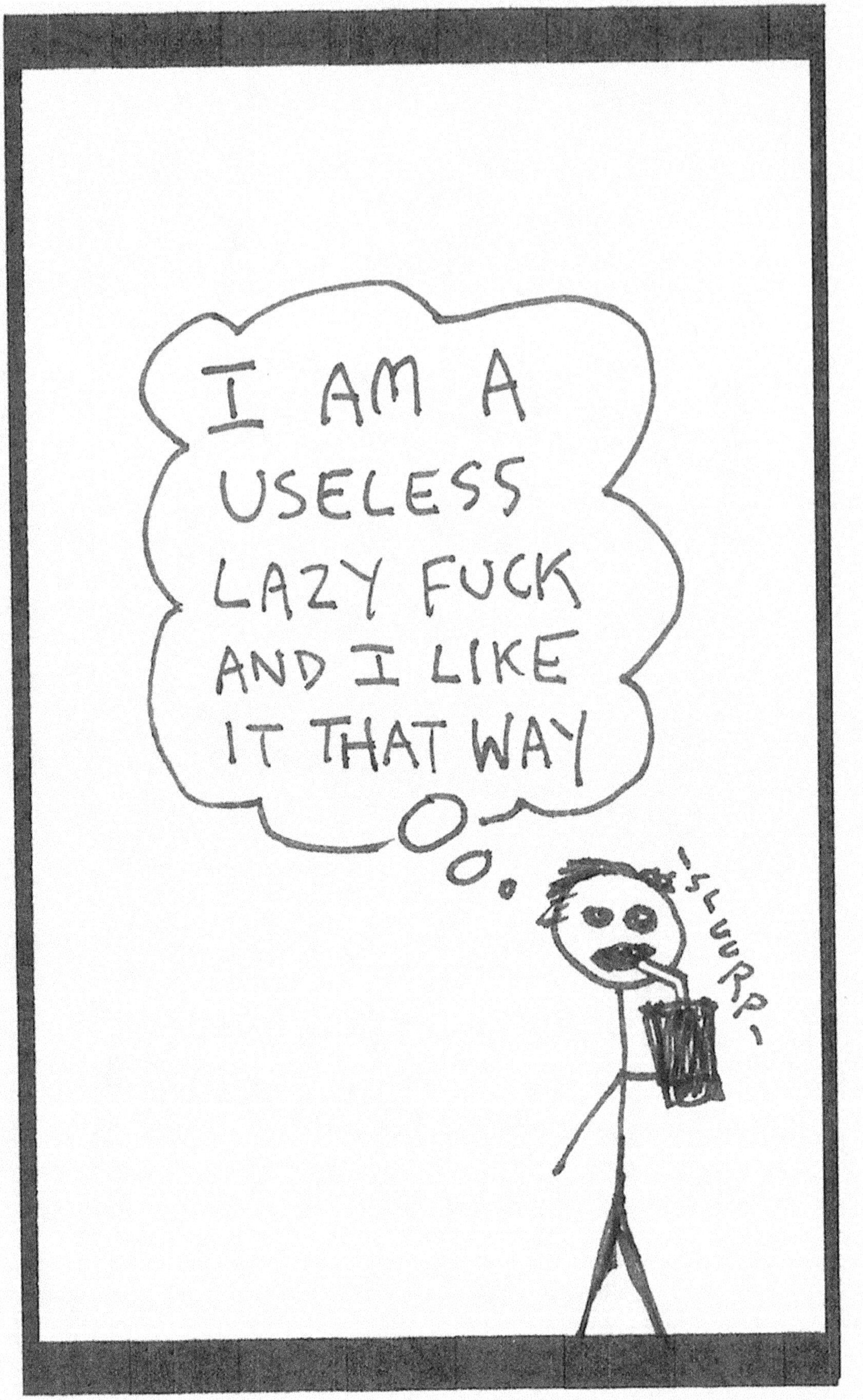
I AM A USELESS LAZY FUCK AND I LIKE IT THAT WAY
-SLURP-
•263• FERRIS

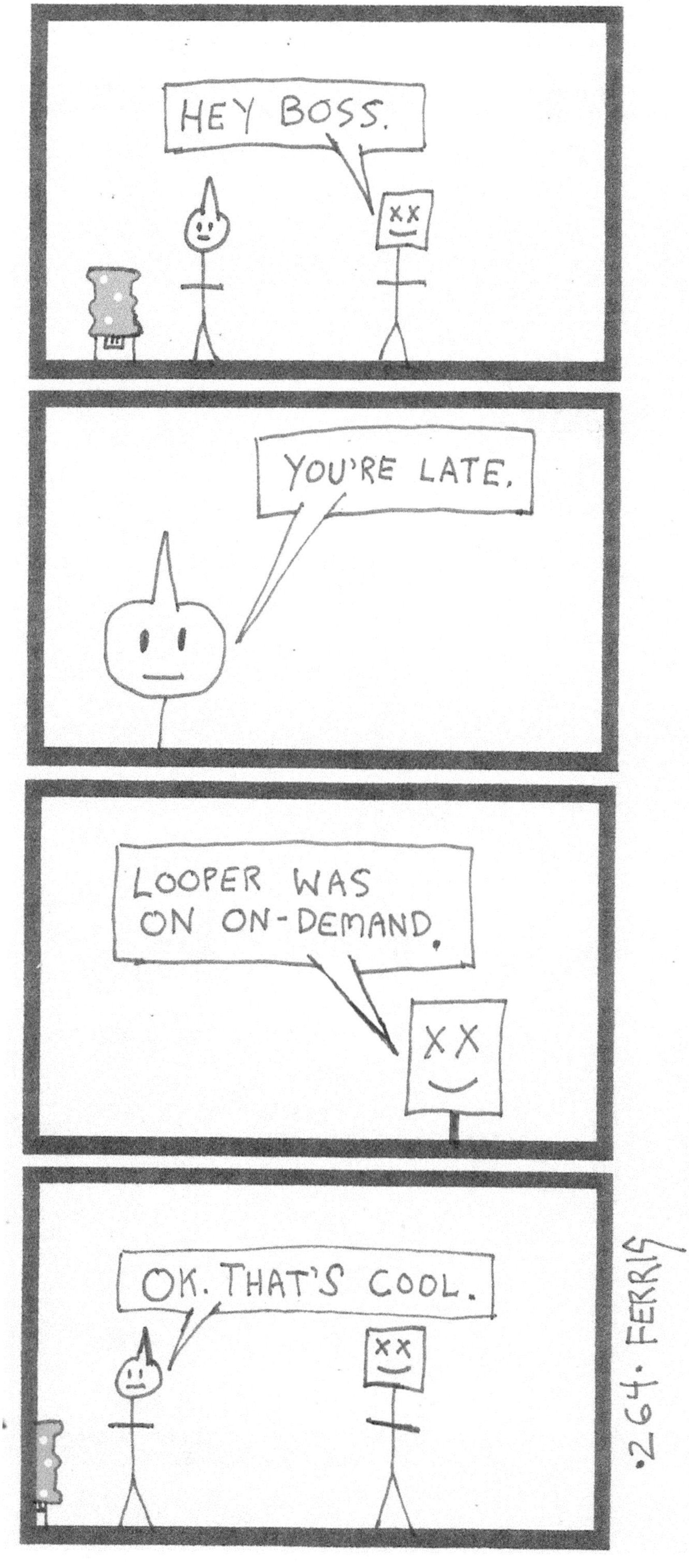
HEY BOSS.
YOU'RE LATE.
LOOPER WAS ON ON-DEMAND.
OK. THAT'S COOL.
·264· FERRIS

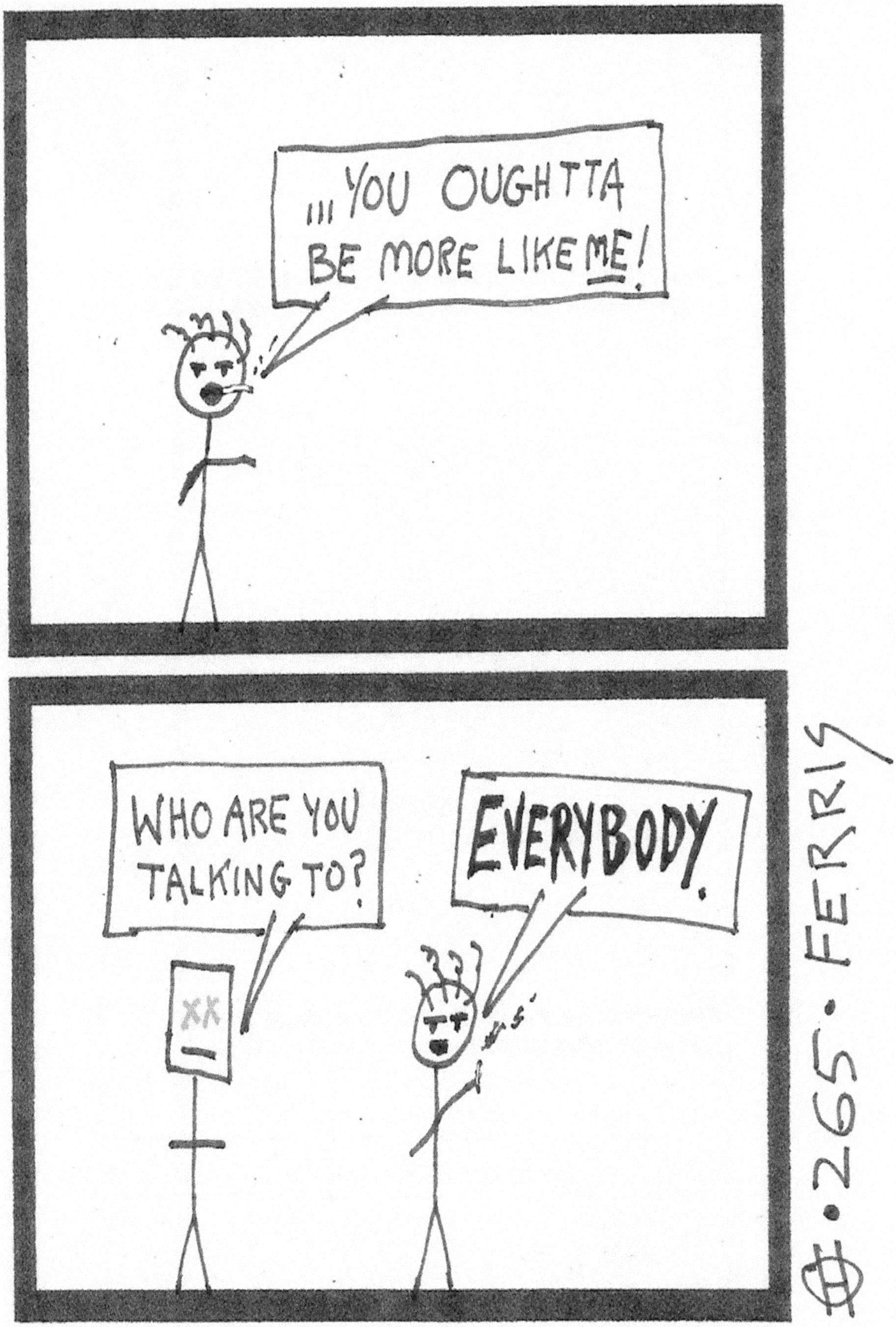
...YOU OUGHTTA BE MORE LIKE ME!
WHO ARE YOU TALKING TO?
EVERYBODY.
© · 265 · FERRIS

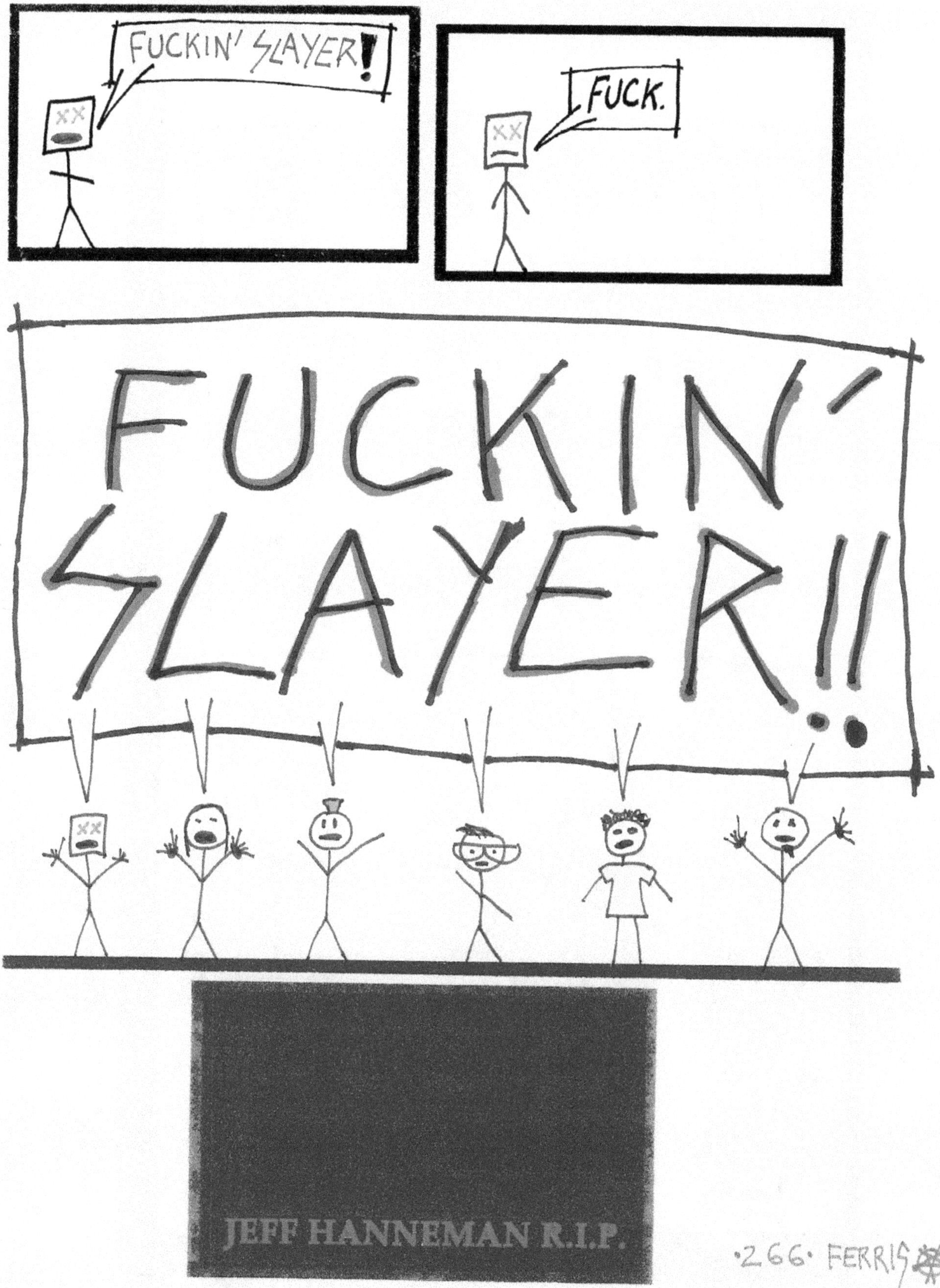
FUCKIN' SLAYER!
FUCK.
FUCKIN' SLAYER!!
JEFF HANNEMAN R.I.P.

·266· FERRIS

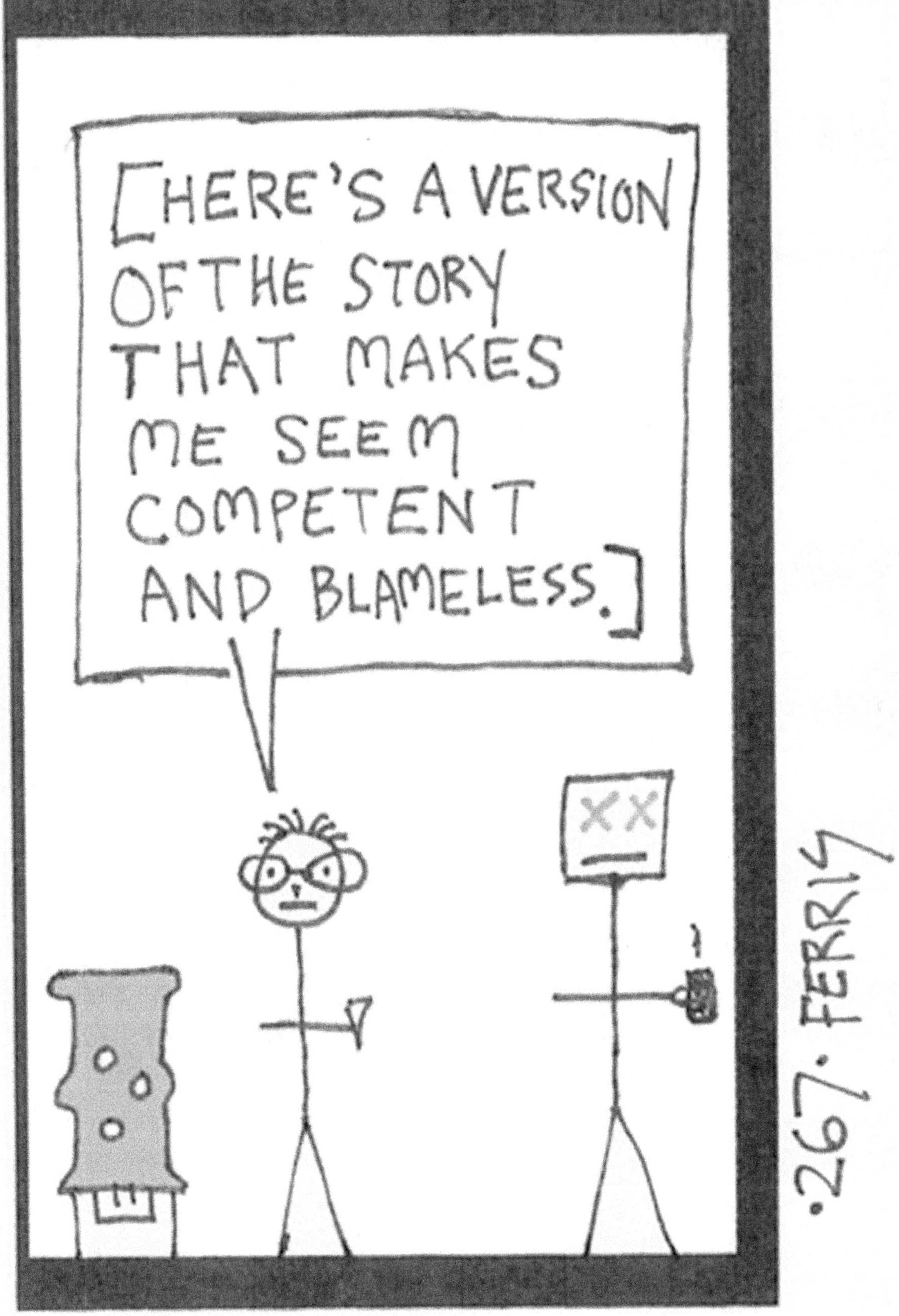
[HERE'S A VERSION OF THE STORY THAT MAKES ME SEEM COMPETENT AND BLAMELESS.]
·267· FERRIS

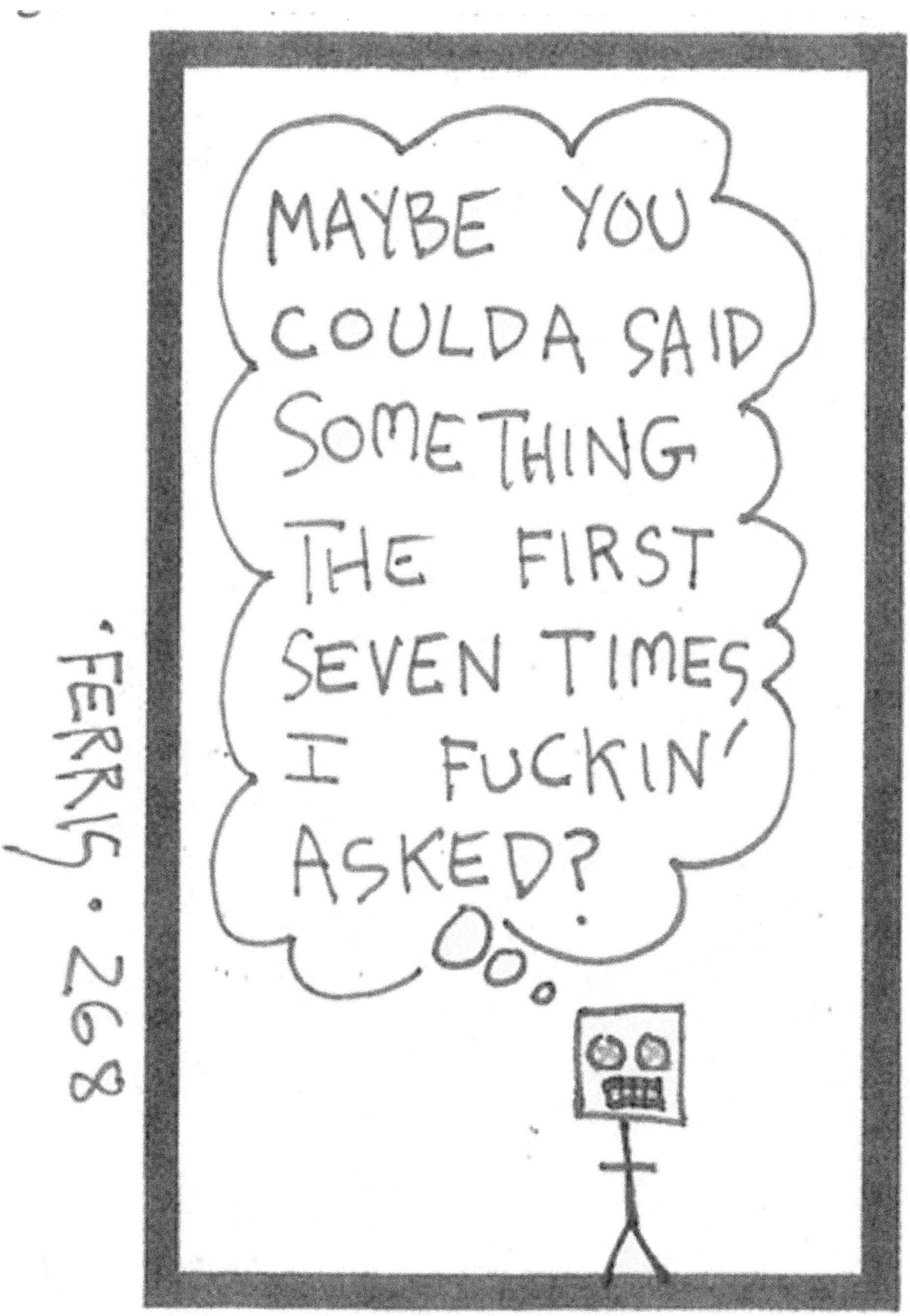
MAYBE YOU COULDA SAID SOMETHING THE FIRST SEVEN TIMES I FUCKIN' ASKED?
FERRIS • 268

SLAYER
SOMEONE SPRAY-PAINTED SLAYER ON THE GARAGE.
UH, YES, SOMEONE DID.
DID YOU SPRAY-PAINT SLAYER ON THE GARAGE?
I'M DEPRESSED. IT'S AN APPROPRIATE TRIBUTE.
LISTENING TO "RAINING BLOOD" FOR SIX HOURS WASN'T ENOUGH?
IF YOU WANT TO COUNT "POSTMORTEM/ RAINING BLOOD" AS ONE SONG, I'LL LET IT SLIDE THIS TIME.
FERRIS. 269 (HUH)

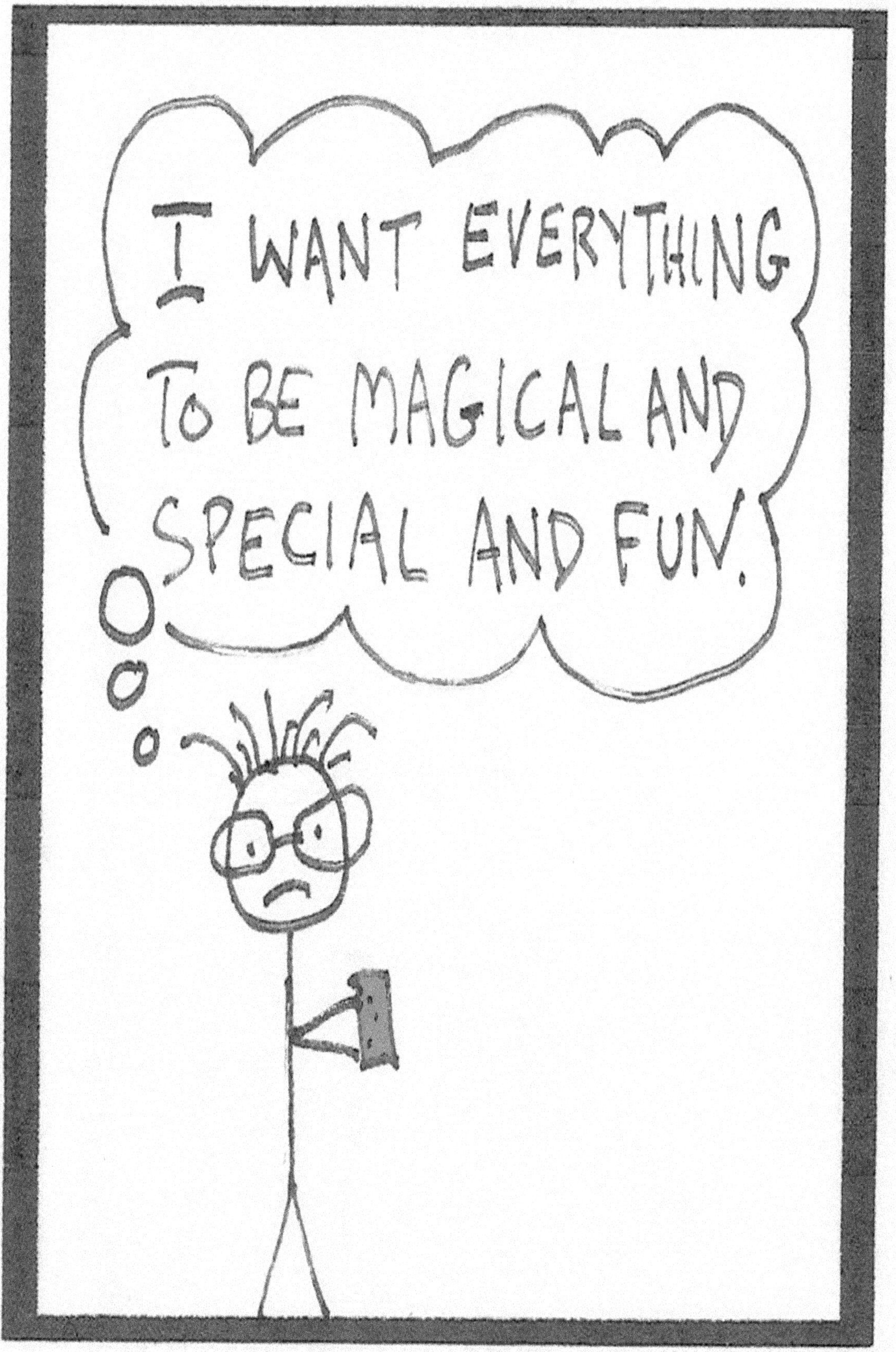
I WANT EVERYTHING TO BE MAGICAL AND SPECIAL AND FUN.

• 270 • FERRIS

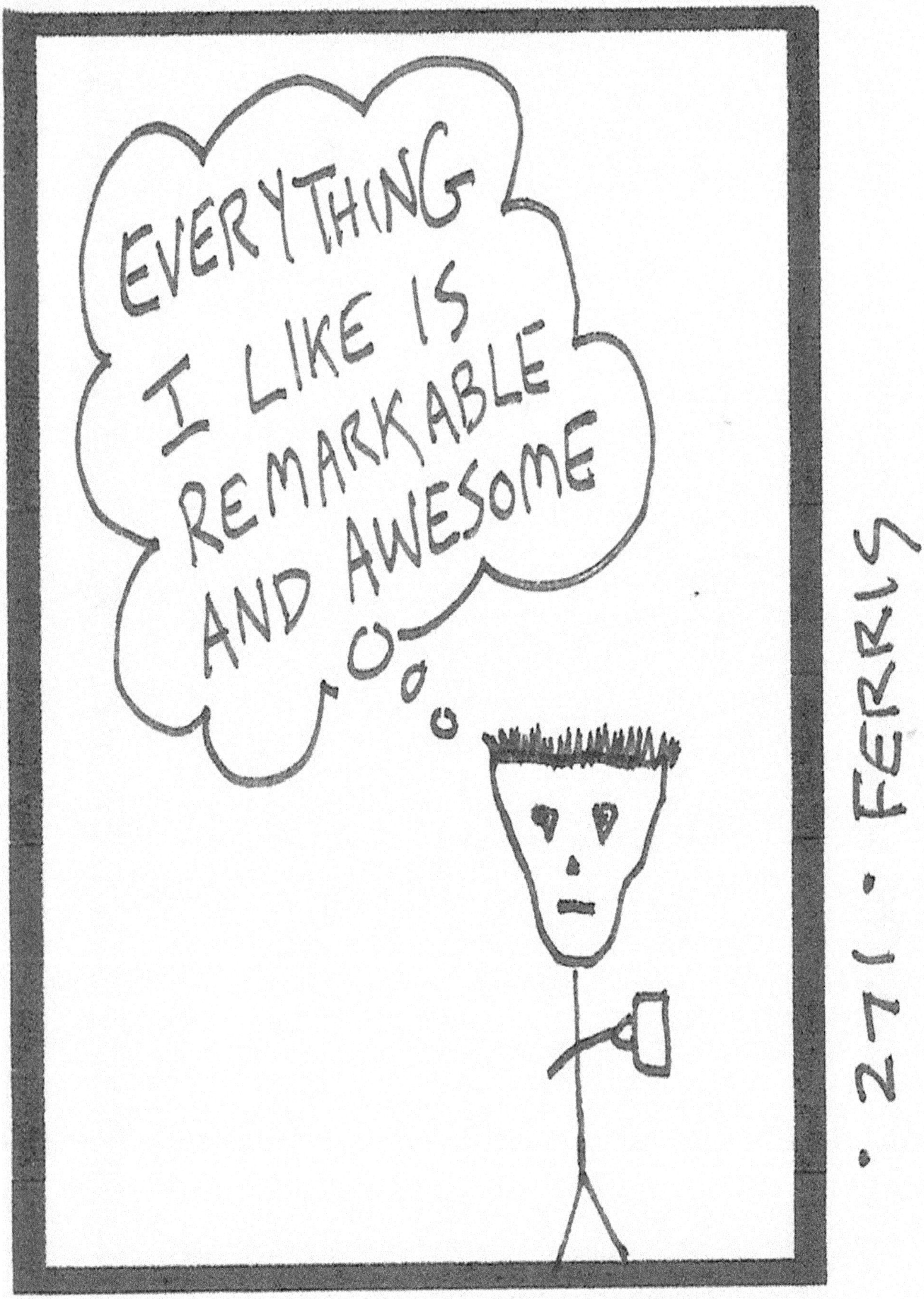
EVERYTHING I LIKE IS REMARKABLE AND AWESOME
• 2011 • FERRIS

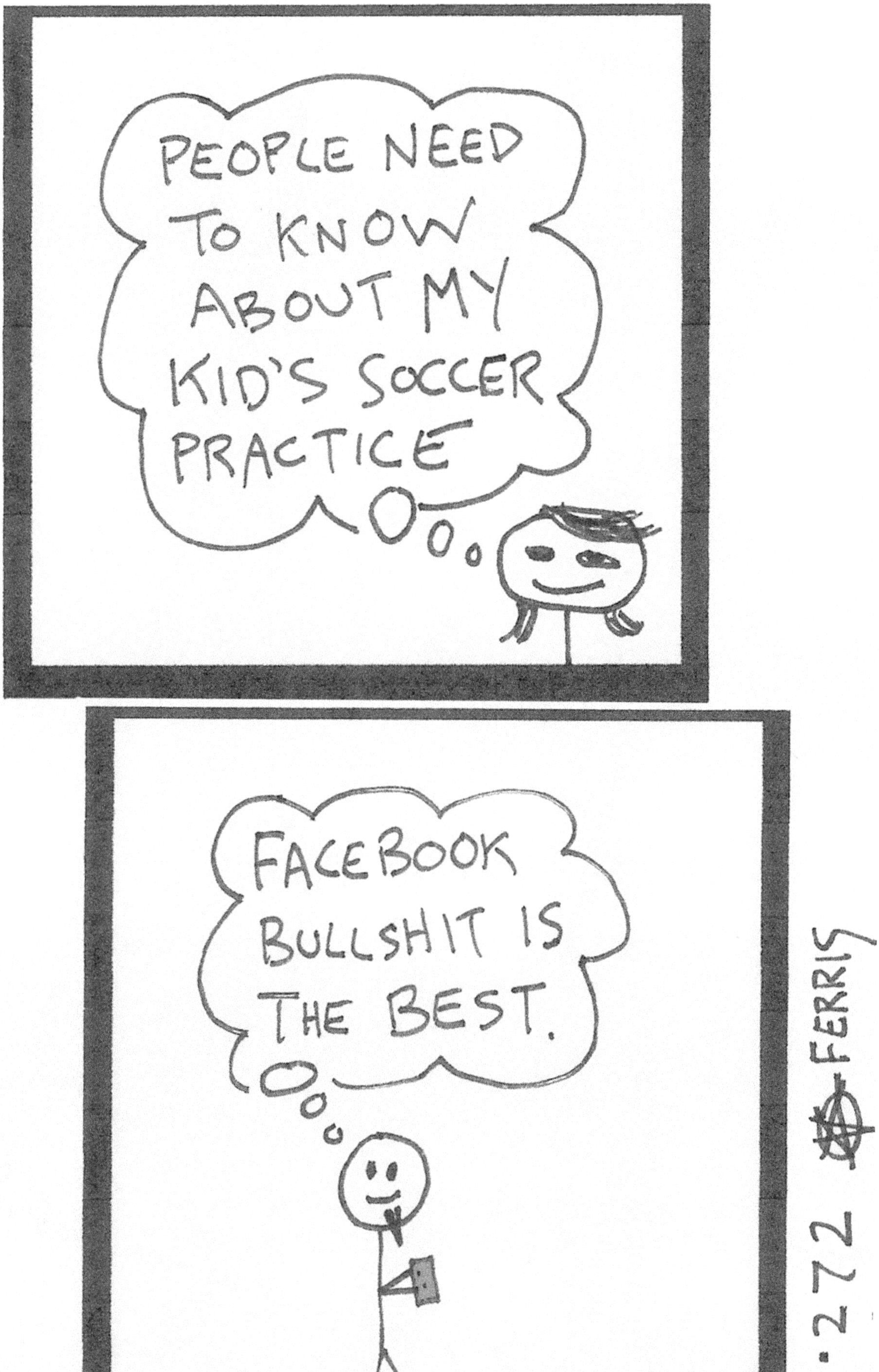
PEOPLE NEED TO KNOW ABOUT MY KID'S SOCCER PRACTICE
FACEBOOK BULLSHIT IS THE BEST.
• 272 FERRIS

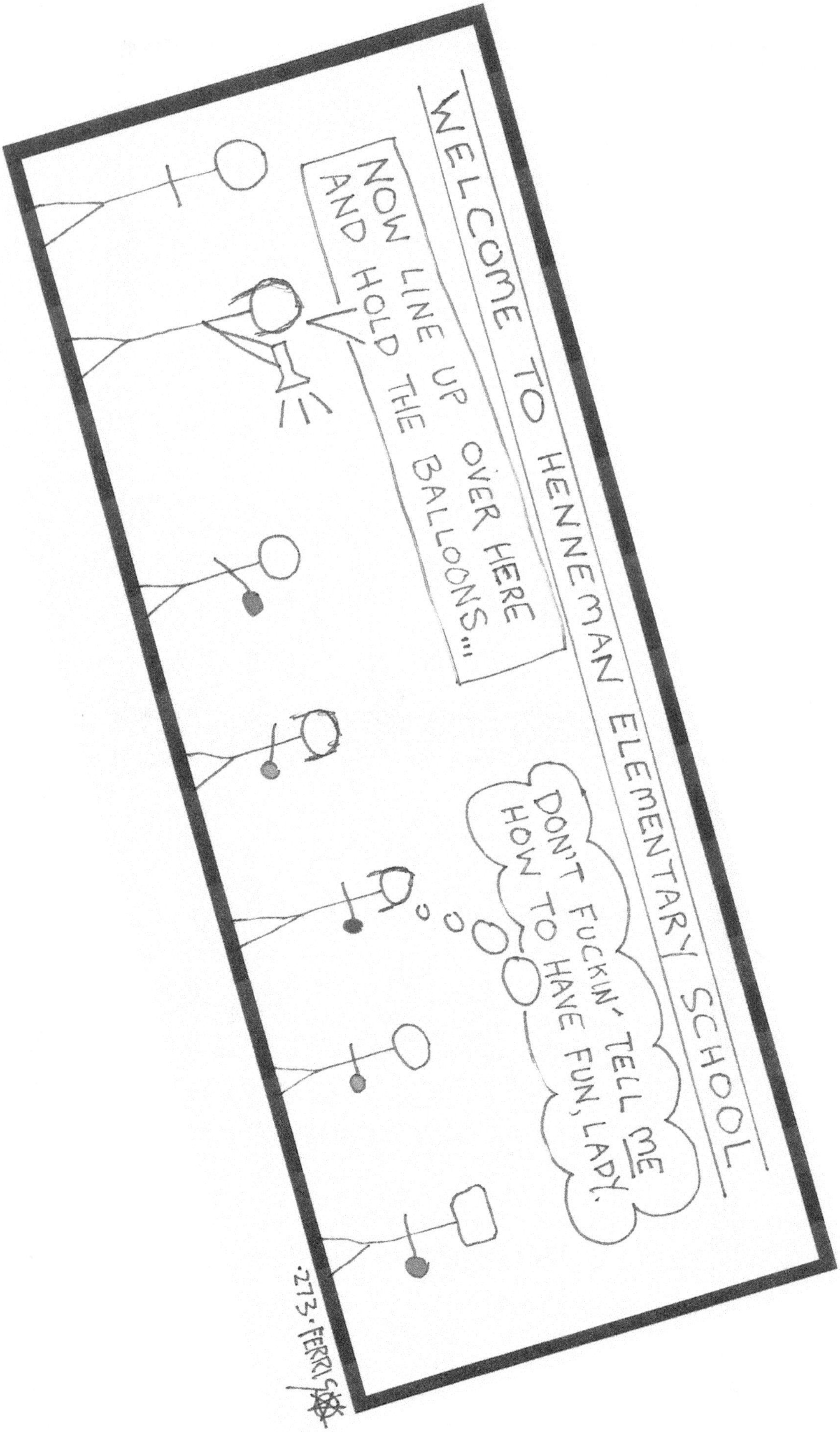
WELCOME TO HENNEMAN ELEMENTARY SCHOOL
NOW LINE UP OVER HERE AND HOLD THE BALLOONS...
DON'T FUCKIN' TELL ME HOW TO HAVE FUN, LADY.
·273·FERRIS

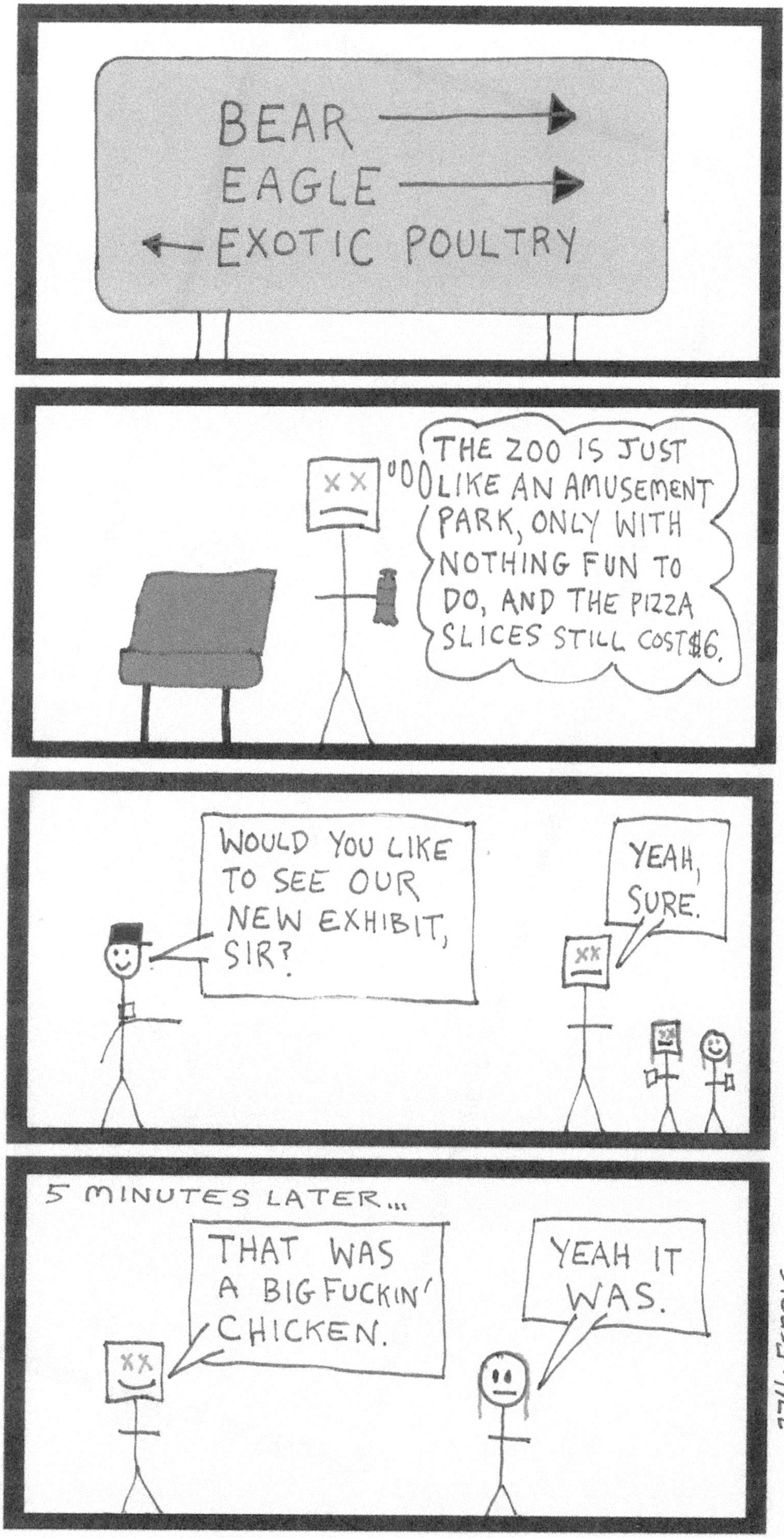
BEAR
EAGLE
EXOTIC POULTRY
THE ZOO IS JUST LIKE AN AMUSEMENT PARK, ONLY WITH NOTHING FUN TO DO, AND THE PIZZA SLICES STILL COST $6.
WOULD YOU LIKE TO SEE OUR NEW EXHIBIT, SIR?
YEAH, SURE.
5 MINUTES LATER...
THAT WAS A BIG FUCKIN' CHICKEN.
YEAH IT WAS.
•274• FERRIS

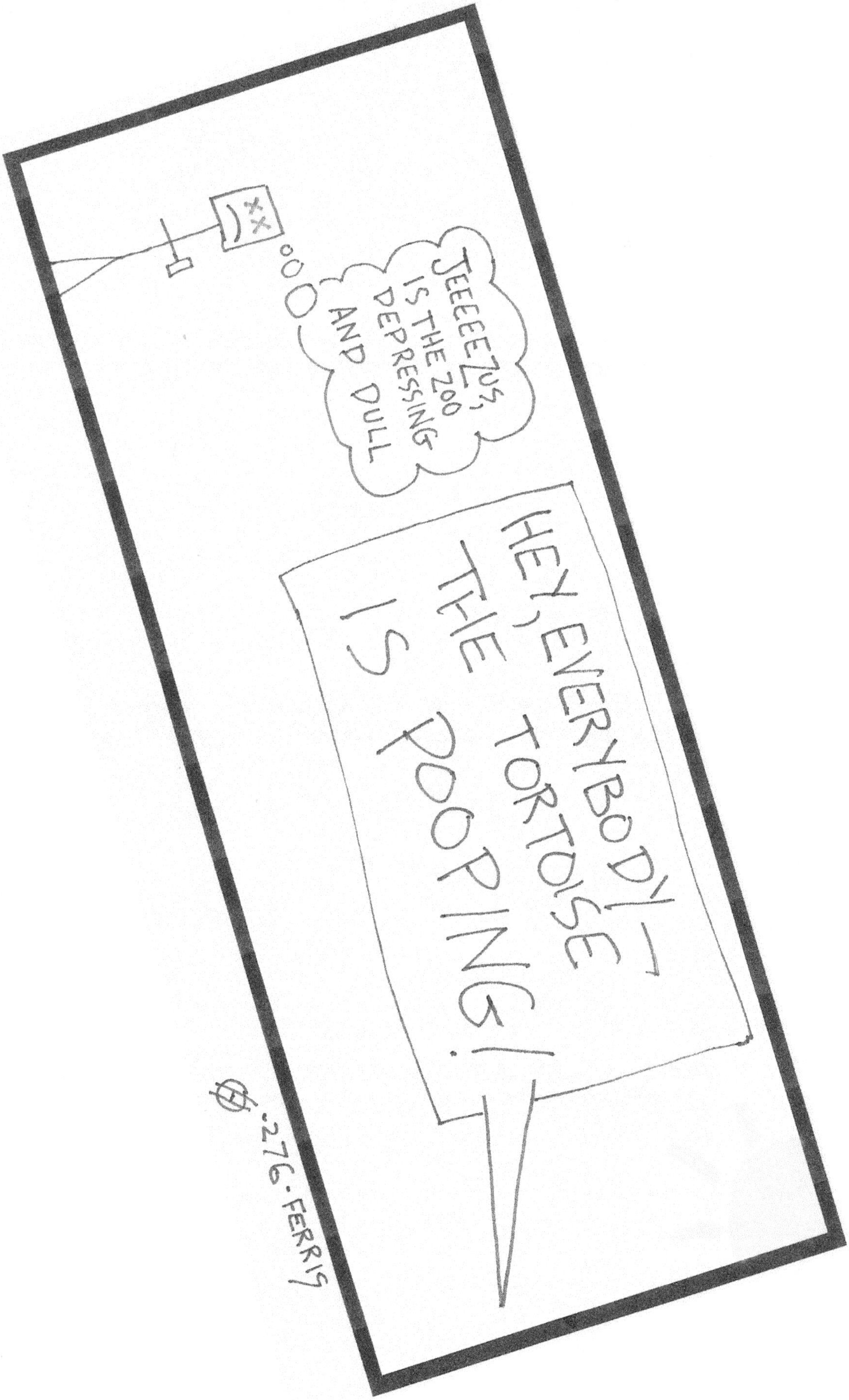
JEEEEEZUS, IS THE ZOO DEPRESSING AND DULL
HEY, EVERYBODY— THE TORTOISE IS POOPING!
·276·FERRIS

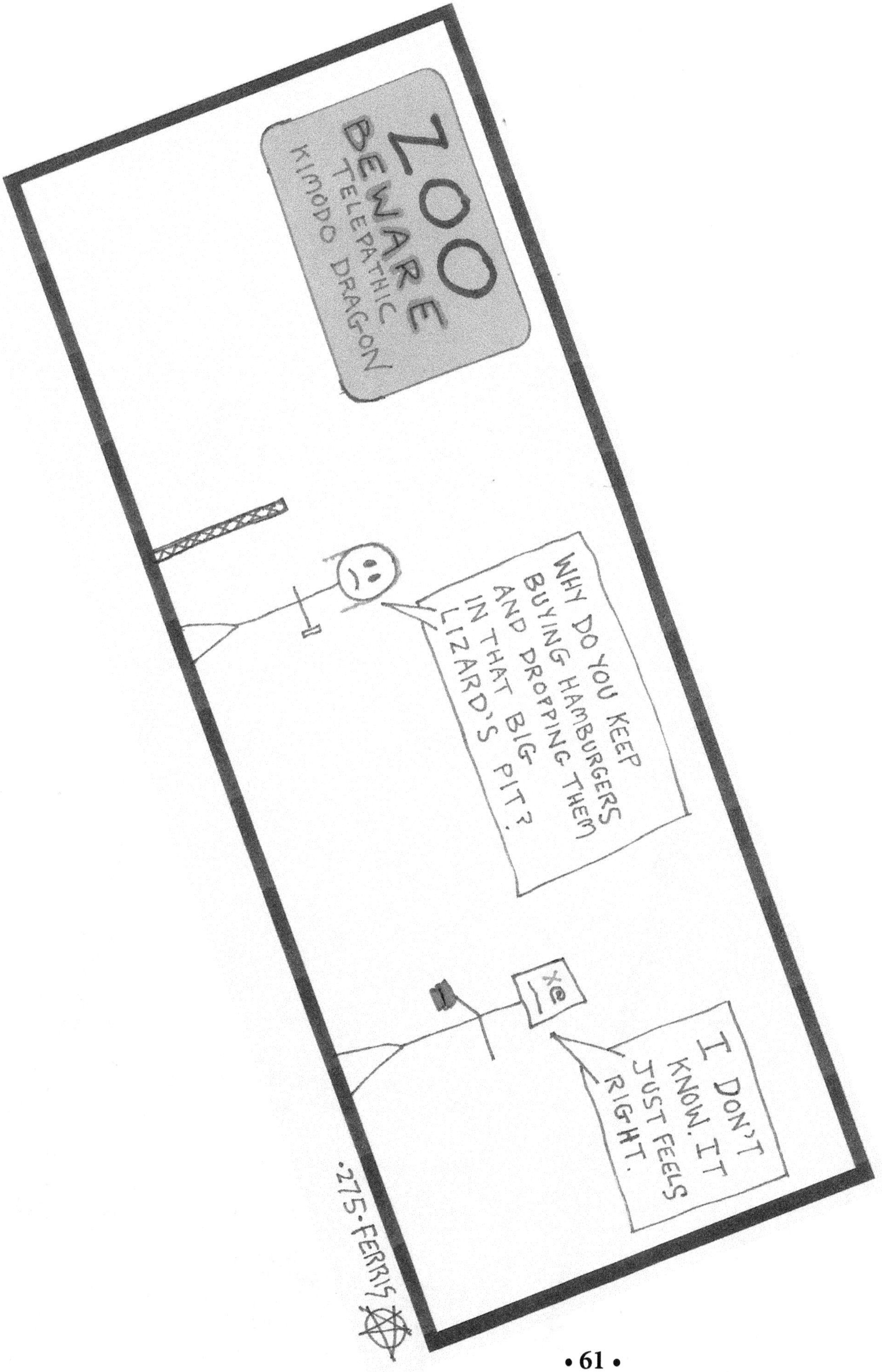
ZOO
BEWARE
TELEPATHIC
KIMODO DRAGON
WHY DO YOU KEEP BUYING HAMBURGERS AND DROPPING THEM IN THAT BIG LIZARD'S PIT?
I DON'T KNOW. IT JUST FEELS RIGHT.
·275·FERRIS

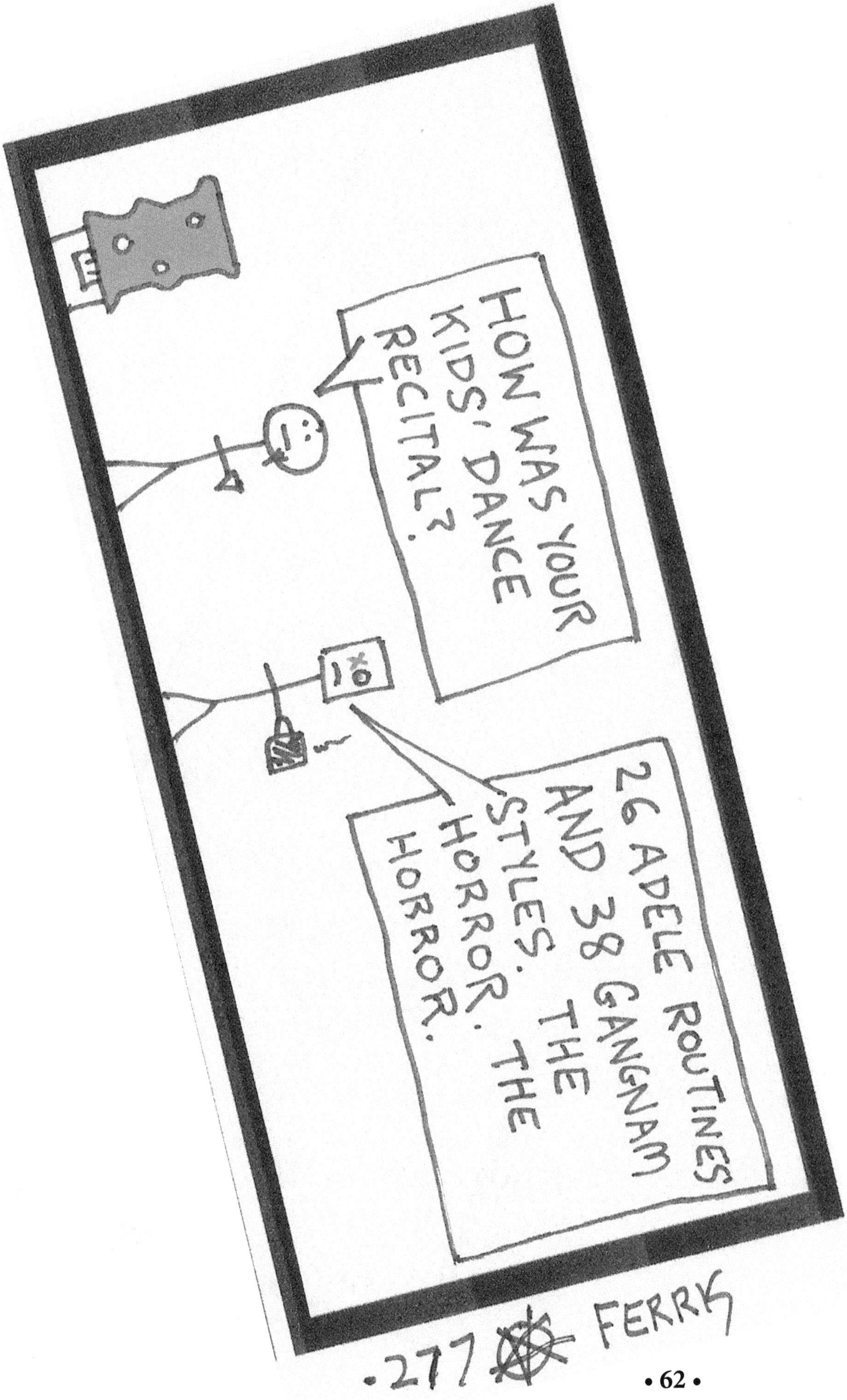
HOW WAS YOUR KIDS' DANCE RECITAL?
26 ADELE ROUTINES AND 38 GANGNAM STYLES. THE HORROR. THE HORROR.
•277 FERRK

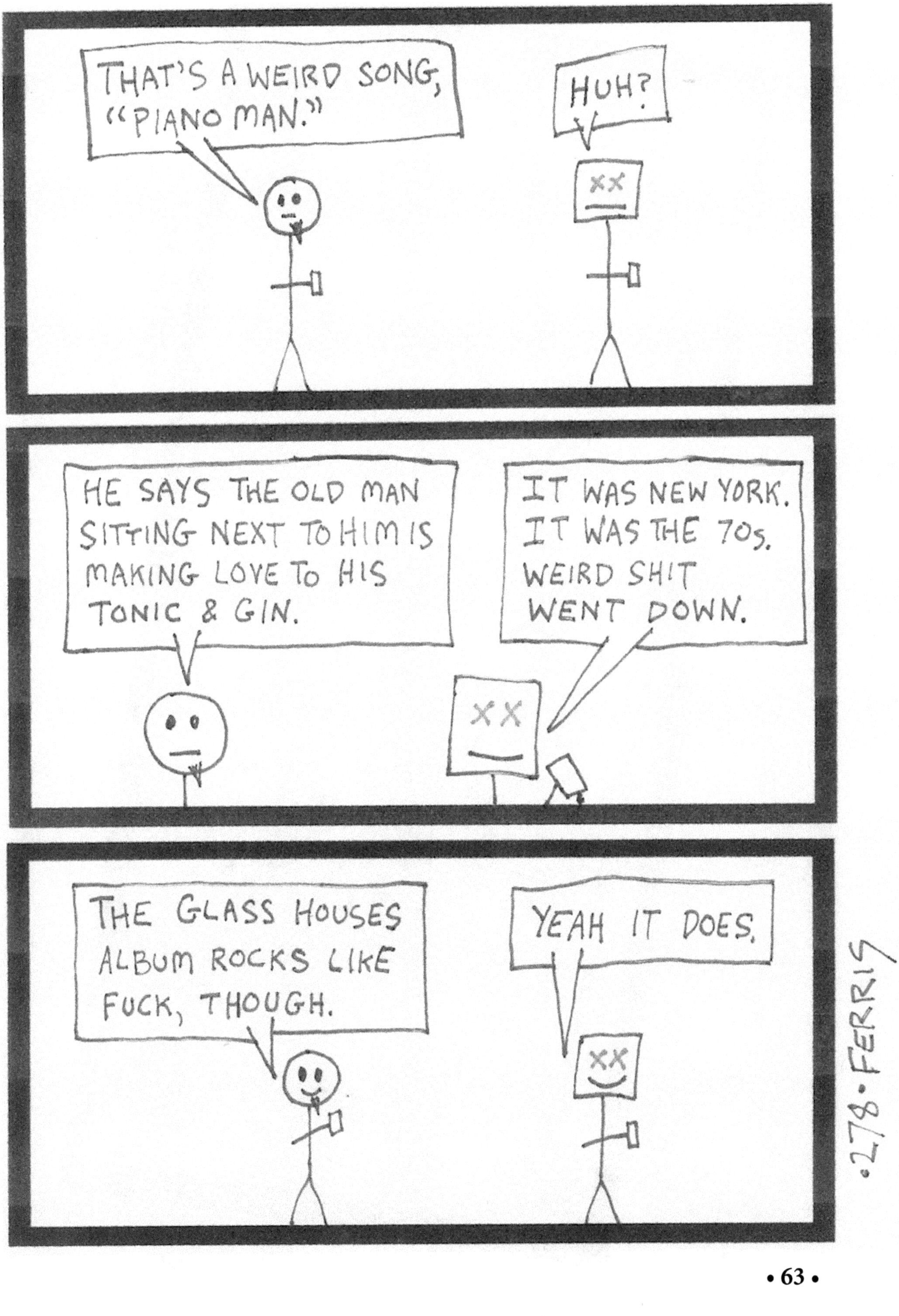
THAT'S A WEIRD SONG, "PIANO MAN."
HUH?
HE SAYS THE OLD MAN SITTING NEXT TO HIM IS MAKING LOVE TO HIS TONIC & GIN.
IT WAS NEW YORK. IT WAS THE 70s. WEIRD SHIT WENT DOWN.
THE GLASS HOUSES ALBUM ROCKS LIKE FUCK, THOUGH.
YEAH IT DOES.
•278•FERRIS

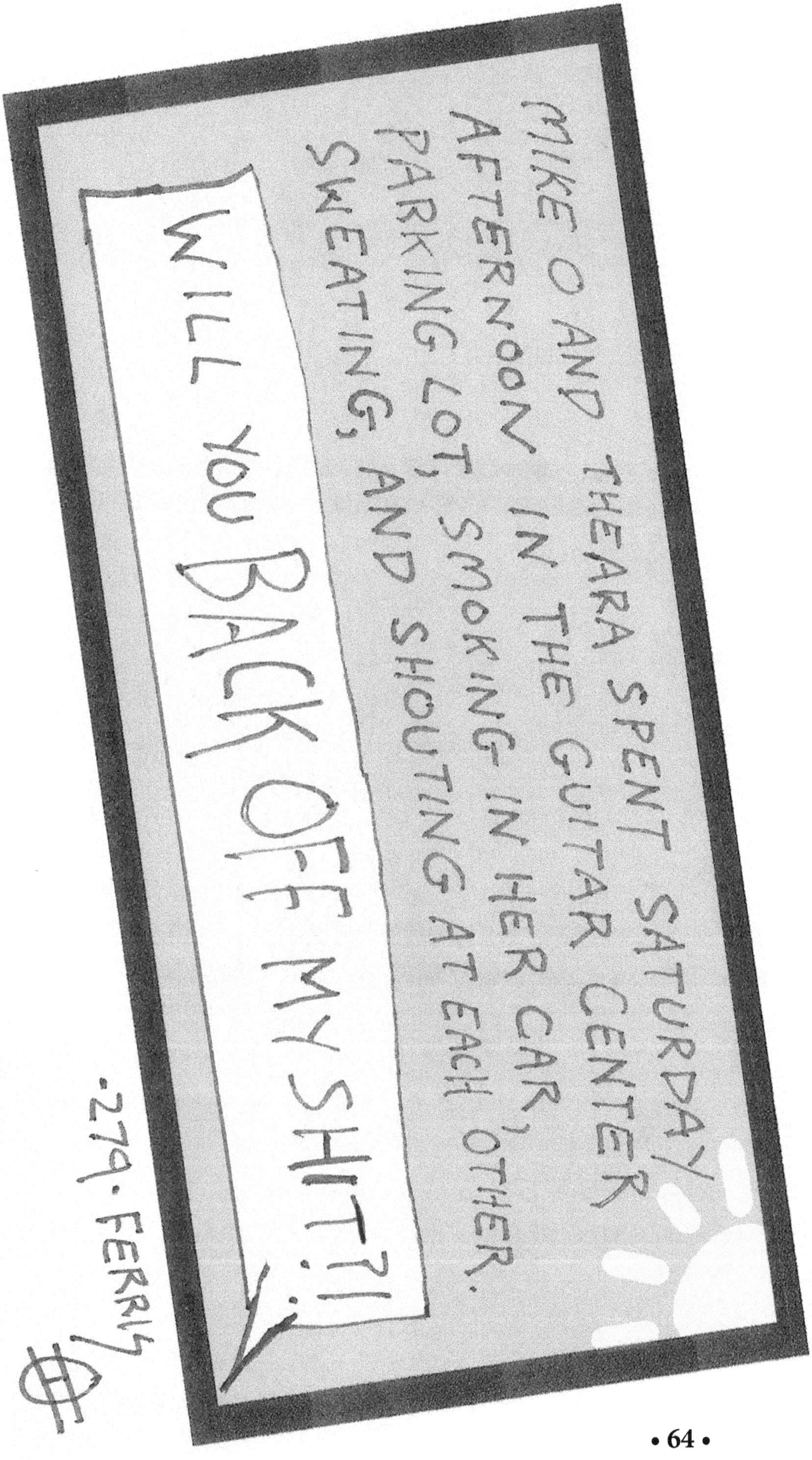
MIKE O AND THEARA SPENT SATURDAY AFTERNOON IN THE GUITAR CENTER PARKING LOT, SMOKING IN HER CAR, SWEATING, AND SHOUTING AT EACH OTHER.
WILL YOU BACK OFF MY SHIT?!
·279· FERRIS

1982....
THIS IS NEW AND SPECIAL!
THIS IS STUPID.
1989....
THIS IS NEW AND SPECIAL!
THIS SUCKS.
1998....
THIS IS NEW AND SPECIAL!
NO IT'S NOT.
2013....
THIS IS NEW AND SPECIAL!
FUCK THIS.
•280•FERRIS

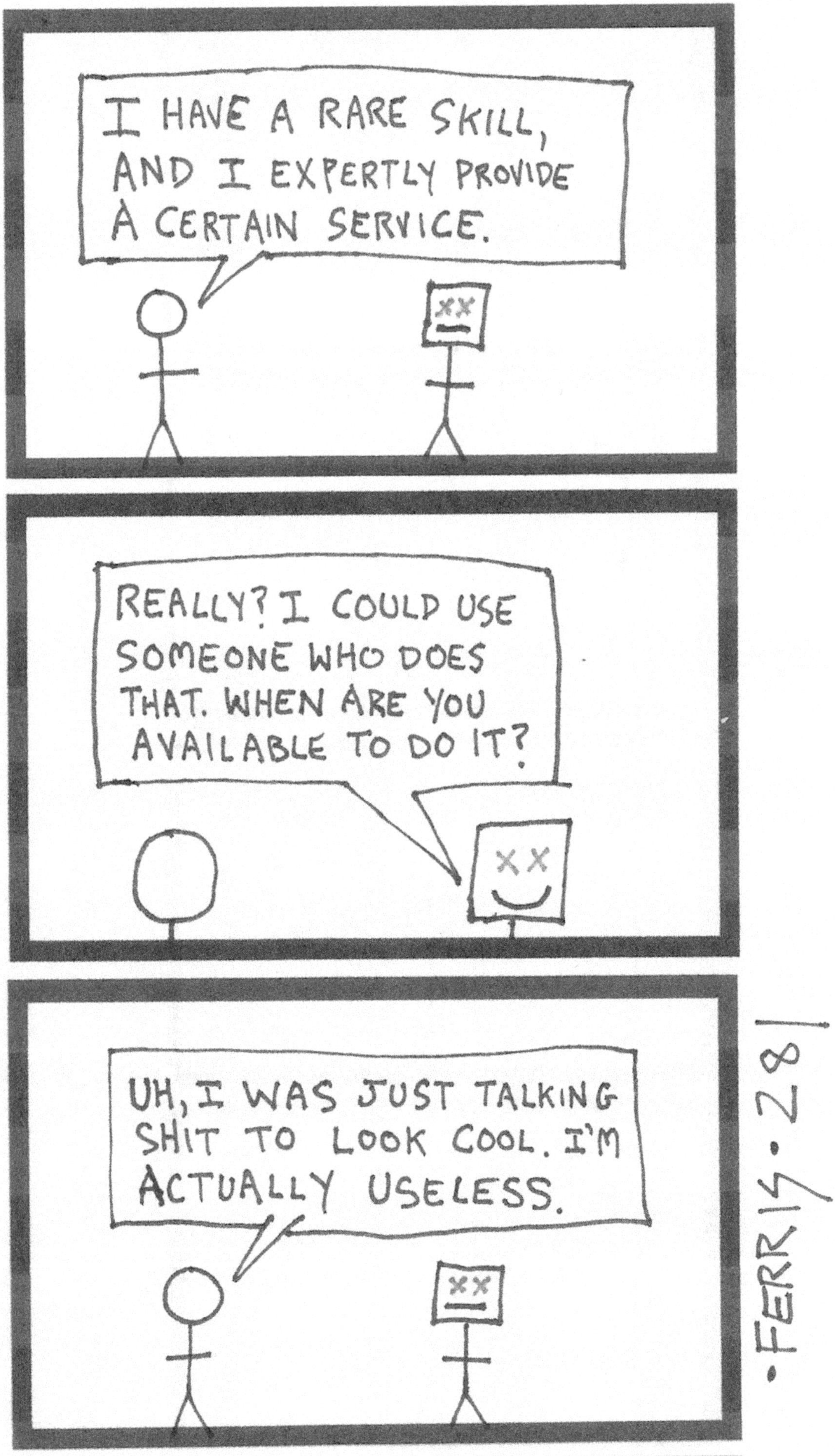
I HAVE A RARE SKILL, AND I EXPERTLY PROVIDE A CERTAIN SERVICE.
REALLY? I COULD USE SOMEONE WHO DOES THAT. WHEN ARE YOU AVAILABLE TO DO IT?
UH, I WAS JUST TALKING SHIT TO LOOK COOL. I'M ACTUALLY USELESS.
• FERRIS • 281

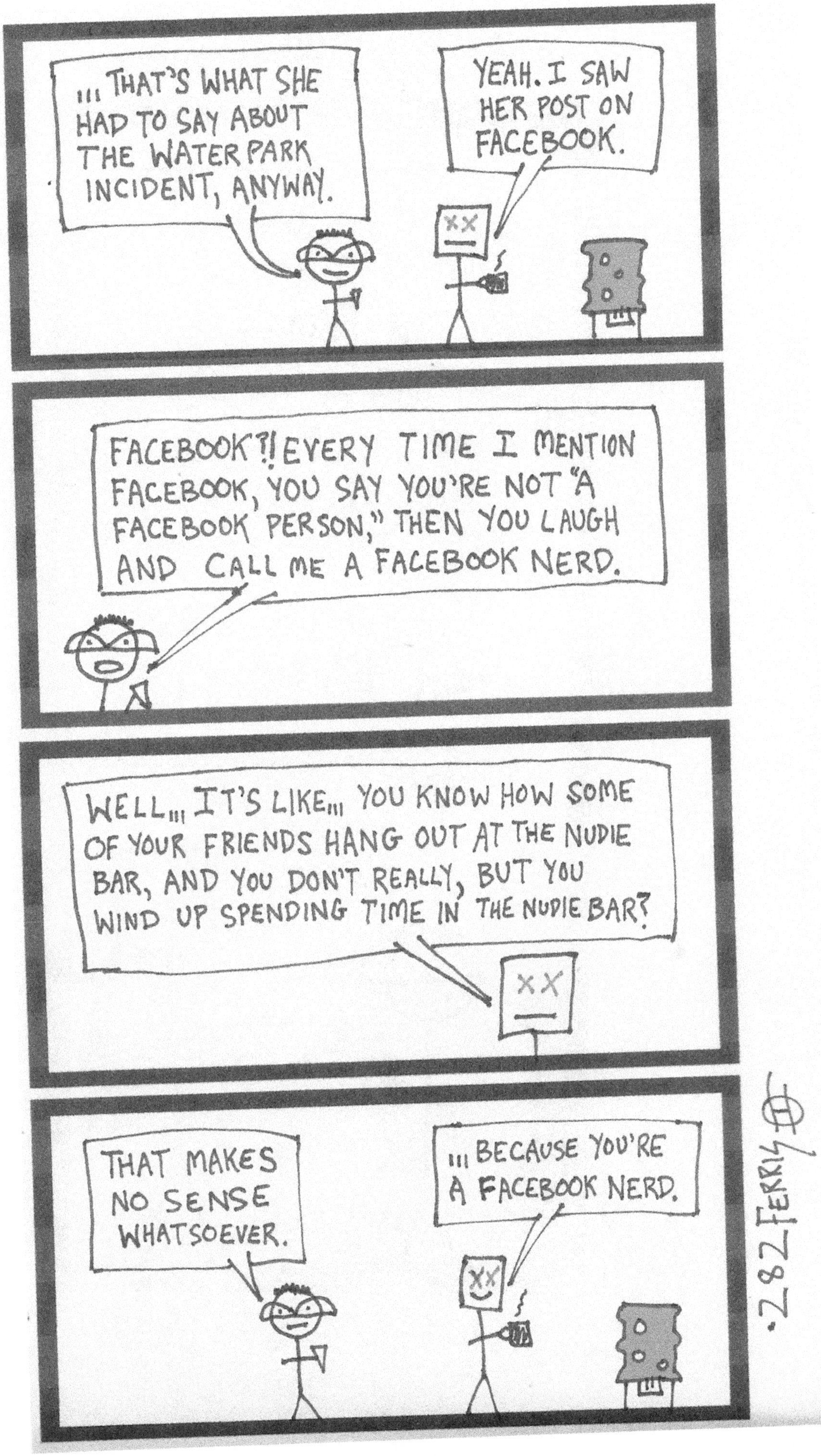
...THAT'S WHAT SHE HAD TO SAY ABOUT THE WATER PARK INCIDENT, ANYWAY.
YEAH. I SAW HER POST ON FACEBOOK.
FACEBOOK?! EVERY TIME I MENTION FACEBOOK, YOU SAY YOU'RE NOT "A FACEBOOK PERSON," THEN YOU LAUGH AND CALL ME A FACEBOOK NERD.
WELL... IT'S LIKE... YOU KNOW HOW SOME OF YOUR FRIENDS HANG OUT AT THE NUDIE BAR, AND YOU DON'T REALLY, BUT YOU WIND UP SPENDING TIME IN THE NUDIE BAR?
THAT MAKES NO SENSE WHATSOEVER.
...BECAUSE YOU'RE A FACEBOOK NERD.
·282 FERRIS

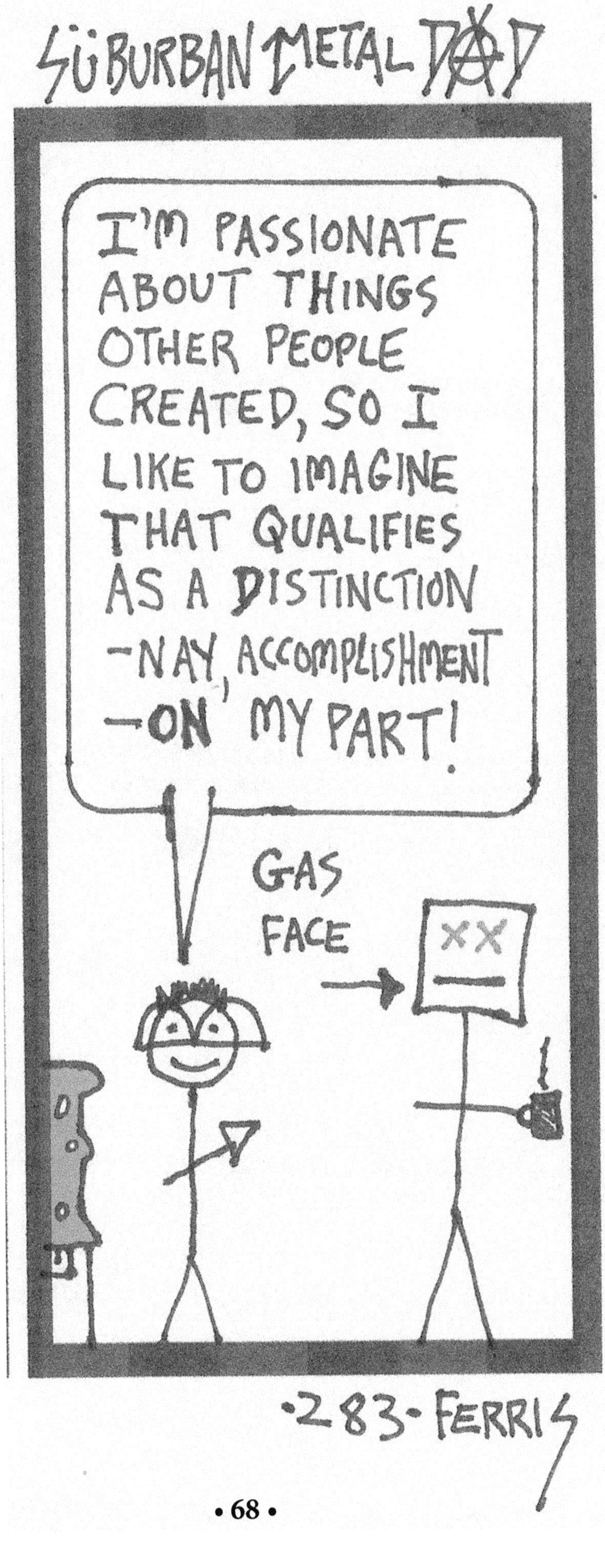
SÜBURBAN METAL DAD
I'M PASSIONATE ABOUT THINGS OTHER PEOPLE CREATED, SO I LIKE TO IMAGINE THAT QUALIFIES AS A DISTINCTION —NAY, ACCOMPLISHMENT —ON MY PART!
GAS FACE
•283• FERRIS

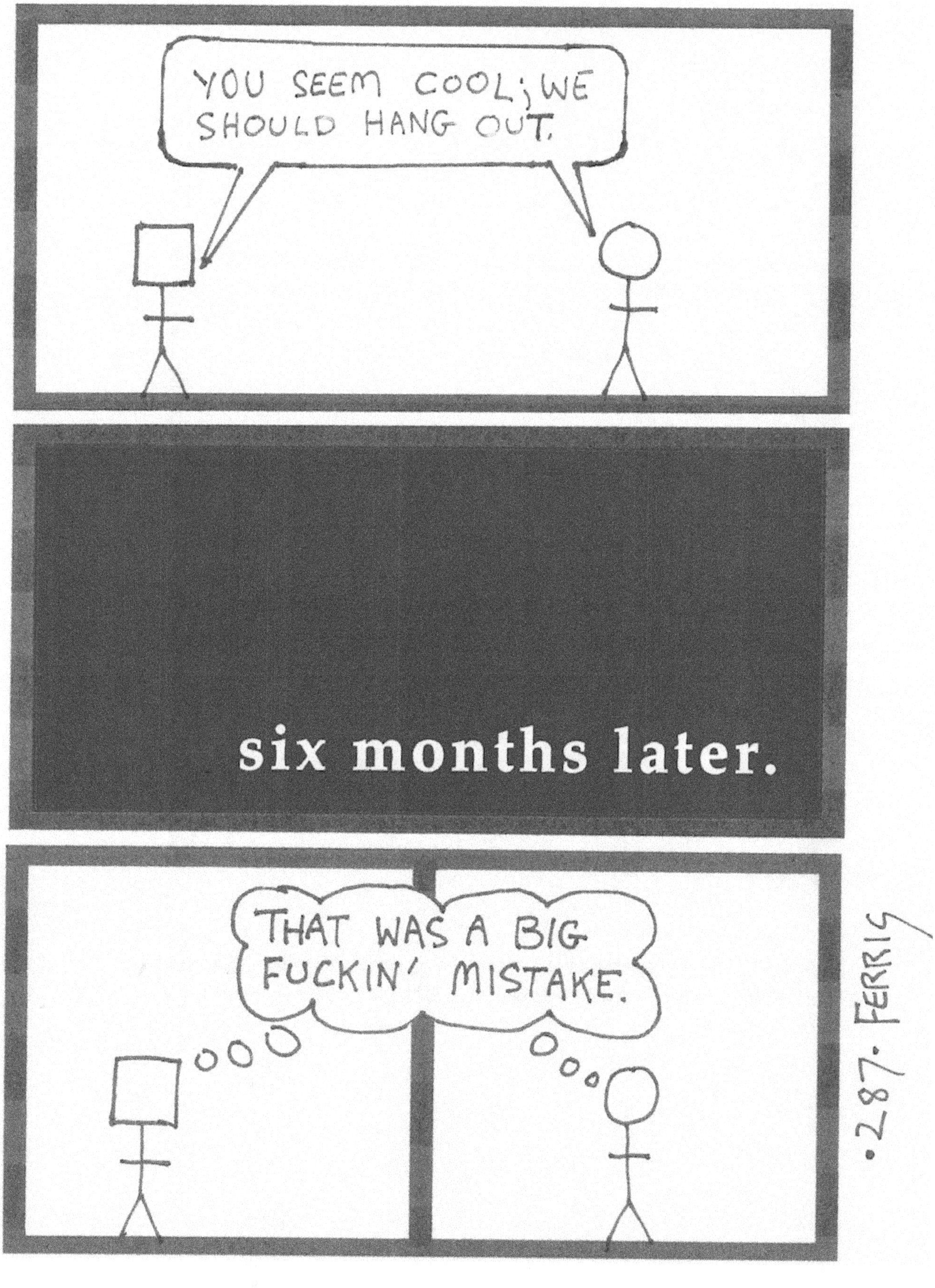
YOU SEEM COOL; WE SHOULD HANG OUT.
six months later.
THAT WAS A BIG FUCKIN' MISTAKE.
•287• FERRIS

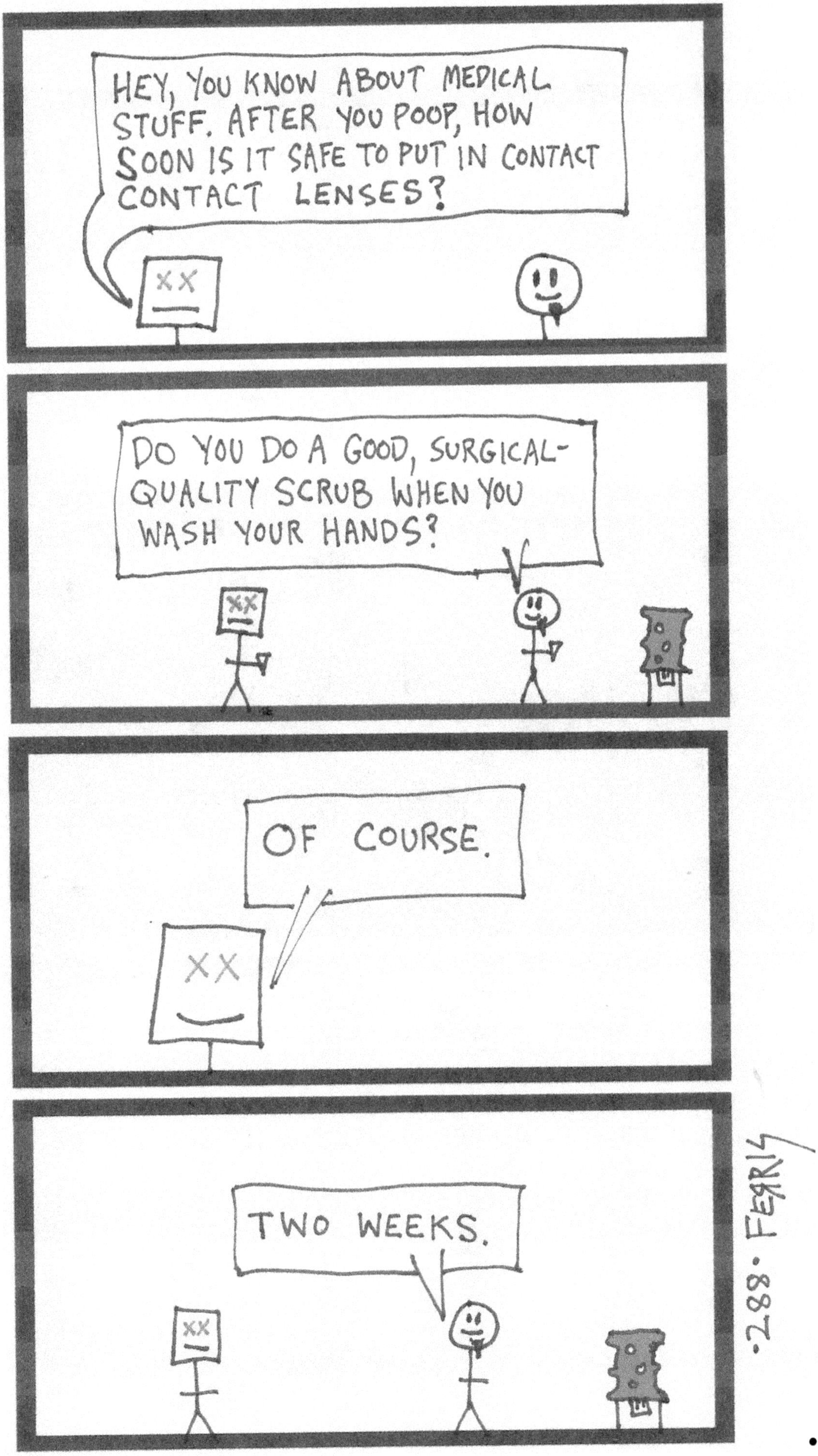
HEY, YOU KNOW ABOUT MEDICAL STUFF. AFTER YOU POOP, HOW SOON IS IT SAFE TO PUT IN CONTACT CONTACT LENSES?
DO YOU DO A GOOD, SURGICAL-QUALITY SCRUB WHEN YOU WASH YOUR HANDS?
OF COURSE.
TWO WEEKS.
·2.88· FERRIS

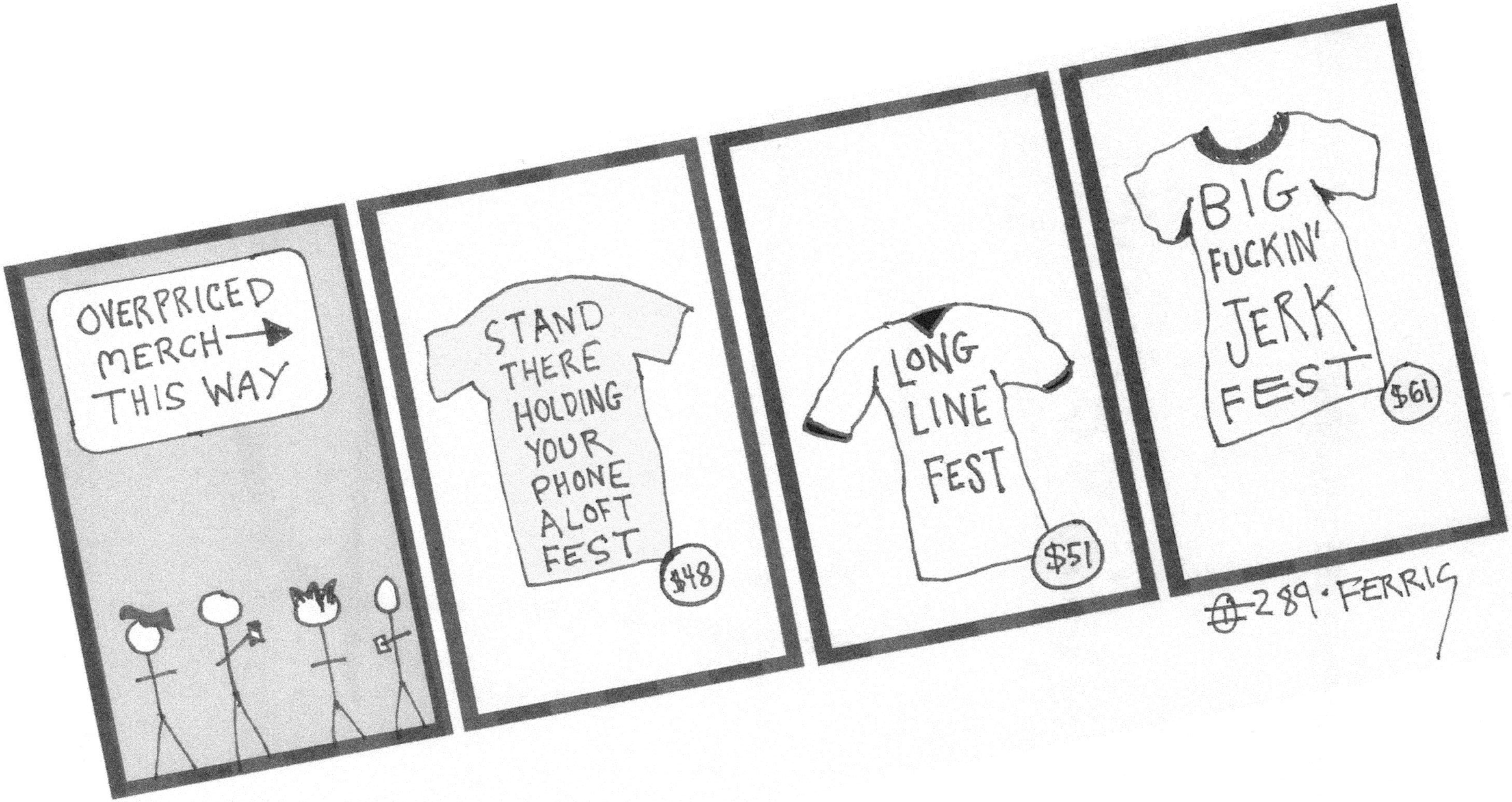
OVERPRICED MERCH → THIS WAY
STAND THERE HOLDING YOUR PHONE ALOFT FEST
$48
LONG LINE FEST
$51
BIG FUCKIN' JERK FEST
$61
289 · FERRIS

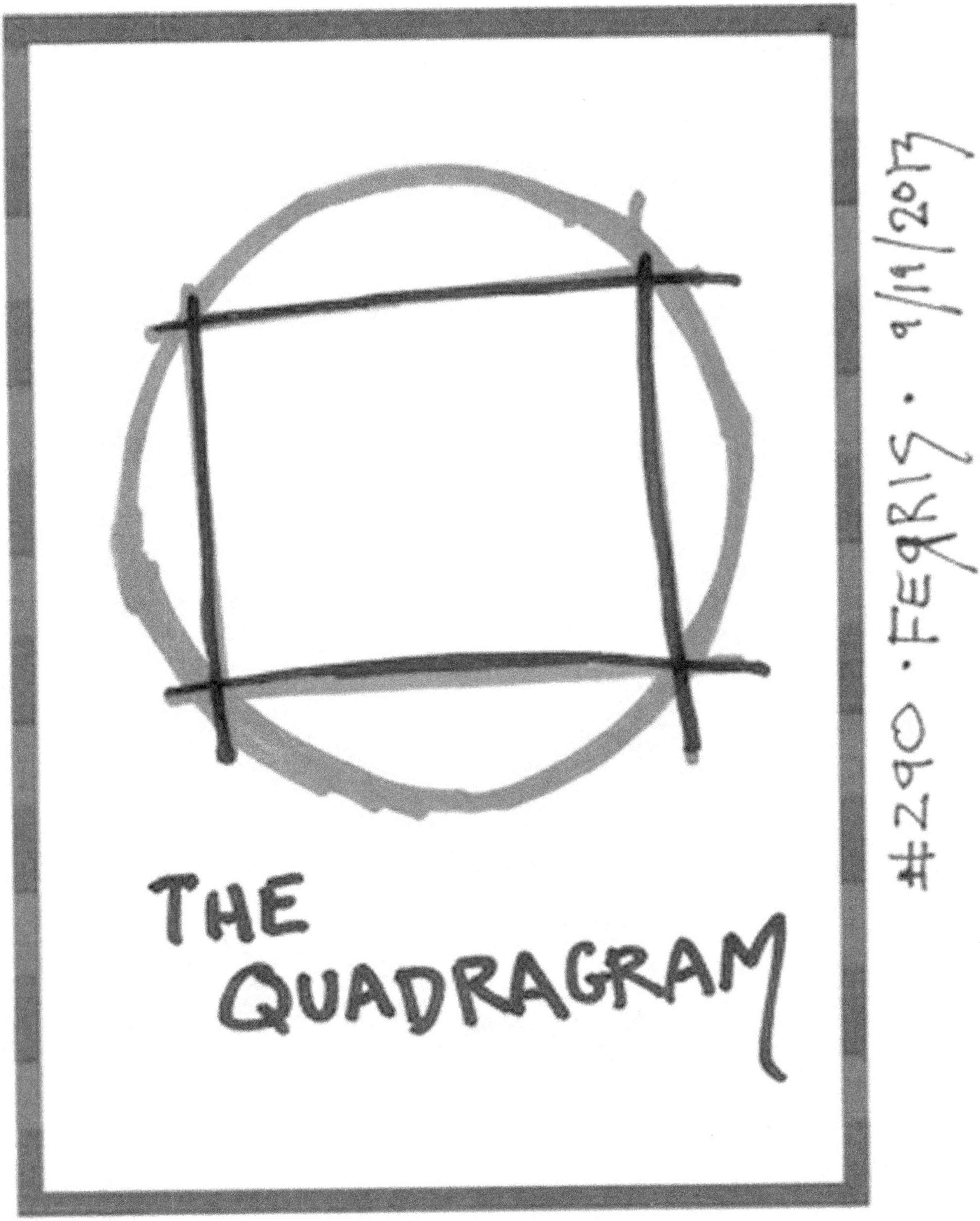
THE QUADRAGRAM
#290 · FERRIS · 9/19/2017

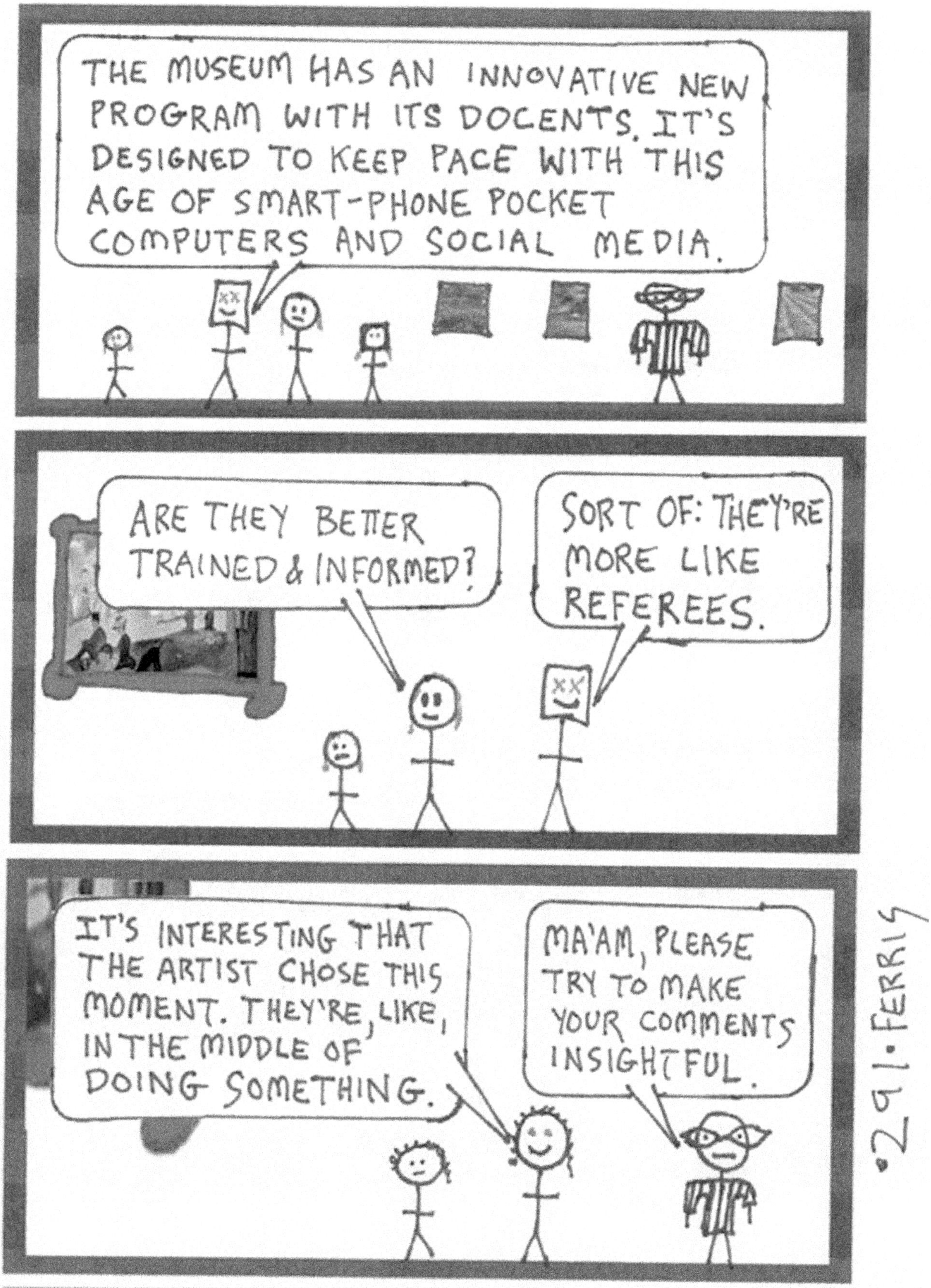
THE MUSEUM HAS AN INNOVATIVE NEW PROGRAM WITH ITS DOCENTS. IT'S DESIGNED TO KEEP PACE WITH THIS AGE OF SMART-PHONE POCKET COMPUTERS AND SOCIAL MEDIA.
ARE THEY BETTER TRAINED & INFORMED?
SORT OF: THEY'RE MORE LIKE REFEREES.
IT'S INTERESTING THAT THE ARTIST CHOSE THIS MOMENT. THEY'RE, LIKE, IN THE MIDDLE OF DOING SOMETHING.
MA'AM, PLEASE TRY TO MAKE YOUR COMMENTS INSIGHTFUL.
©291 • FERRIS

AS THIS GUITAR T-SHIRT CLEARLY DEMONSTRATES, I'M PART OF THIS ART THING TOO, MAN!
FENDER
I'M SORRY, SIR: YOU CAN'T TAKE NOTES IN HERE.
•292•FERRIS

NO DECONSTRUCTION
MA'AM, WE ASK THAT YOU DON'T INTERPRET THE ART FOR OTHER PATRONS.
NOW THIS ONE...
I'M SORRY, SIR: YOU CAN'T MAKE OBSERVATIONS IN HERE.
·293 FERRIS

this is not an empty page

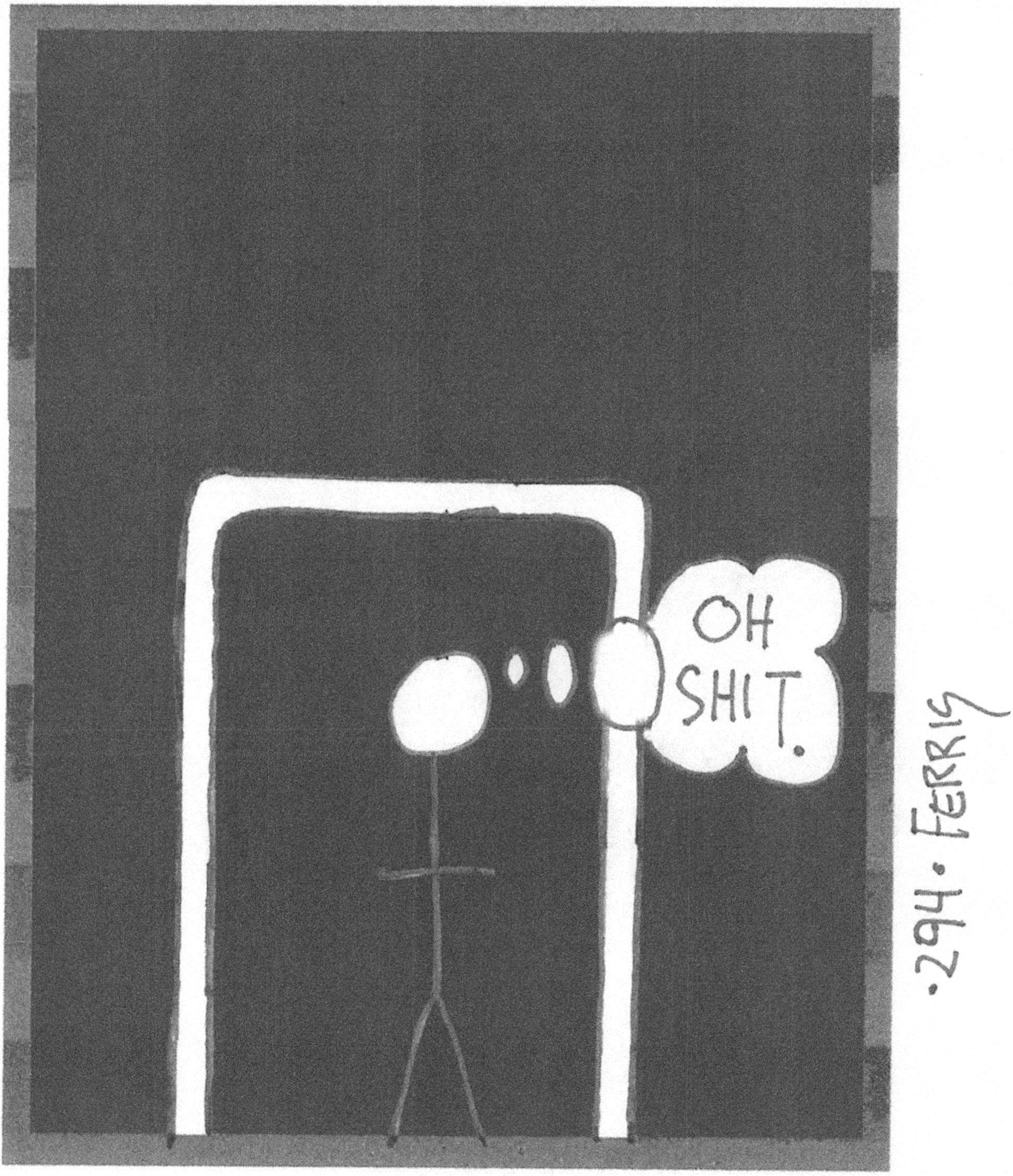
OH SHIT.
•294• FERRIS

"grab the shaft."

"move the head joint."

"put your lips over the hole."

(flute lesson)

295. FERRIS

EXCLUSIVE RECAP OF THE BRAINSTORMING SESSIONS THAT CULMINATED IN THE YAHOO! MAIL REDESIGN
DUH
DUH DUH DUH
DUH
UH-DUH
UH-DUH
DUH DUH!
·296.66· FERRIS

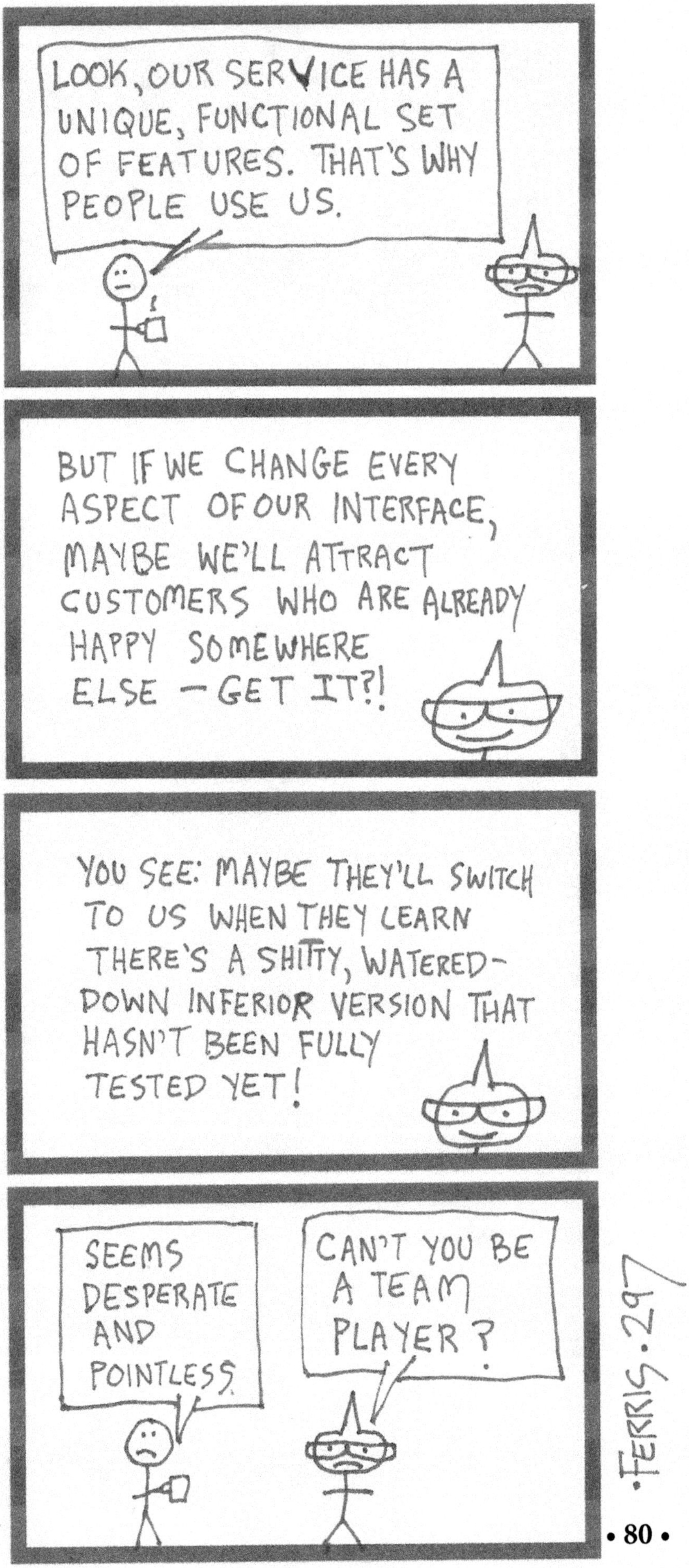
LOOK, OUR SERVICE HAS A UNIQUE, FUNCTIONAL SET OF FEATURES. THAT'S WHY PEOPLE USE US.
BUT IF WE CHANGE EVERY ASPECT OF OUR INTERFACE, MAYBE WE'LL ATTRACT CUSTOMERS WHO ARE ALREADY HAPPY SOMEWHERE ELSE — GET IT?!
YOU SEE: MAYBE THEY'LL SWITCH TO US WHEN THEY LEARN THERE'S A SHITTY, WATERED-DOWN INFERIOR VERSION THAT HASN'T BEEN FULLY TESTED YET!
SEEMS DESPERATE AND POINTLESS
CAN'T YOU BE A TEAM PLAYER?
·FERRIS·297

OHIO

MORON SLOWPOKE

THE NO PASSING LANE STATE

FERRIS 298

"SMD #298: Ohio License Plate."

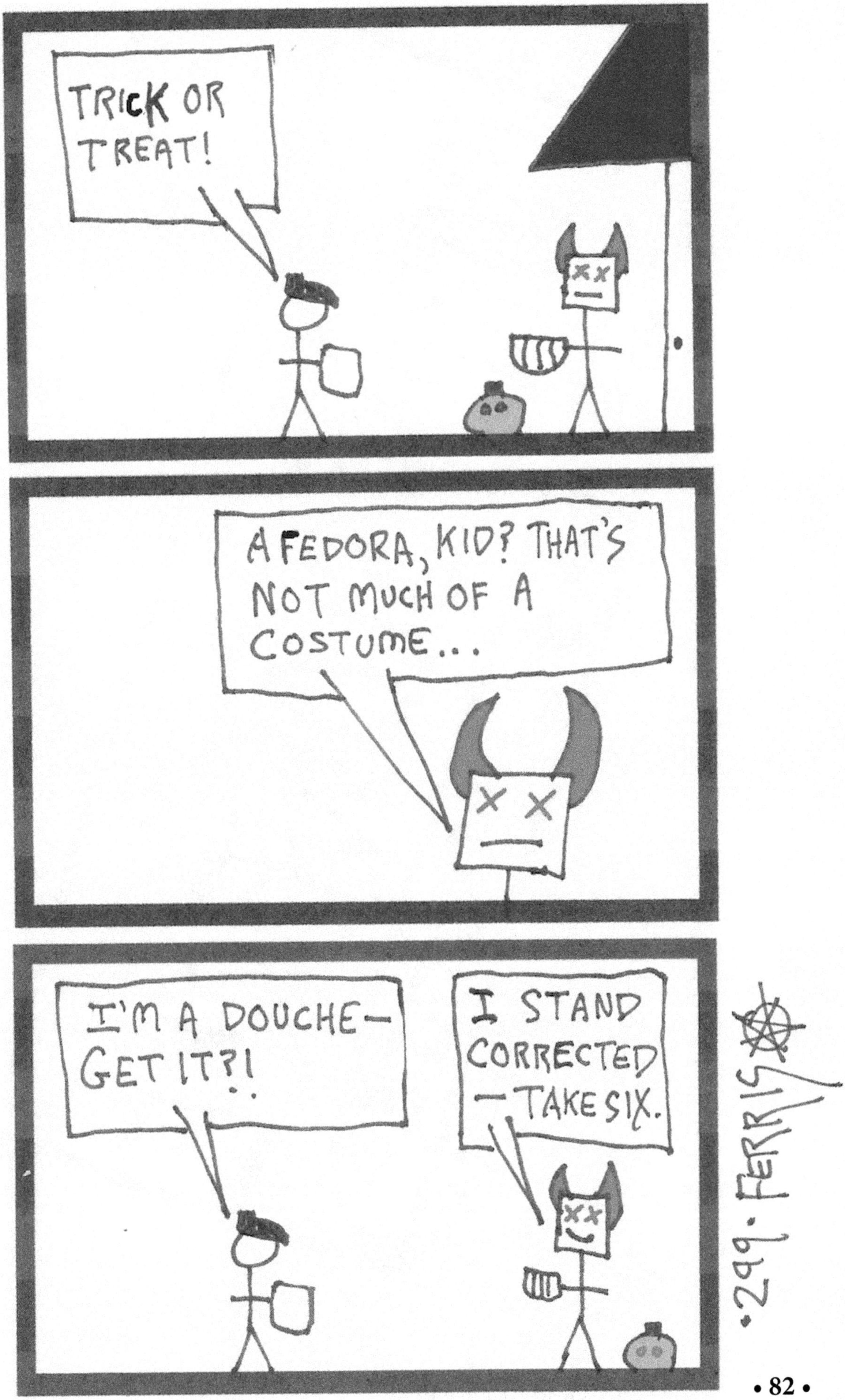
TRICK OR TREAT!
A FEDORA, KID? THAT'S NOT MUCH OF A COSTUME...
I'M A DOUCHE— GET IT?!
I STAND CORRECTED — TAKE SIX.
•299• FERRIS

BOOMF!
WHAT ARE YOU?
A SUCCUBUS.
TAKE WHATEVER YOU WANT.
I'LL SEE YOU LATER, THEN.
300·FERRIS

HOW DO WE DO TRICK-OR-TREATING?
YOU WALK UP TO HOUSES, RING THE BELL, AND SAY "TRICK OR TREAT."
IS IT LEGAL?
OF COURSE IT'S LEGAL.
I WOULDN'T WANT TO BE ACCUSED OF TWERKING.
•FERRIS #301

# YEAR

# IV

# (ZoSo)

[2014]

WELCOME TO HELL, SLAPPY.
AW, SHIT; THE NUNS WERE RIGHT.
FIRST FOR YOUR AFTERLIFE OF RELENTLESS TORMENT, YOU'RE GOING TO WAL-MART ON A SATURDAY AFTERNOON!!!
CAN I JUST HAVE A WHITE-HOT POKER JAMMED UP MY ASS FOR ALL ETERNITY INSTEAD?
NO! YOU'RE NOT GETTING OF THAT EASY! WELCOME TO HELL! IT'S WAL-MART FOR YOU!
I KNEW I SHOULD HAVE COURTESY FLUSHED.
·FERRIS #302

BOK
BOK
BOK
BAW
BA-GAWK
EDWARD CHICKENHANDS
FERRIS #303

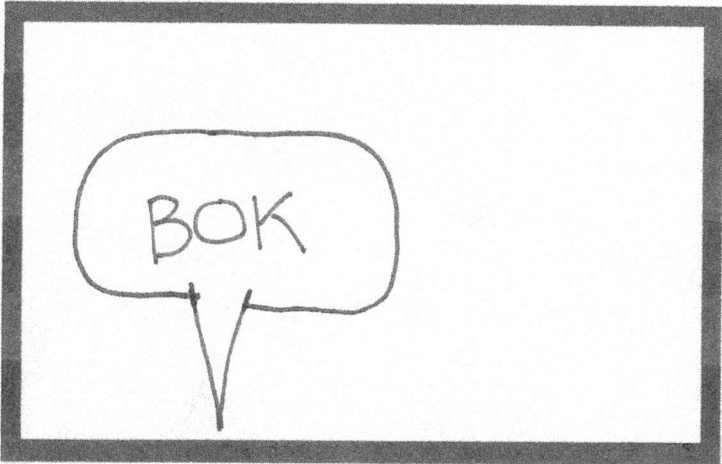

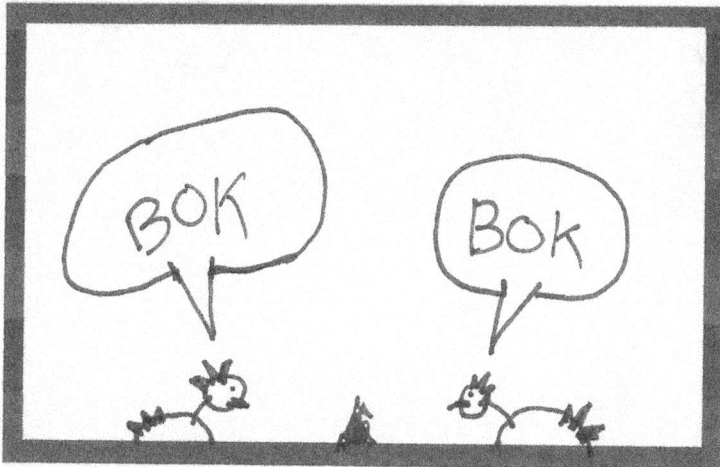

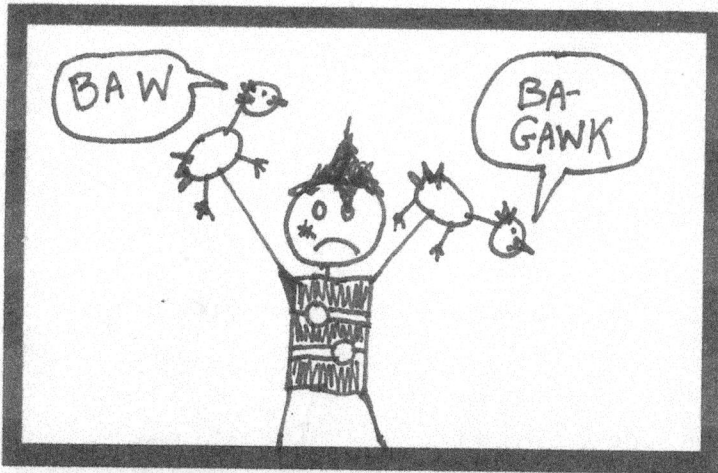

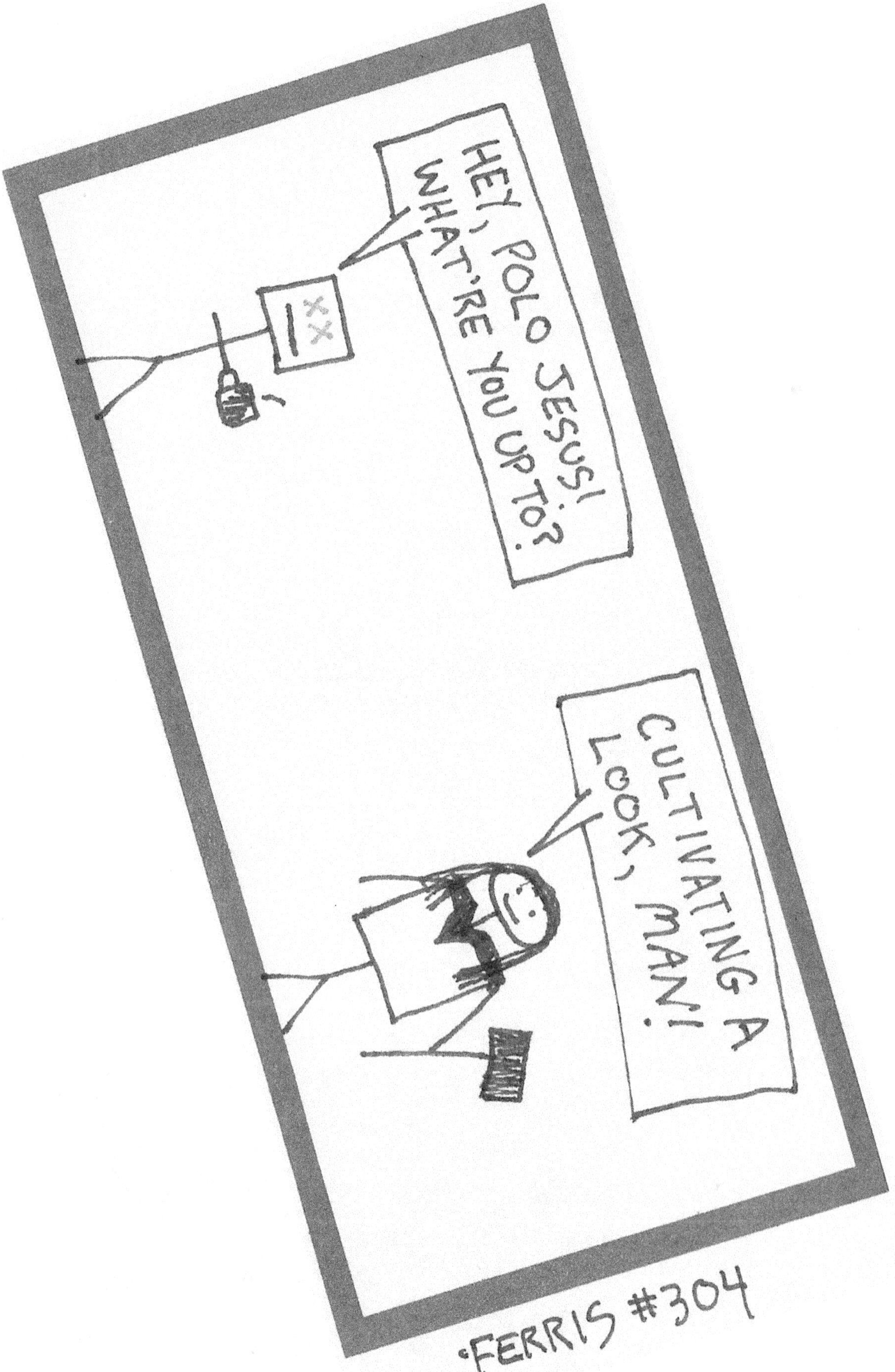
HEY, POLO JESUS! WHAT'RE YOU UP TO?
CULTIVATING A LOOK, MAN!
FERRIS #304

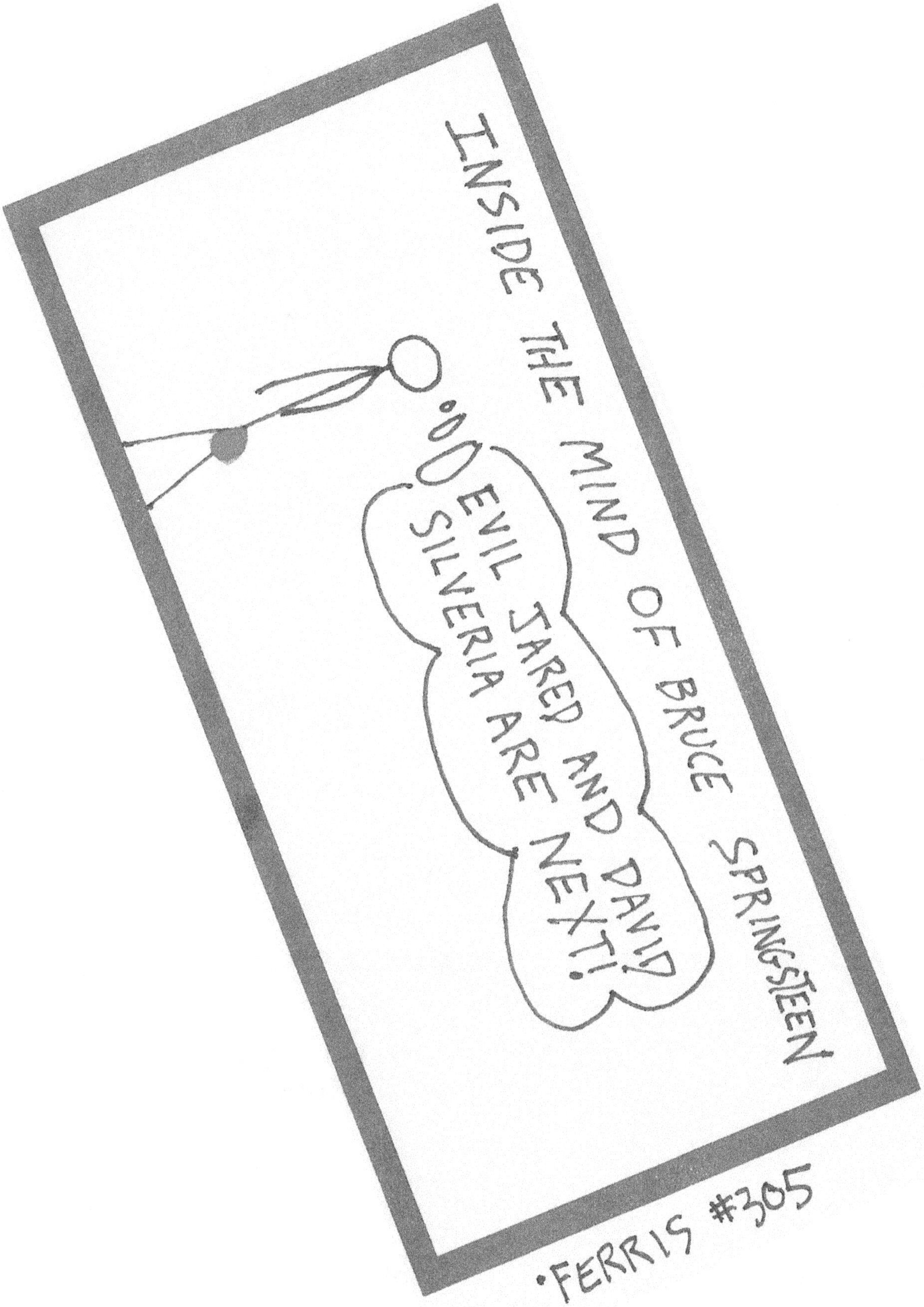
INSIDE THE MIND OF BRUCE SPRINGSTEEN
EVIL JARED AND DAVID SILVERIA ARE NEXT!
•FERRIS #305

**This one was particularly funny and timely.**

DID YOU UNFRIEND ME ON FACEBOOK?!
YEAH, I CAN'T DEAL WITH YOUR PUSSY FRIENDS.
YOU'RE COOL, THOUGH.
FERRIS #306.66

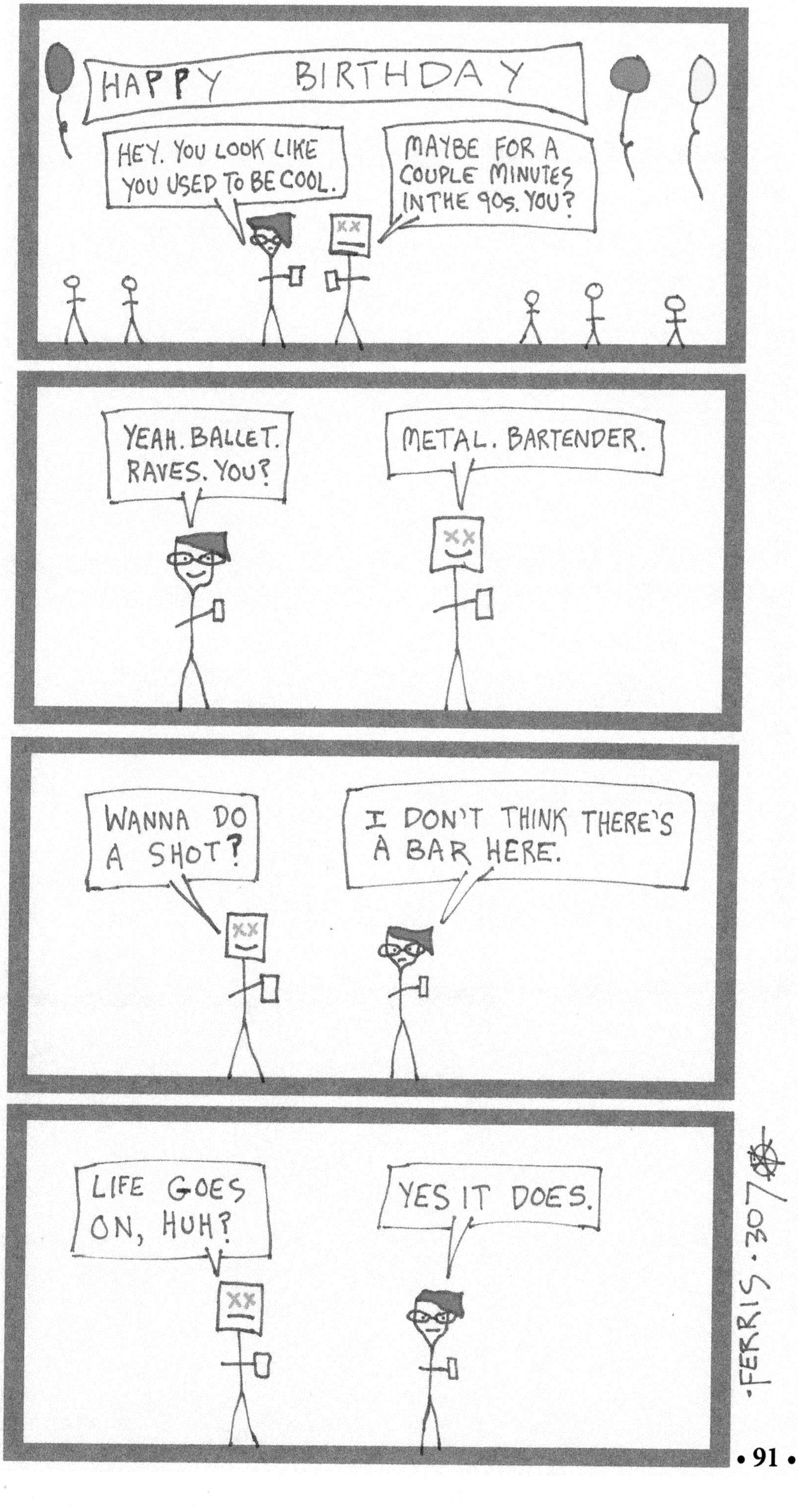
HAPPY BIRTHDAY
HEY. YOU LOOK LIKE YOU USED TO BE COOL.
MAYBE FOR A COUPLE MINUTES IN THE 90s. YOU?
YEAH. BALLET. RAVES. YOU?
METAL. BARTENDER.
WANNA DO A SHOT?
I DON'T THINK THERE'S A BAR HERE.
LIFE GOES ON, HUH?
YES IT DOES.
FERRIS · 307

GET INVOLVED IN MY BULLSHIT! GET INVOLVED IN MY BULLSHIT!
HEY, DO YOU WANNA CHECK OUT SOME OF MY BULLSHIT?
GEE, MAN, I DON'T KNOW, I'M KINDA BUSY.
·308 FERRIS

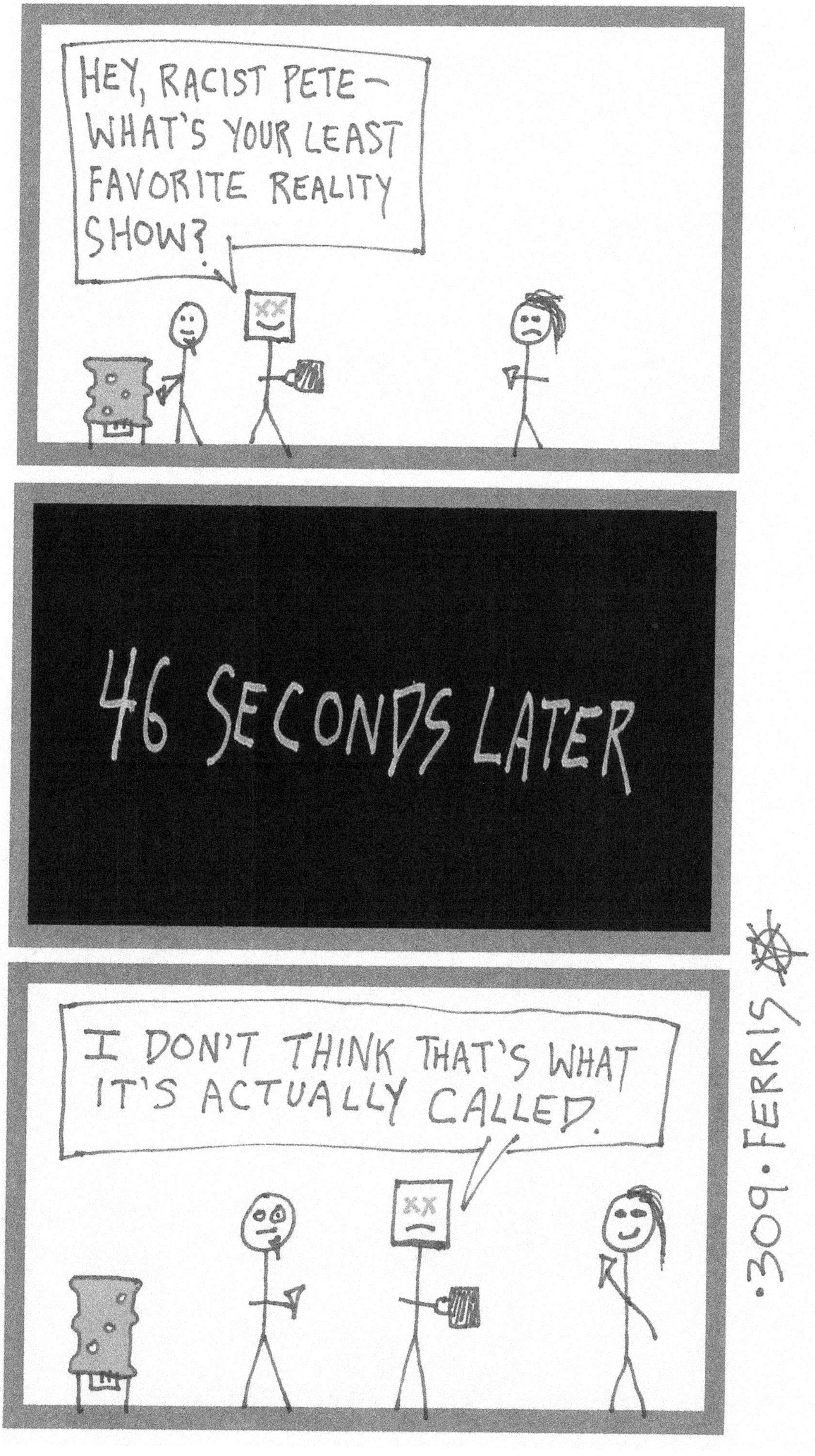
HEY, RACIST PETE— WHAT'S YOUR LEAST FAVORITE REALITY SHOW?
46 SECONDS LATER
I DON'T THINK THAT'S WHAT IT'S ACTUALLY CALLED.
•309•FERRIS

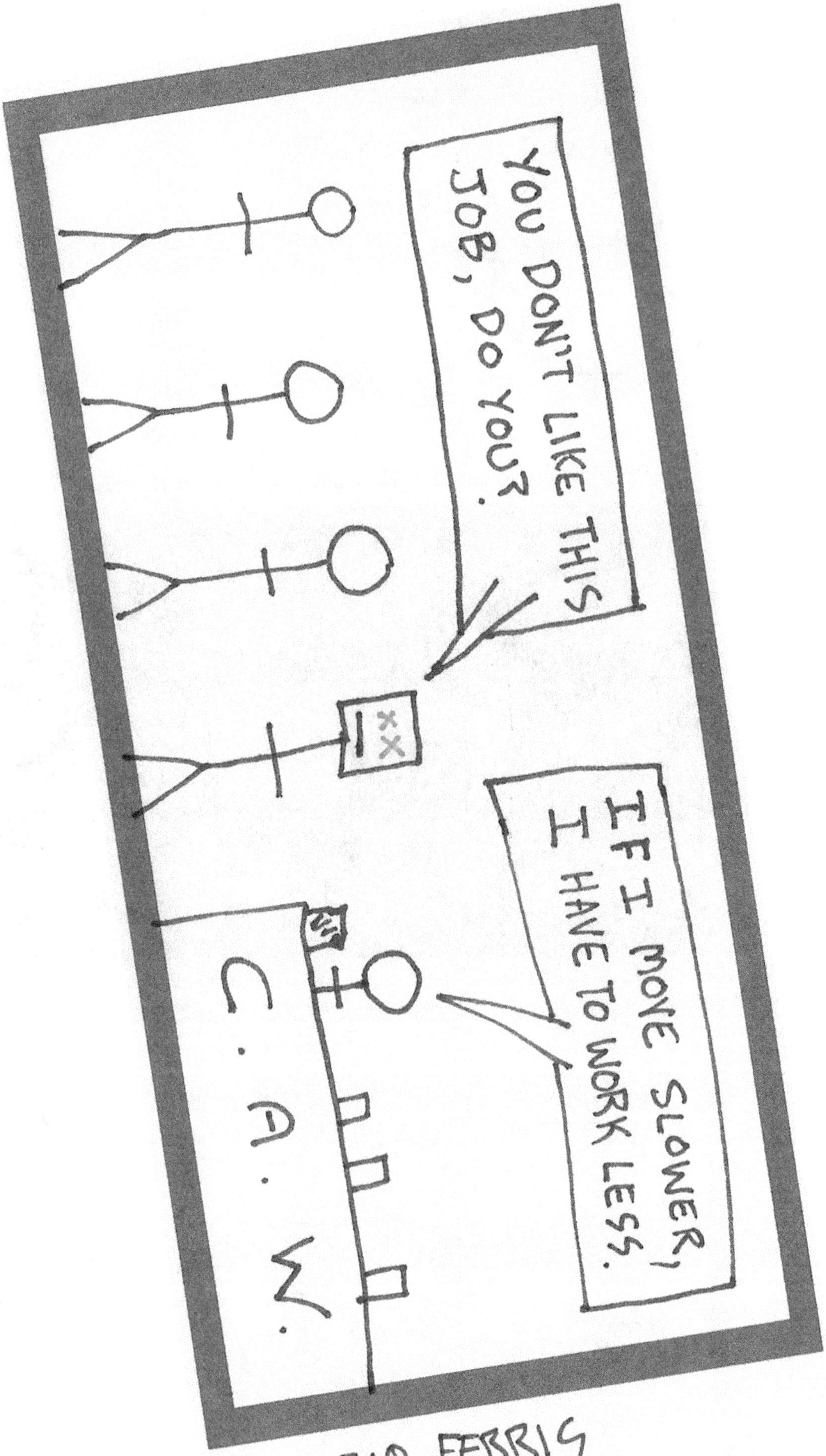
YOU DON'T LIKE THIS JOB, DO YOU?
IF I MOVE SLOWER, I HAVE TO WORK LESS.
C.A.W.

•310• FERRIS

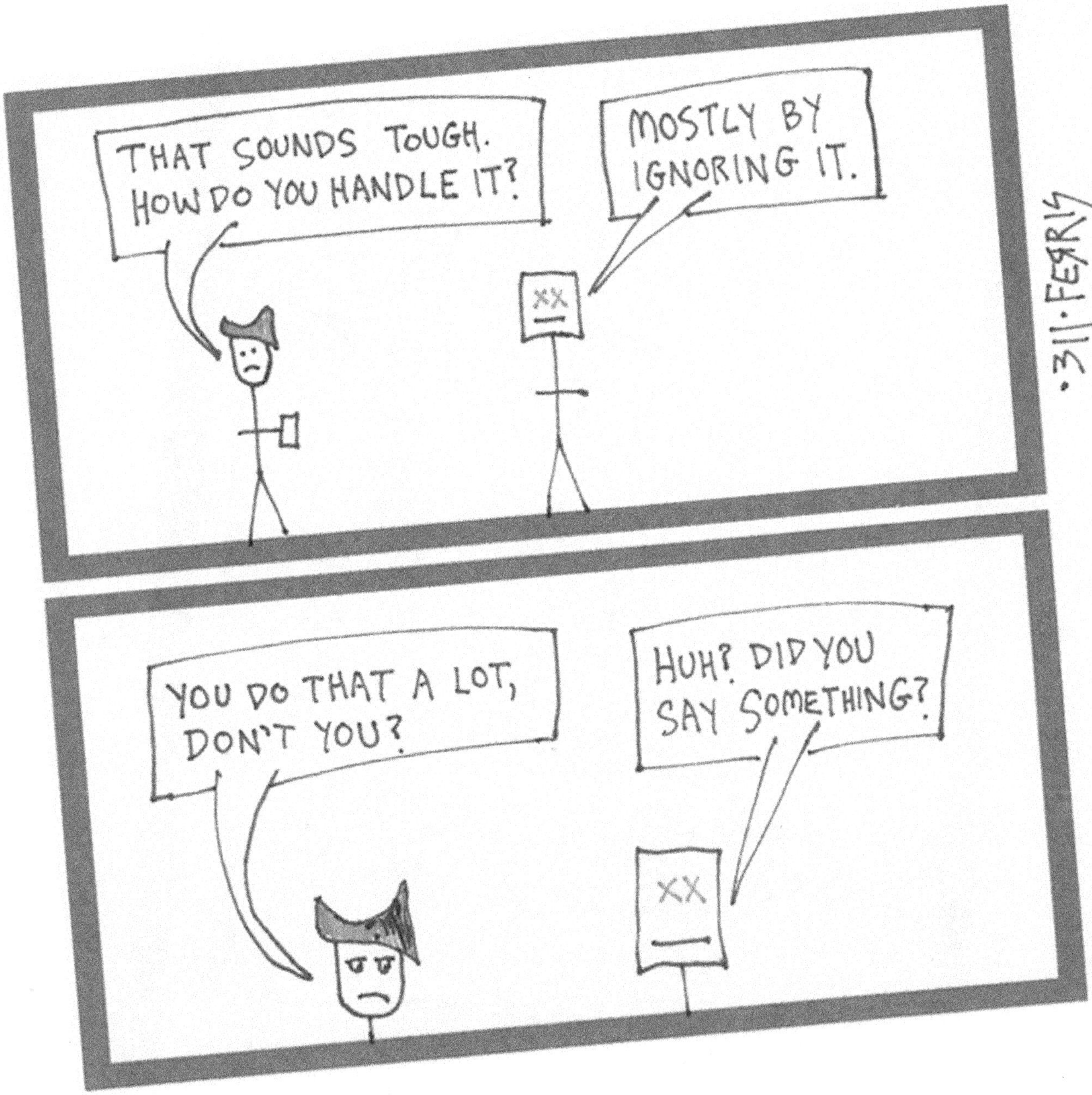
THAT SOUNDS TOUGH. HOW DO YOU HANDLE IT?
MOSTLY BY IGNORING IT.
YOU DO THAT A LOT, DON'T YOU?
HUH? DID YOU SAY SOMETHING?
•311•FERRIS

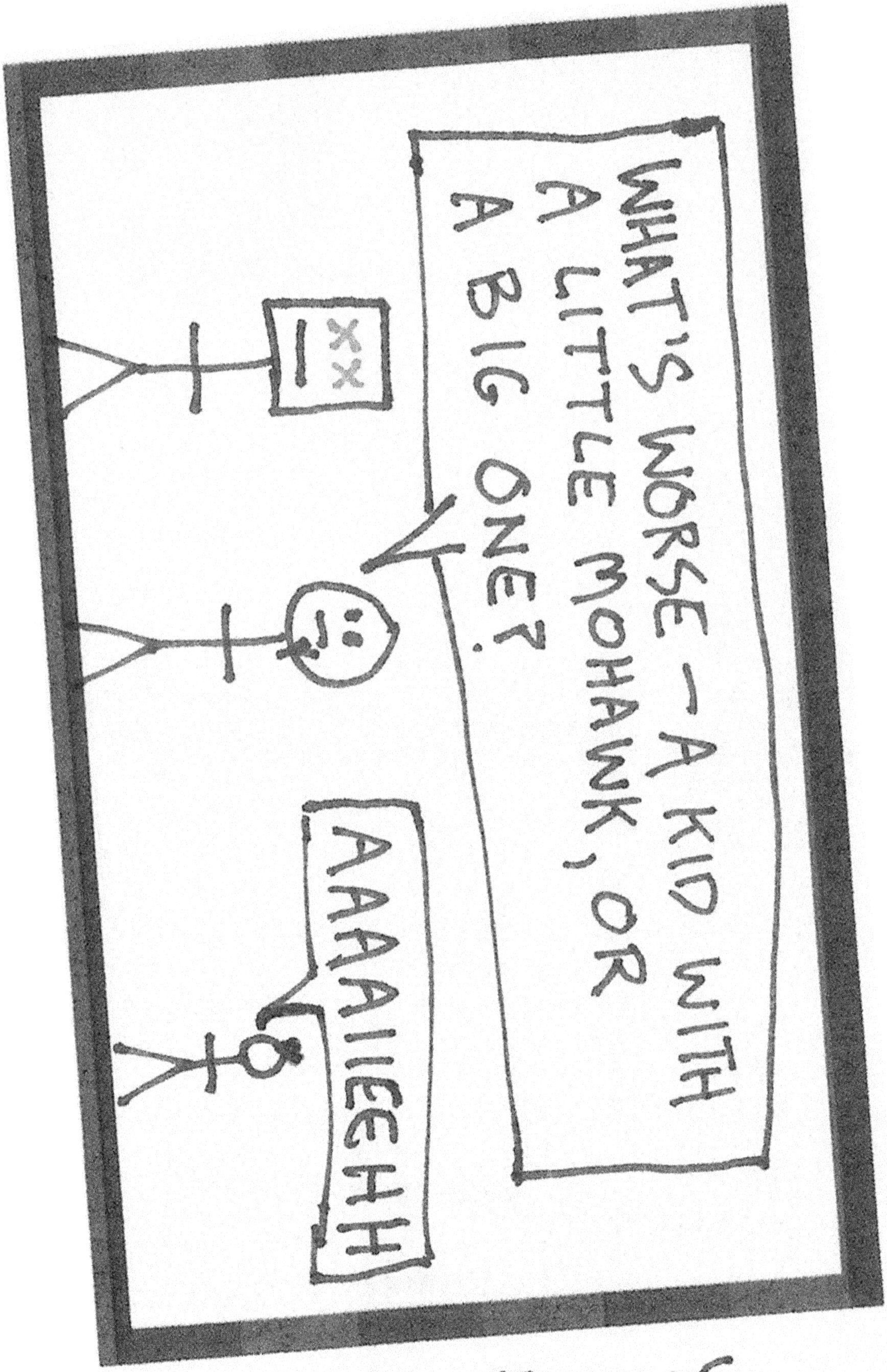
WHAT'S WORSE — A KID WITH A LITTLE MOHAWK, OR A BIG ONE?
AAAAIIEEHH

·312·FERRIS

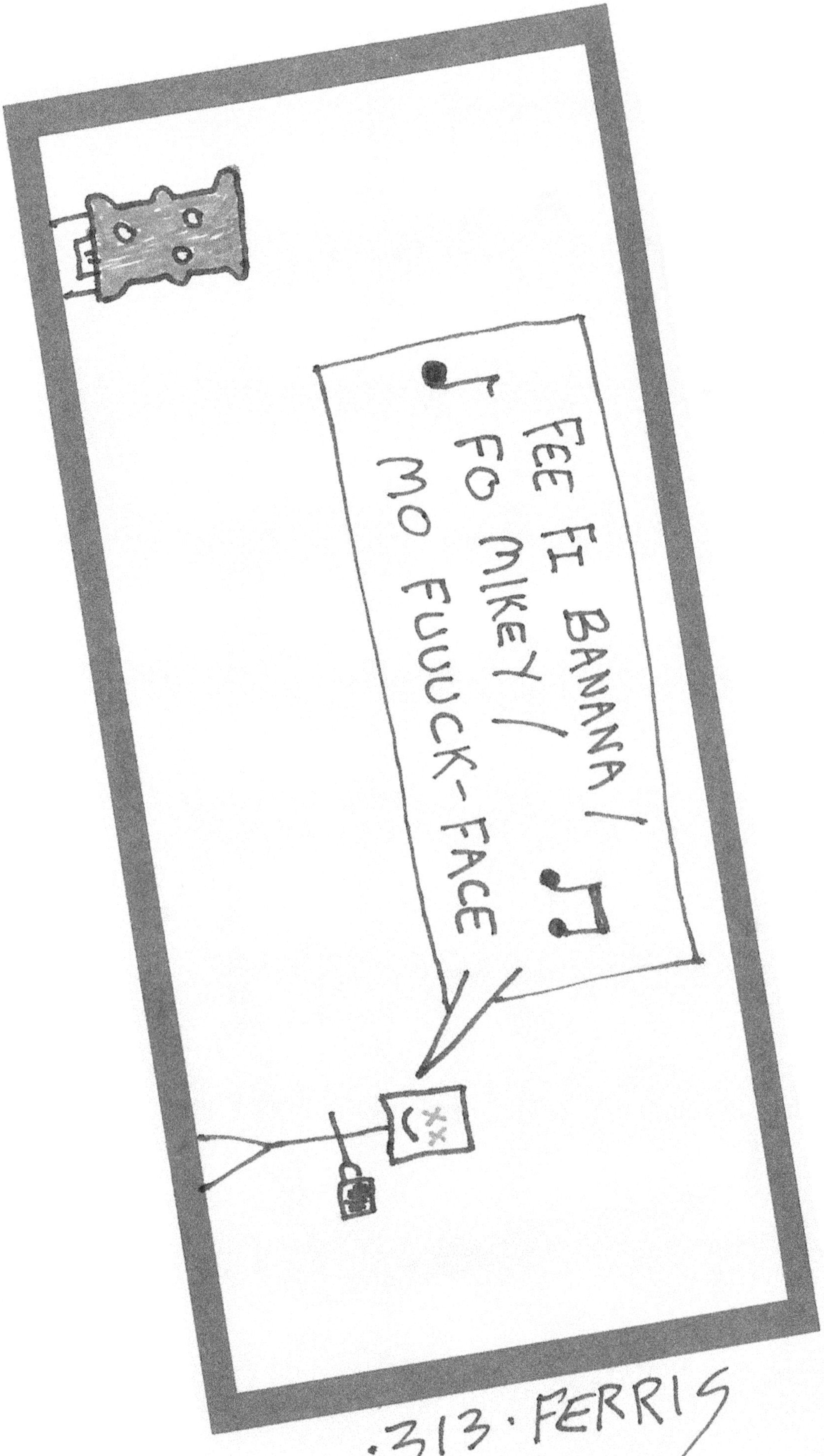
FEE FI BANANA / FO MIKEY / MO FUUUCK-FACE
·313· FERRIS

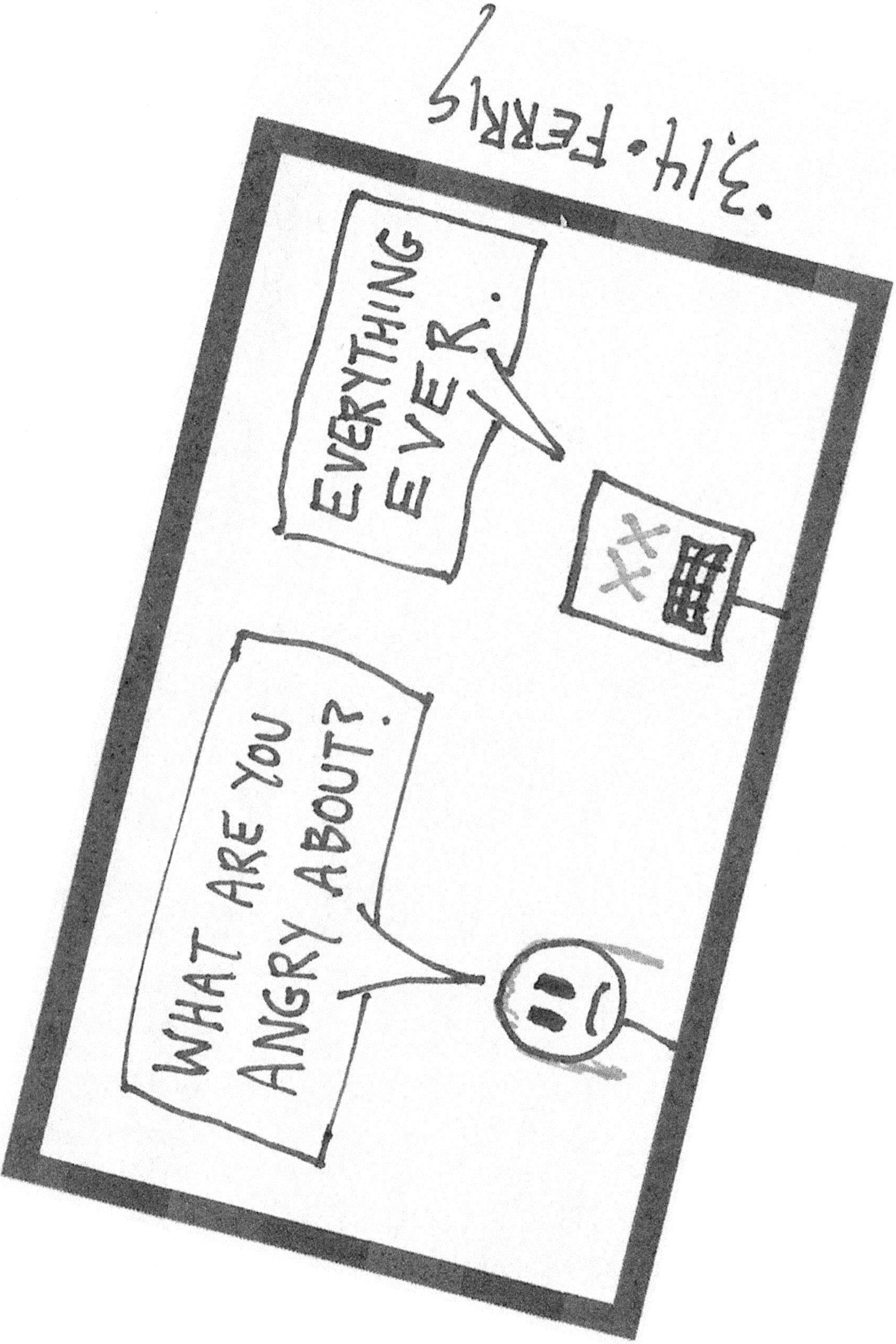
3.14 • FERRIS
WHAT ARE YOU ANGRY ABOUT?
EVERYTHING EVER.

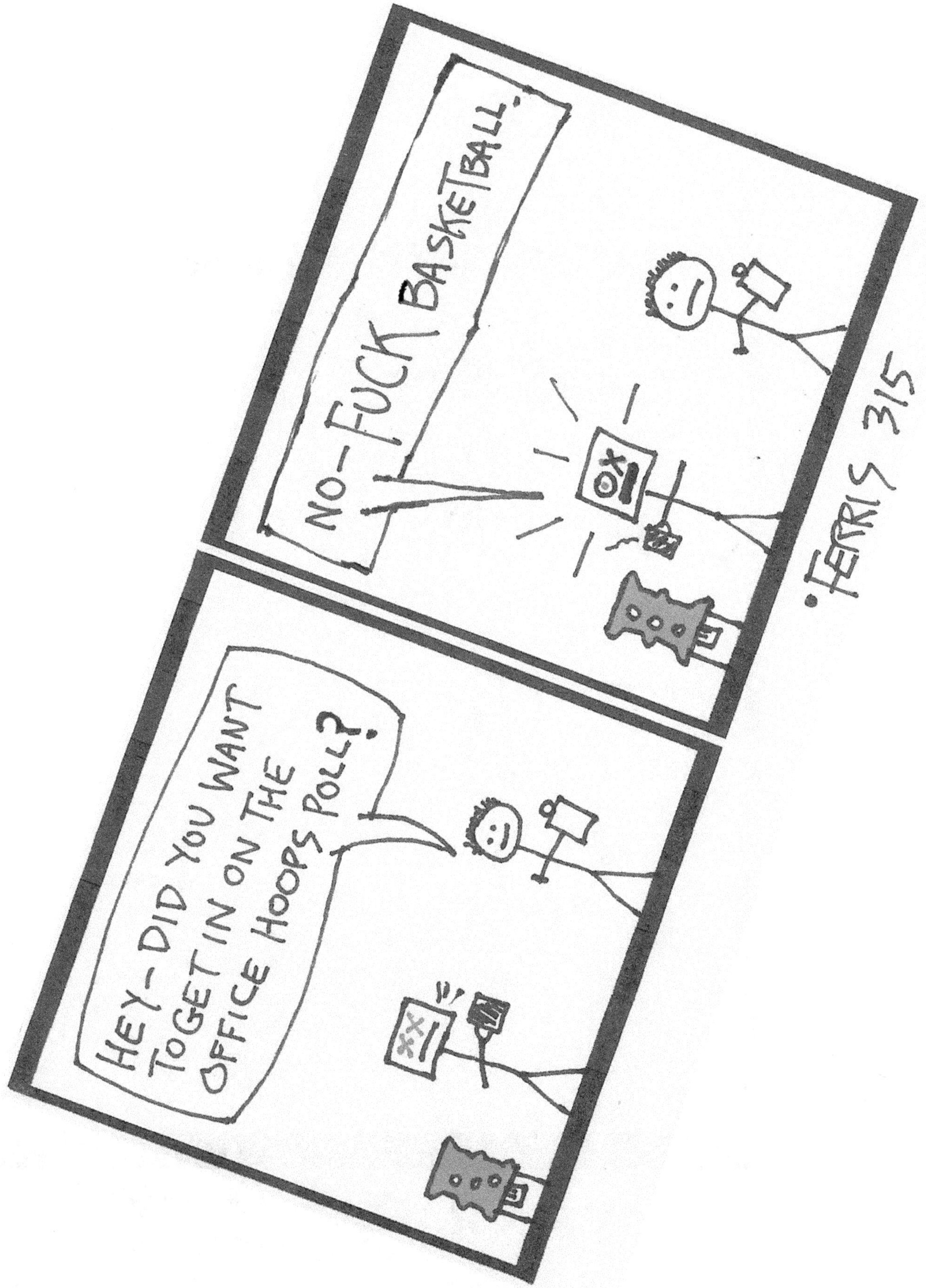
HEY-DID YOU WANT TOGET IN ON THE OFFICE HOOPS POLL?
NO-FUCK BASKETBALL.
FERRIS 3/15

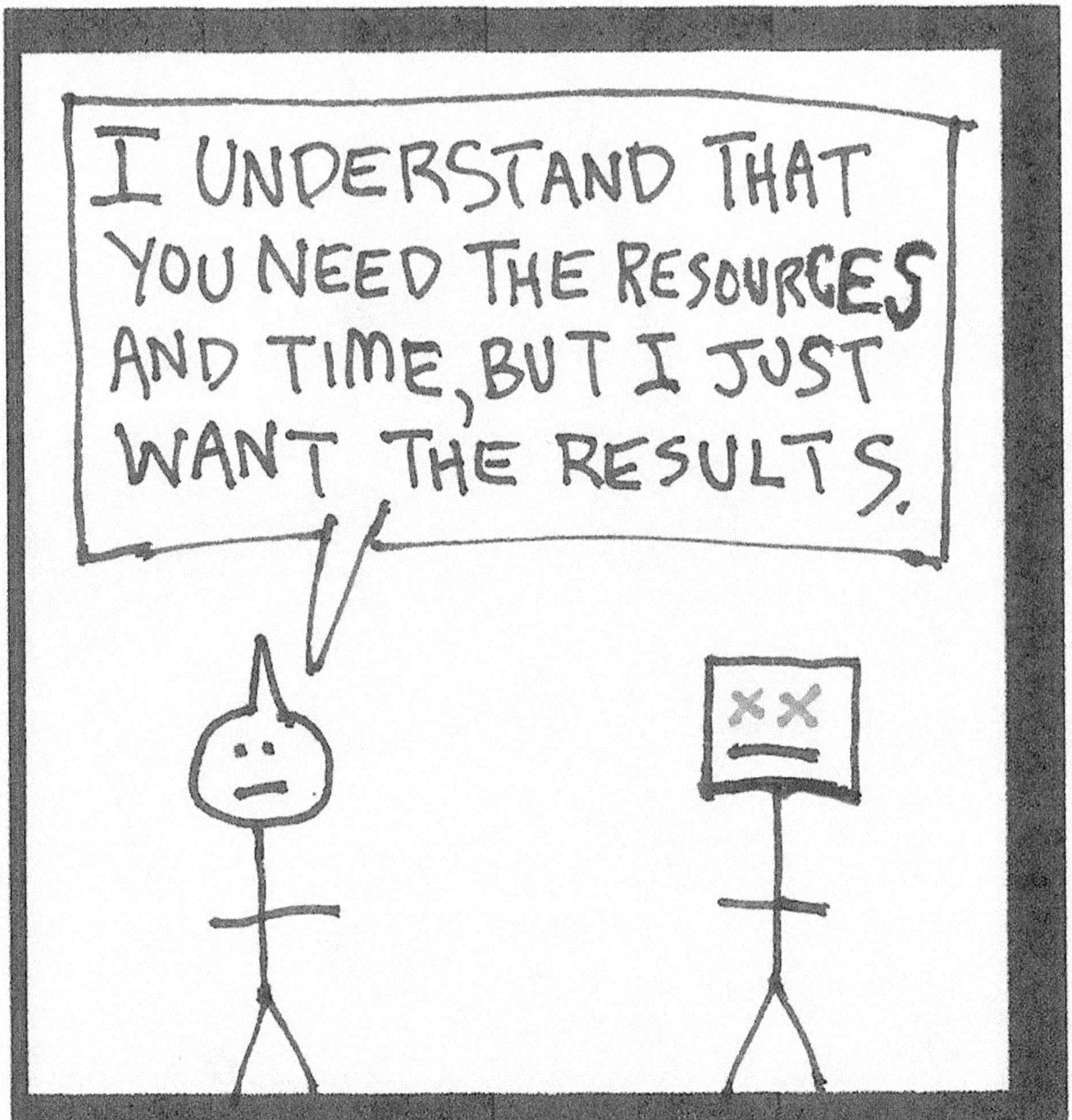
I UNDERSTAND THAT YOU NEED THE RESOURCES AND TIME, BUT I JUST WANT THE RESULTS.

•FERRIS 316.66

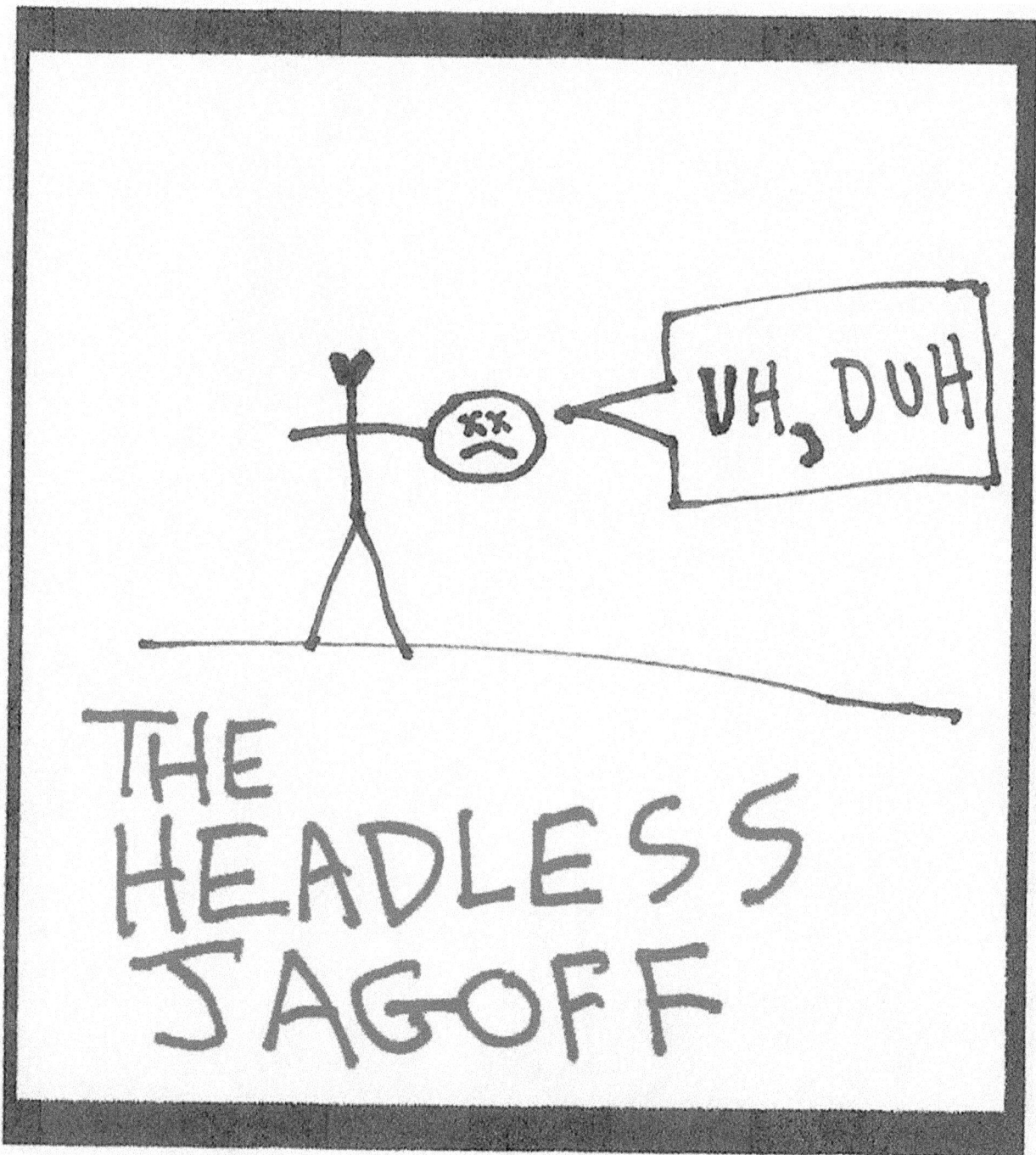
THE HEADLESS JAGOFF

•FERRIS 317

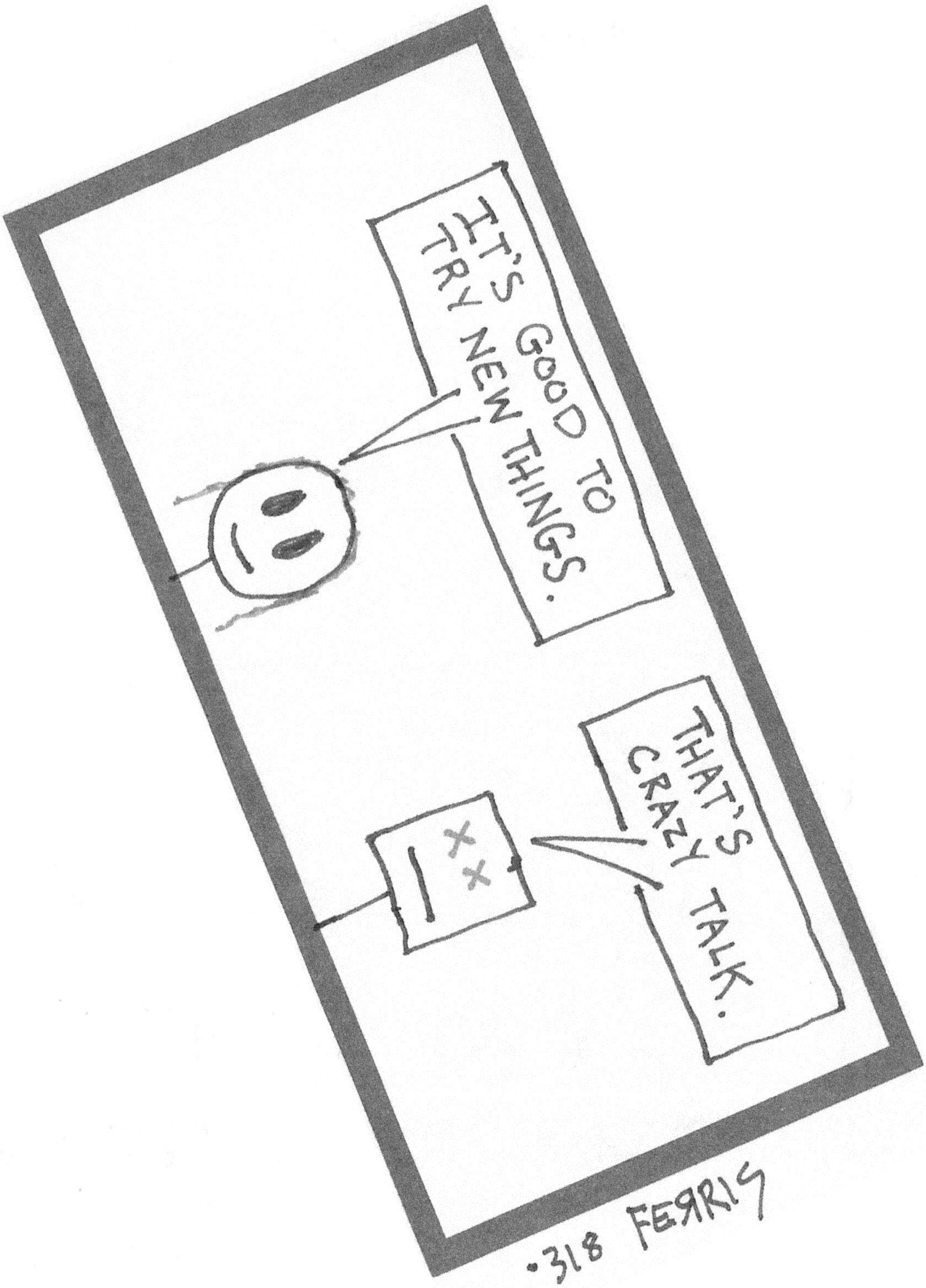
IT'S GOOD TO TRY NEW THINGS.
THAT'S CRAZY TALK.
•318 FERRIS

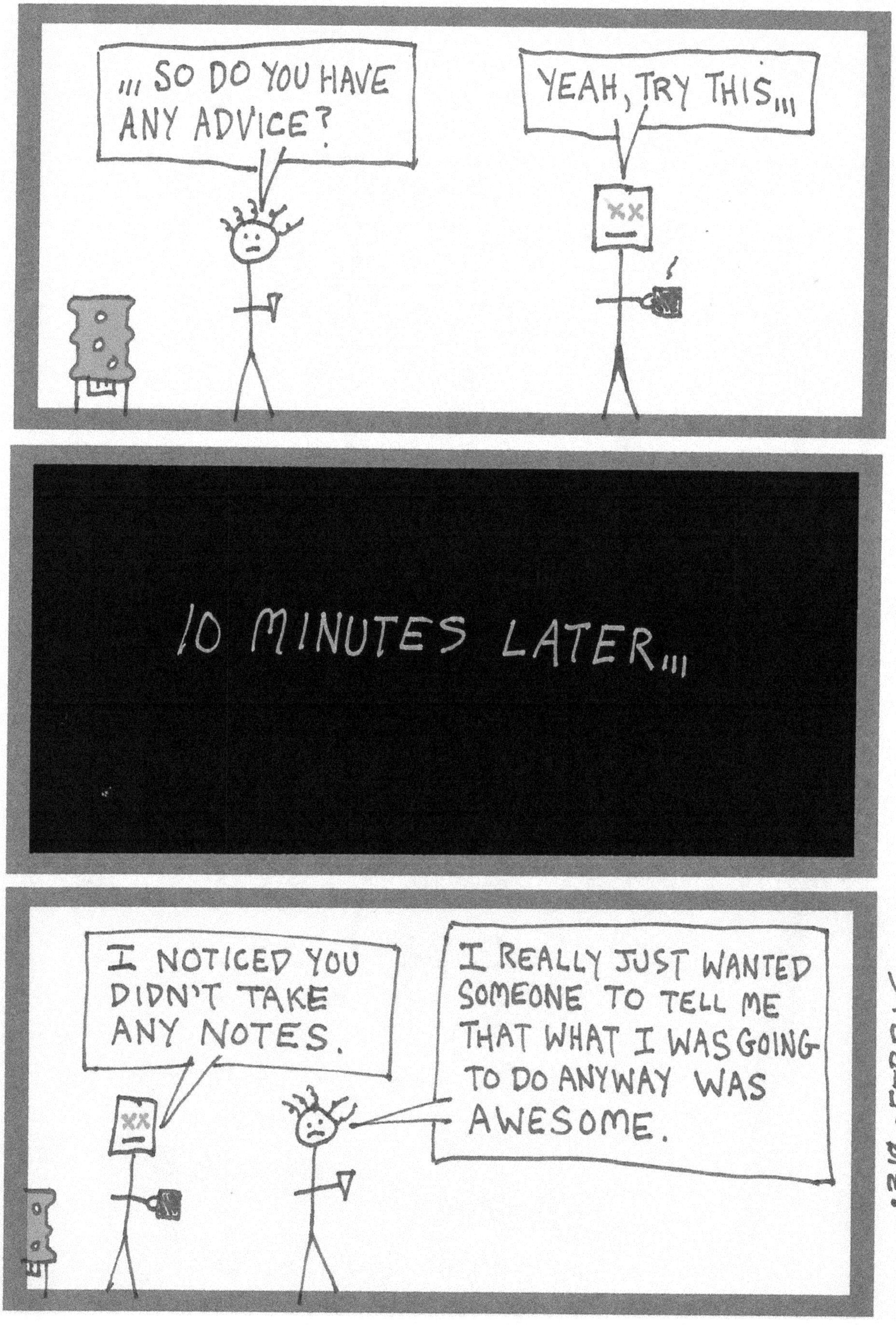

... SO DO YOU HAVE ANY ADVICE?
YEAH, TRY THIS...
10 MINUTES LATER...
I NOTICED YOU DIDN'T TAKE ANY NOTES.
I REALLY JUST WANTED SOMEONE TO TELL ME THAT WHAT I WAS GOING TO DO ANYWAY WAS AWESOME.
FERRIS

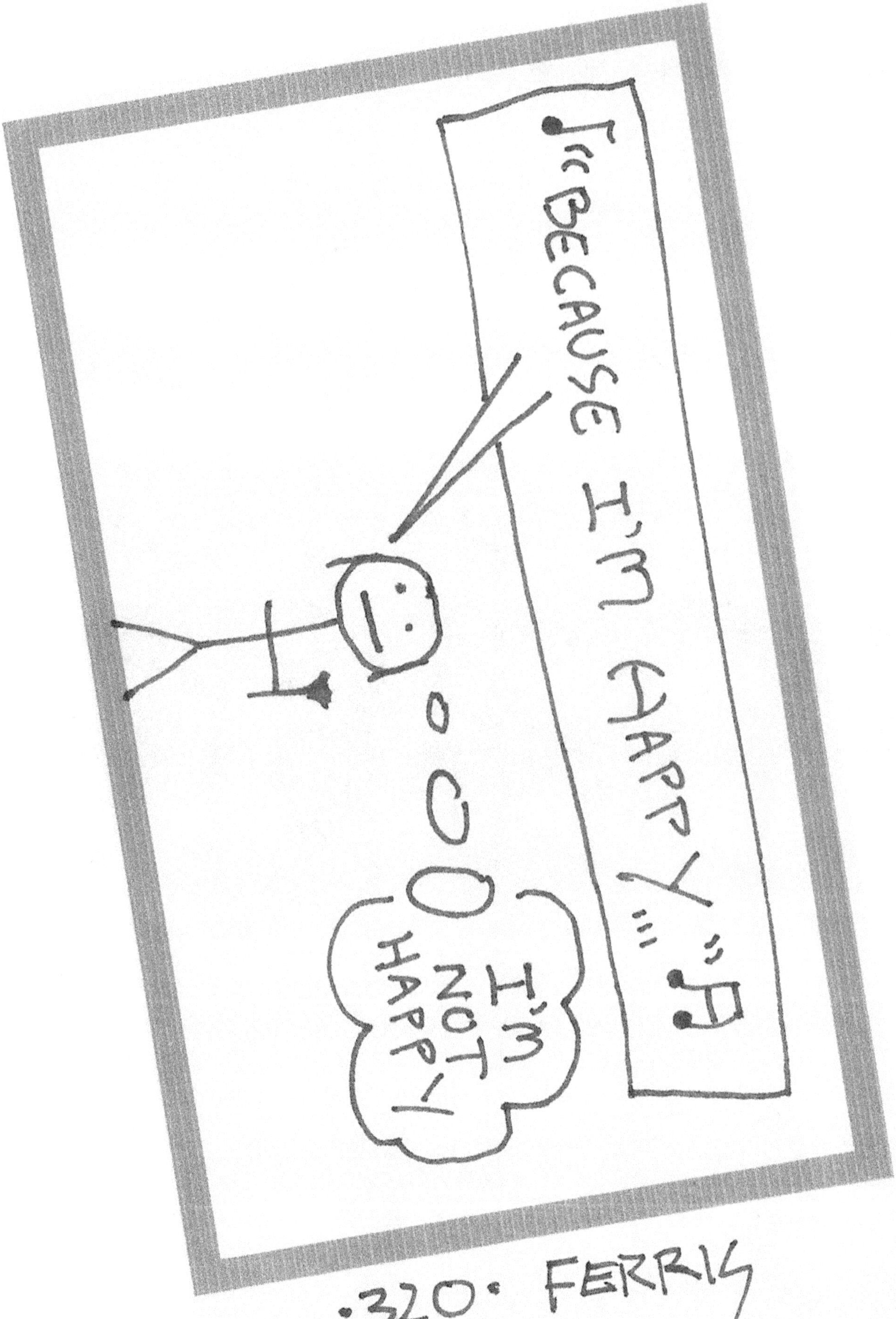
"BECAUSE I'M HAPPY..."
I'M NOT HAPPY

•320• FERRIS

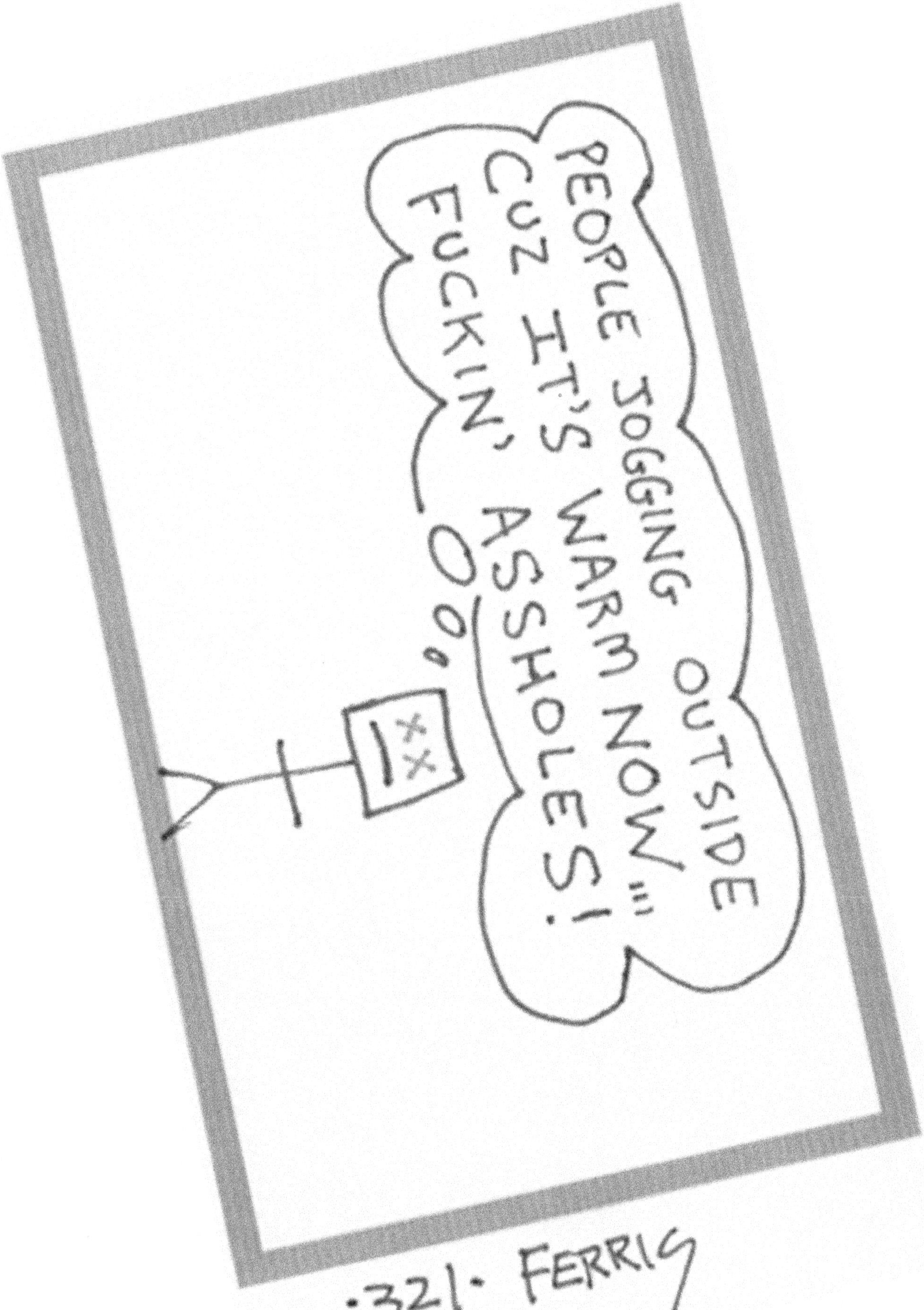
PEOPLE JOGGING OUTSIDE CUZ IT'S WARM NOW... FUCKIN' ASSHOLES!
·321· FERRIS

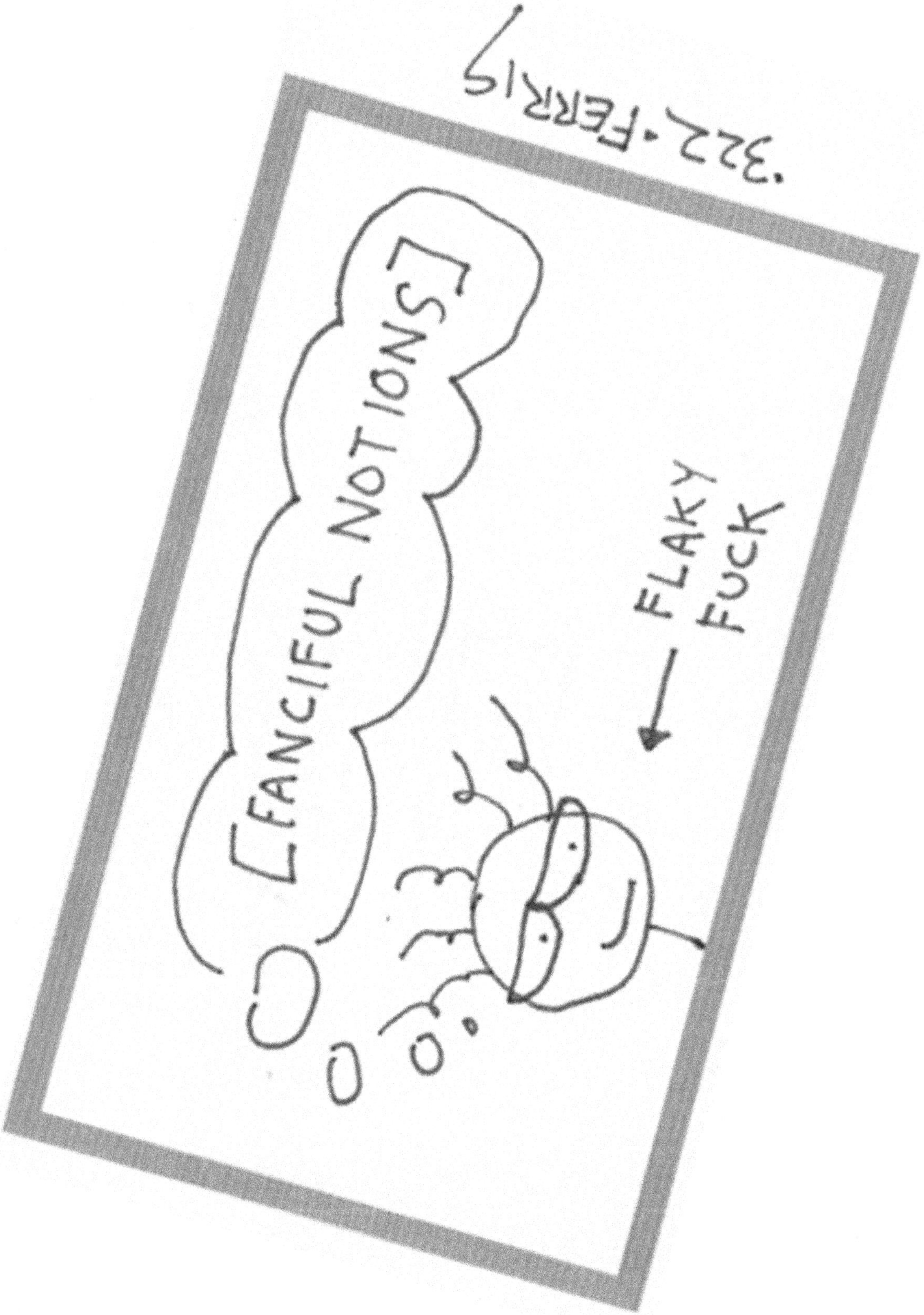
322 • FERRIS
[FANCIFUL NOTIONS]
FLAKY FUCK

FUCK THAT SHIT.

·323·FERRIS

DO YOU WANT TO SEE MY NEW AVATAR?
YEAH, SURE.
WHAT'S THAT?
IT'S THE VIEW OF ME DISAPPEARING UP MY OWN ASS!
IT'S DARK UP THERE.
I DON'T TAKE ELABORATE SELFIES BECAUSE I'M HAPPY AND CONTENT.
FERRIS #324

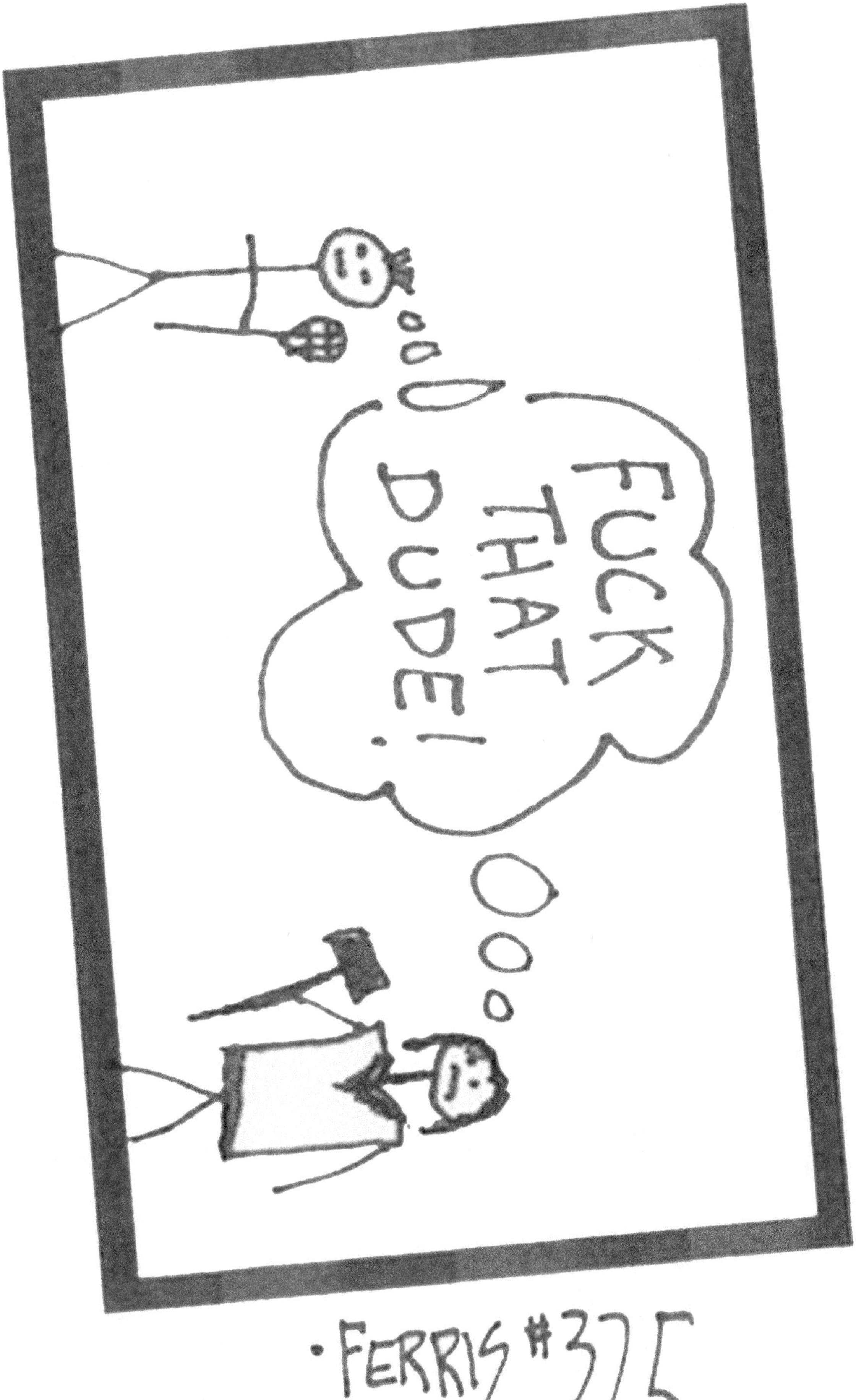
FUCK THAT DUDE!

·FERRIS #325

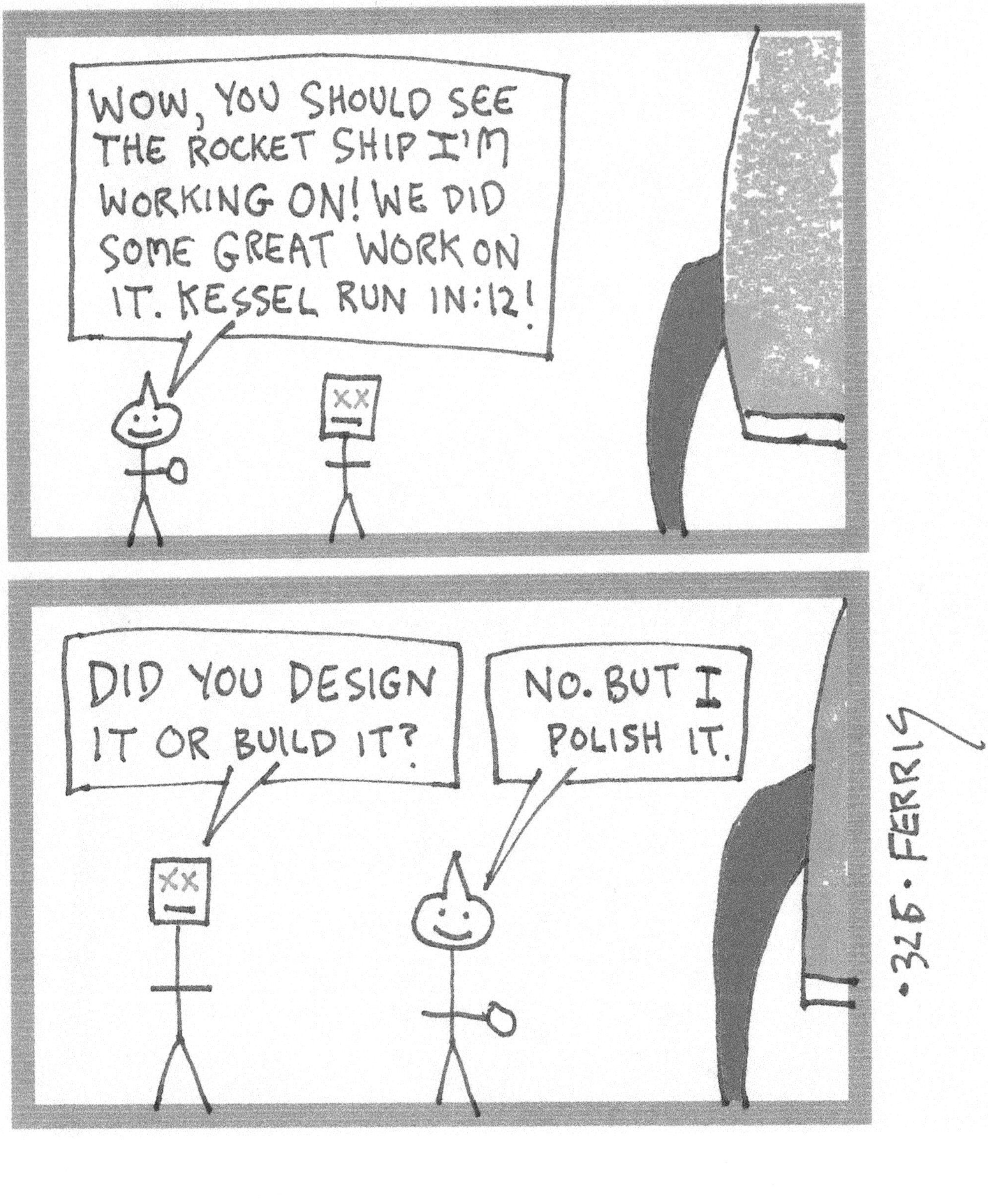
WOW, YOU SHOULD SEE THE ROCKET SHIP I'M WORKING ON! WE DID SOME GREAT WORK ON IT. KESSEL RUN IN :12!
DID YOU DESIGN IT OR BUILD IT?
NO. BUT I POLISH IT.
•326• FERRIS

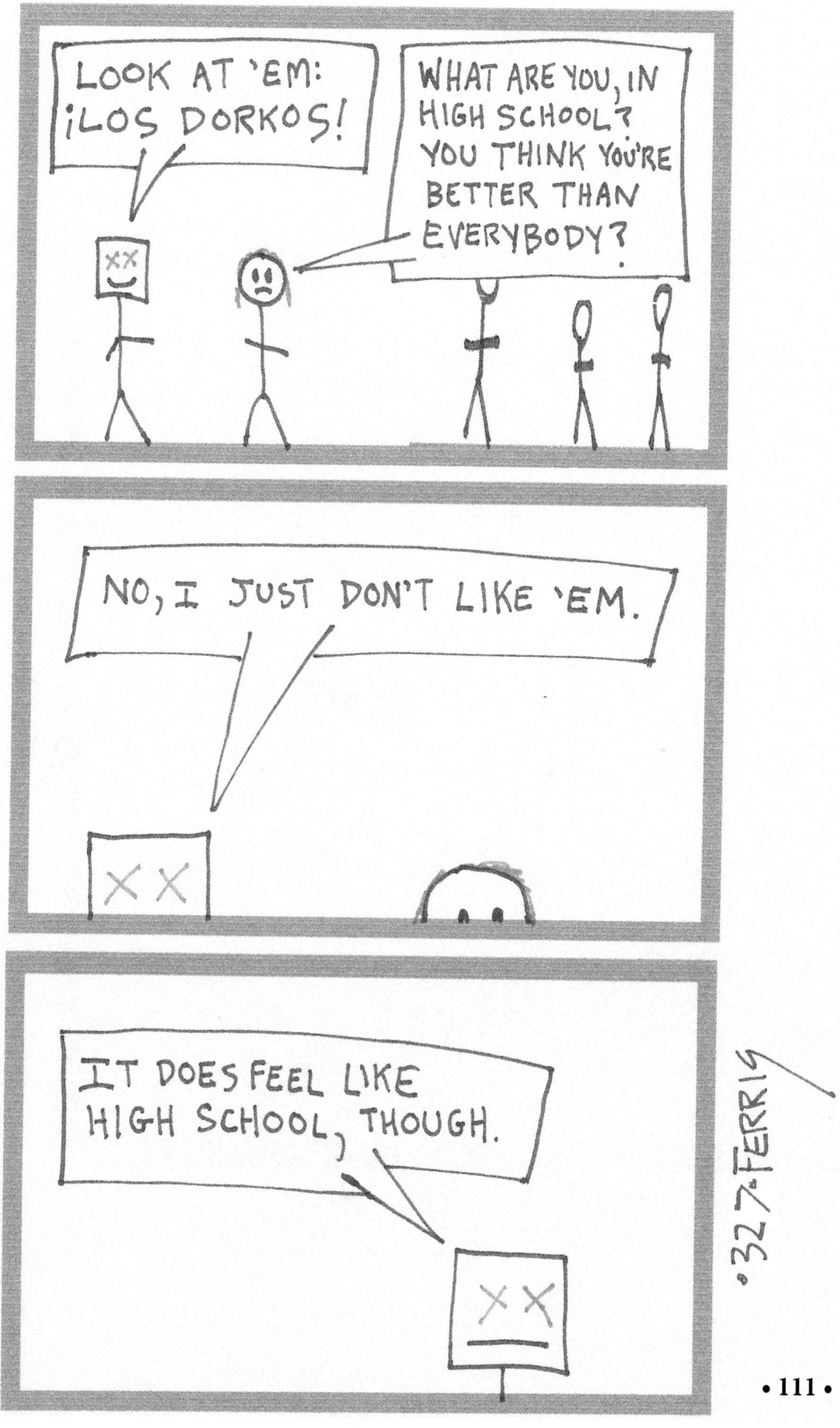
LOOK AT 'EM: ¡LOS DORKOS!
WHAT ARE YOU, IN HIGH SCHOOL? YOU THINK YOU'RE BETTER THAN EVERYBODY?
NO, I JUST DON'T LIKE 'EM.
IT DOES FEEL LIKE HIGH SCHOOL, THOUGH.
327.FERRIS

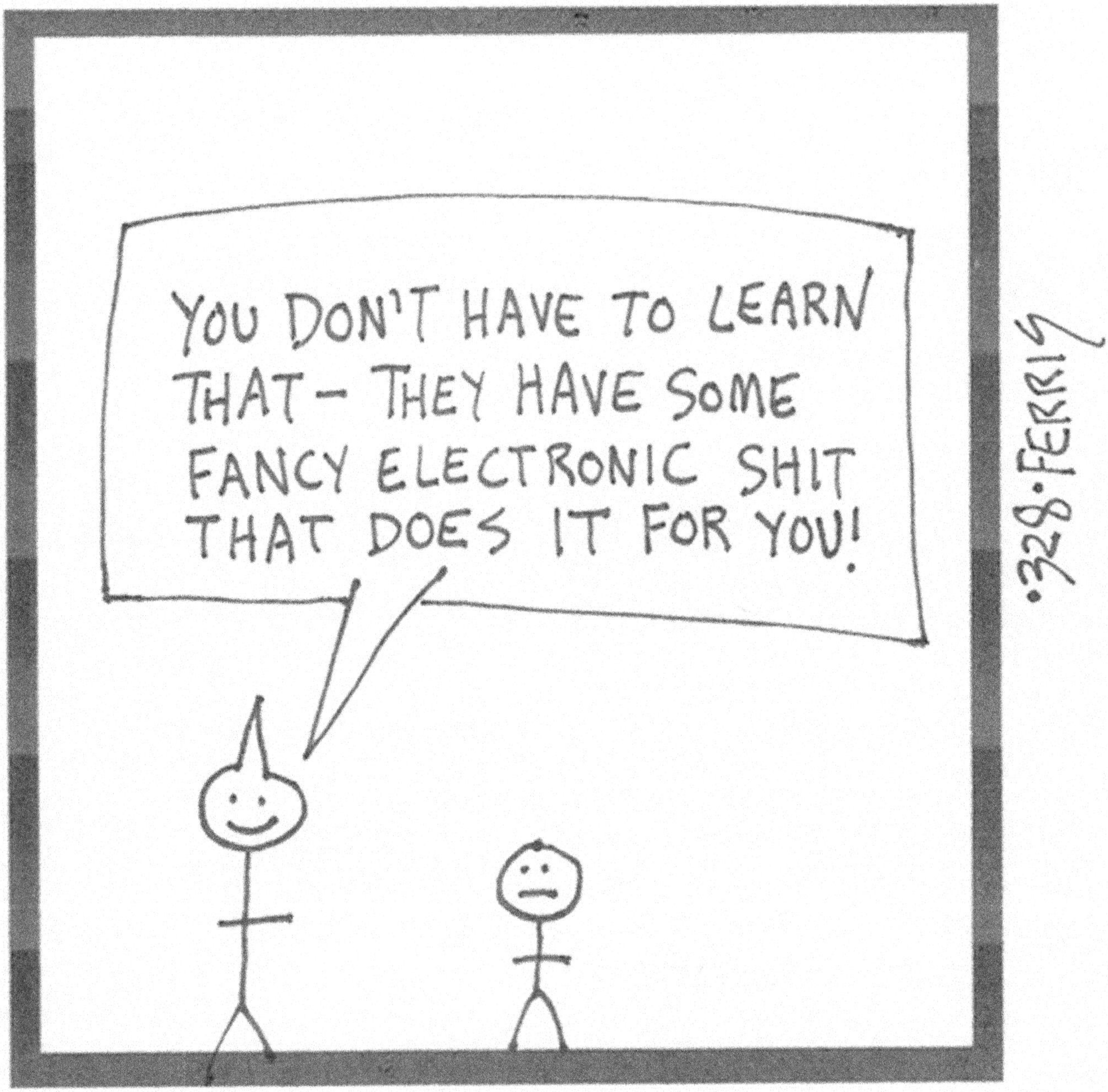
YOU DON'T HAVE TO LEARN THAT- THEY HAVE SOME FANCY ELECTRONIC SHIT THAT DOES IT FOR YOU!
•328•FERRIS

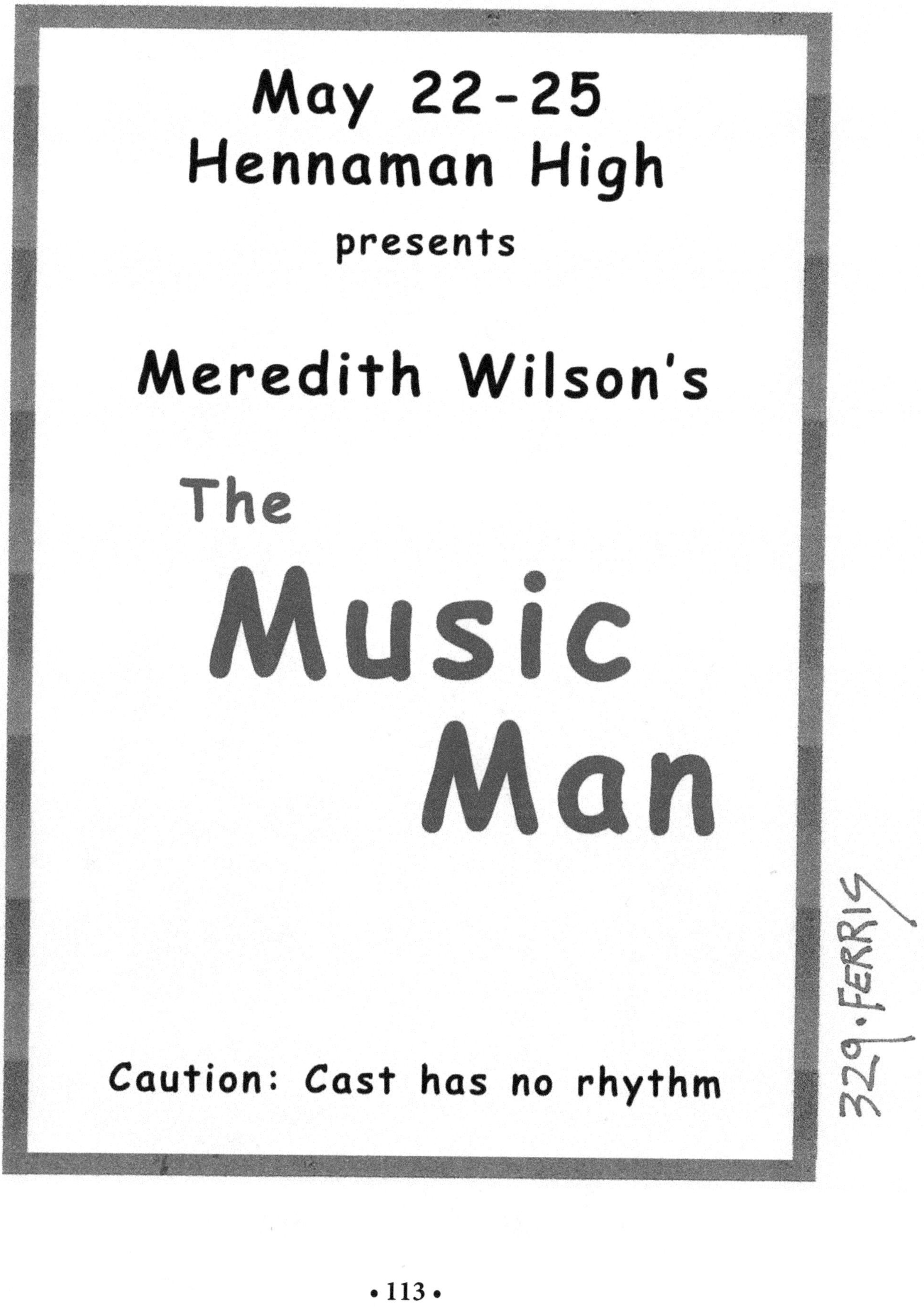
May 22-25
Hennaman High
presents
Meredith Wilson's
The
Music
Man
Caution: Cast has no rhythm
329•FERRIS

ALL THESE PEOPLE DRIVING AROUND, DOING ERRANDS BECAUSE IT'S SATURDAY AFTERNOON, AND THEY DON'T HAVE TO WORK — FUCKIN' ASSHOLES!
·330·FERRIS

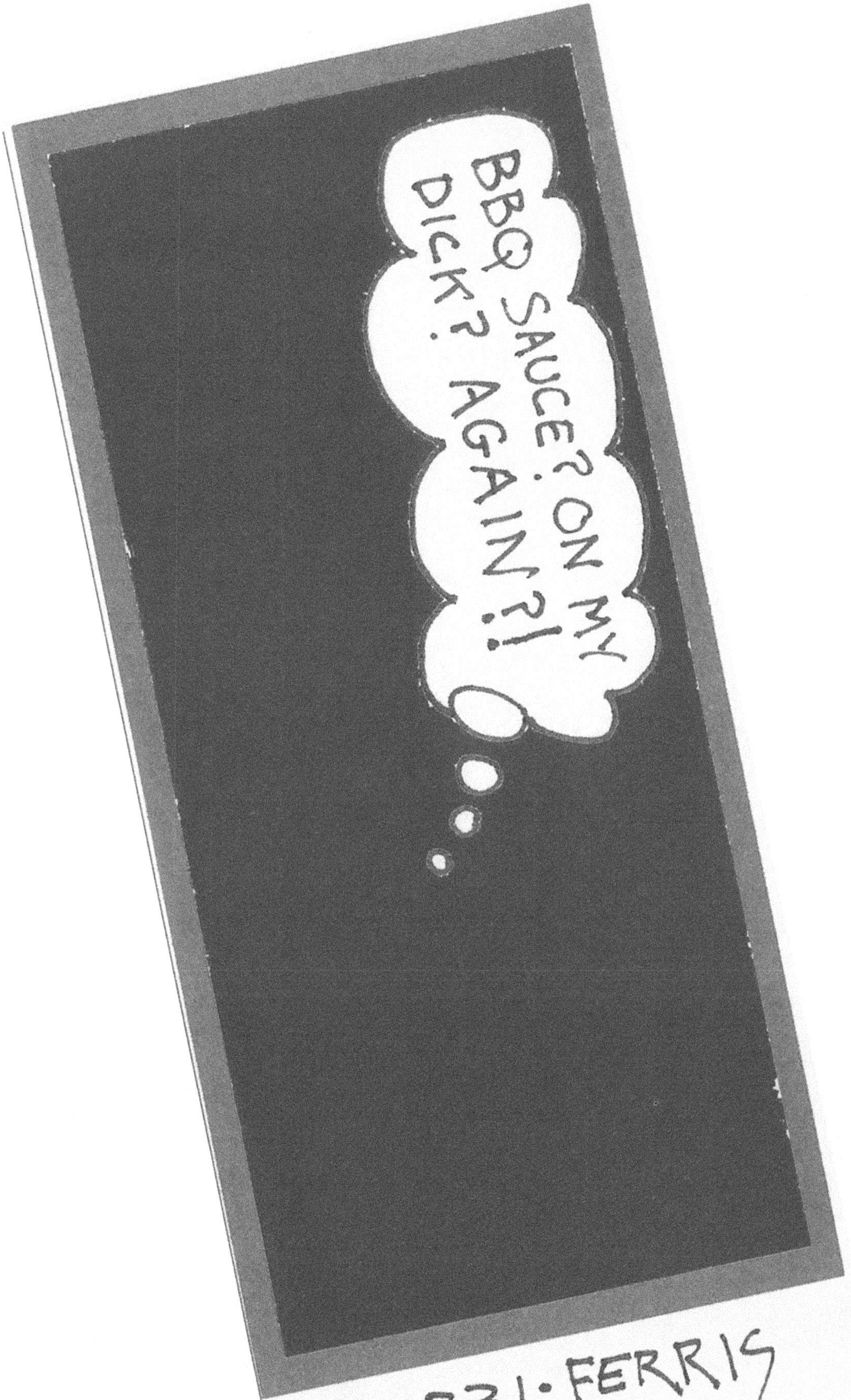


•331• FERRIS

332. FERRIS

15 MINUTES LATER...
THAT WAS A FUCKIN' SHITSHOW.

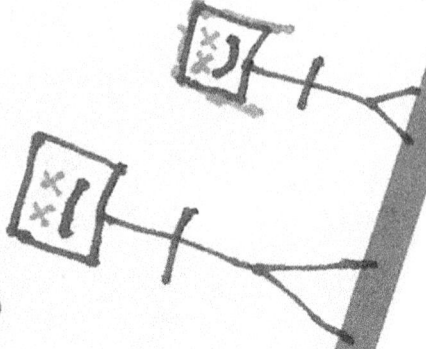

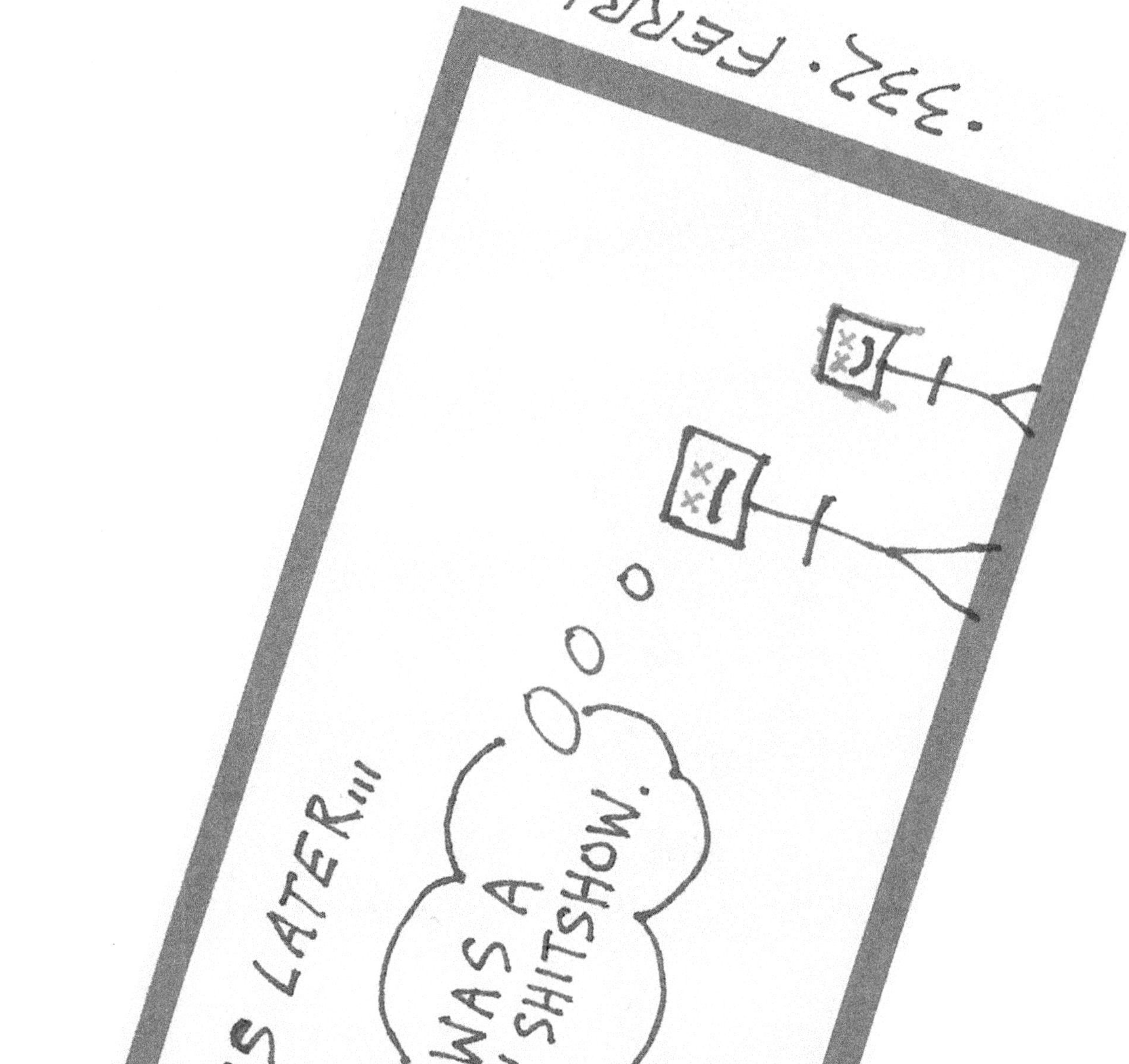

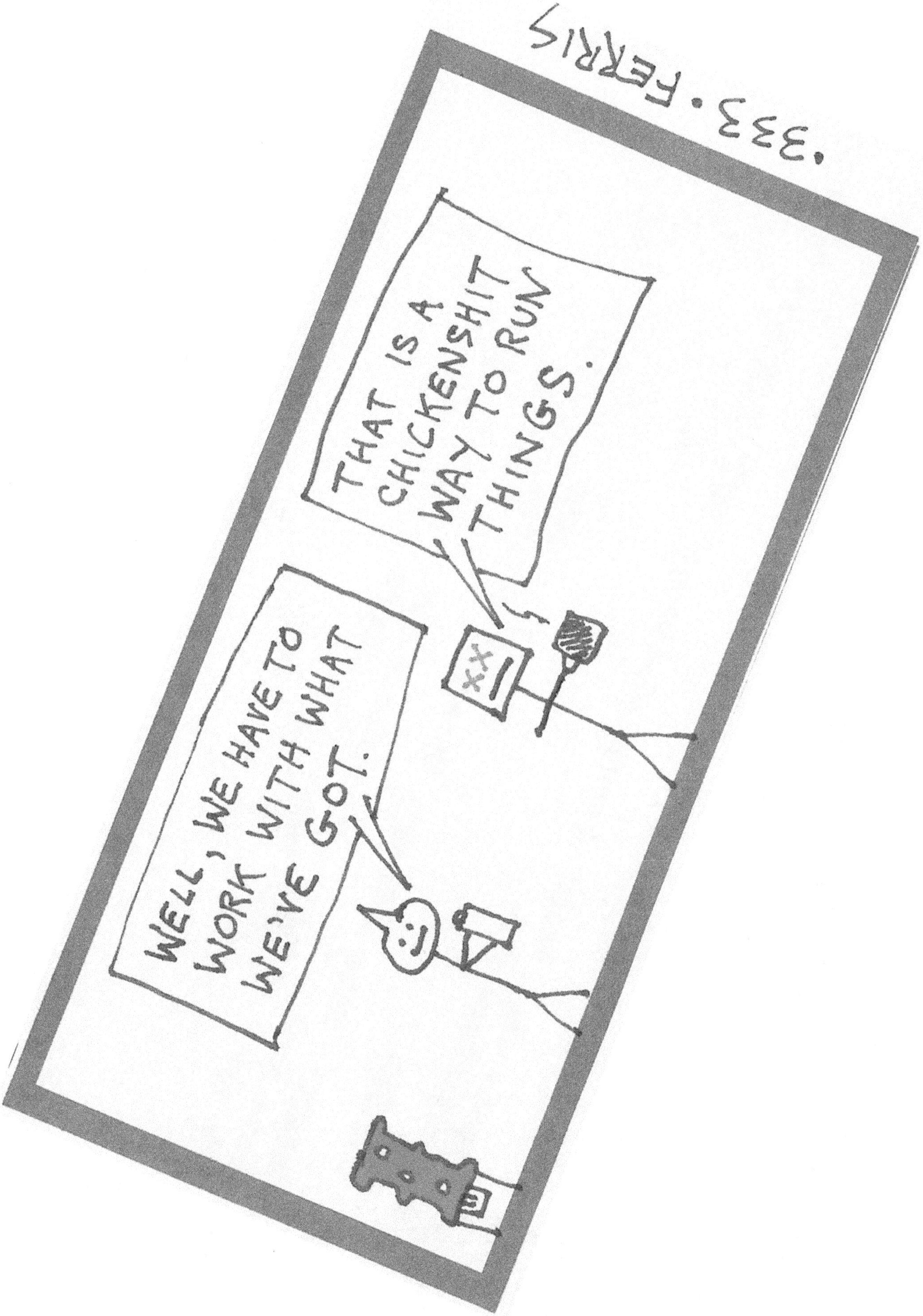

•333 • FERRIS
WELL, WE HAVE TO WORK WITH WHAT WE'VE GOT.
THAT IS A CHICKENSHIT WAY TO RUN THINGS.

THE NEIGHBOR KIDS DON'T DRIVE YOU CRAZY?
GOOD TUNES ON THE STEREO. I GOT BEER. THEY'RE EASY TO TUNE OUT.

•334• FERRIS

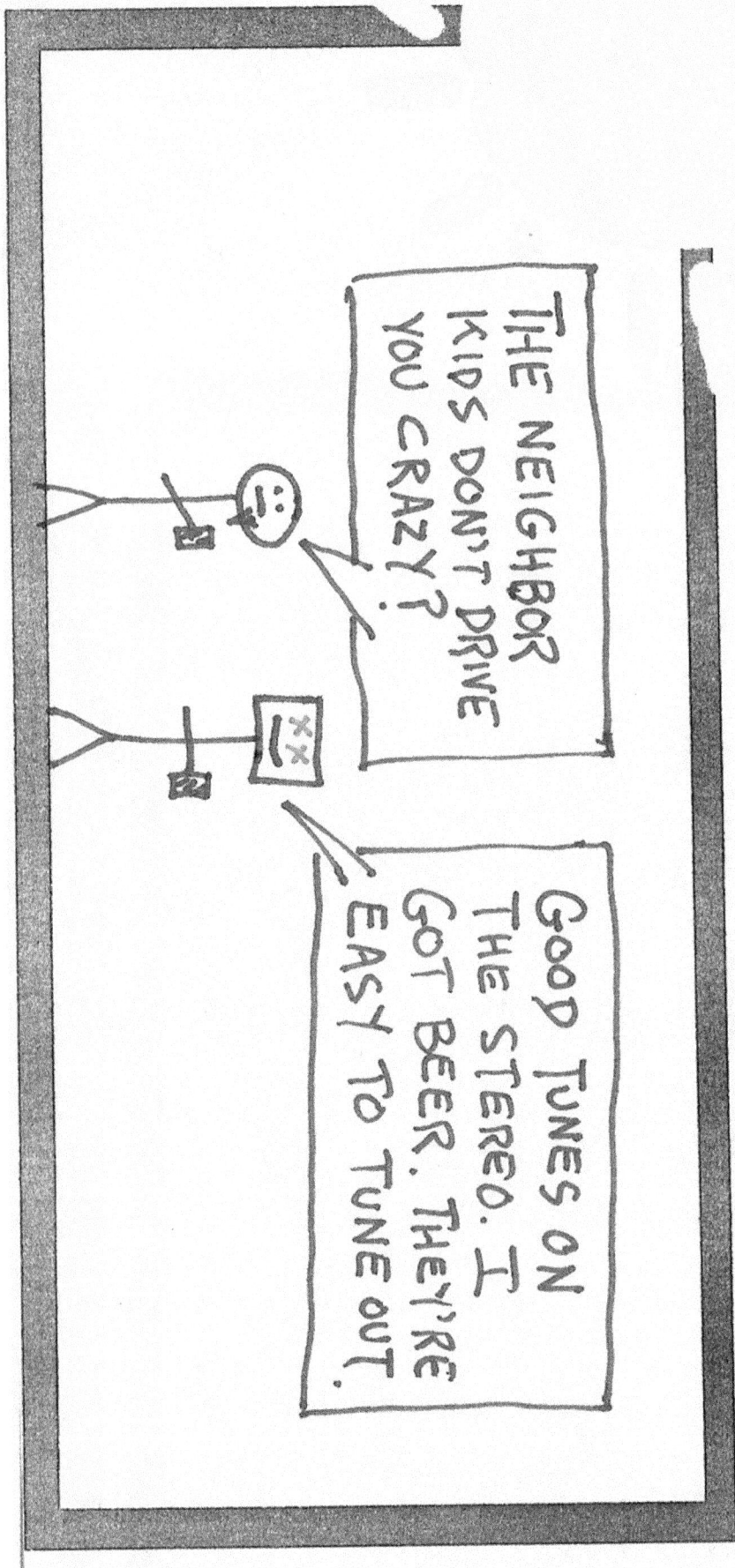

**there is no #335. my bad.**

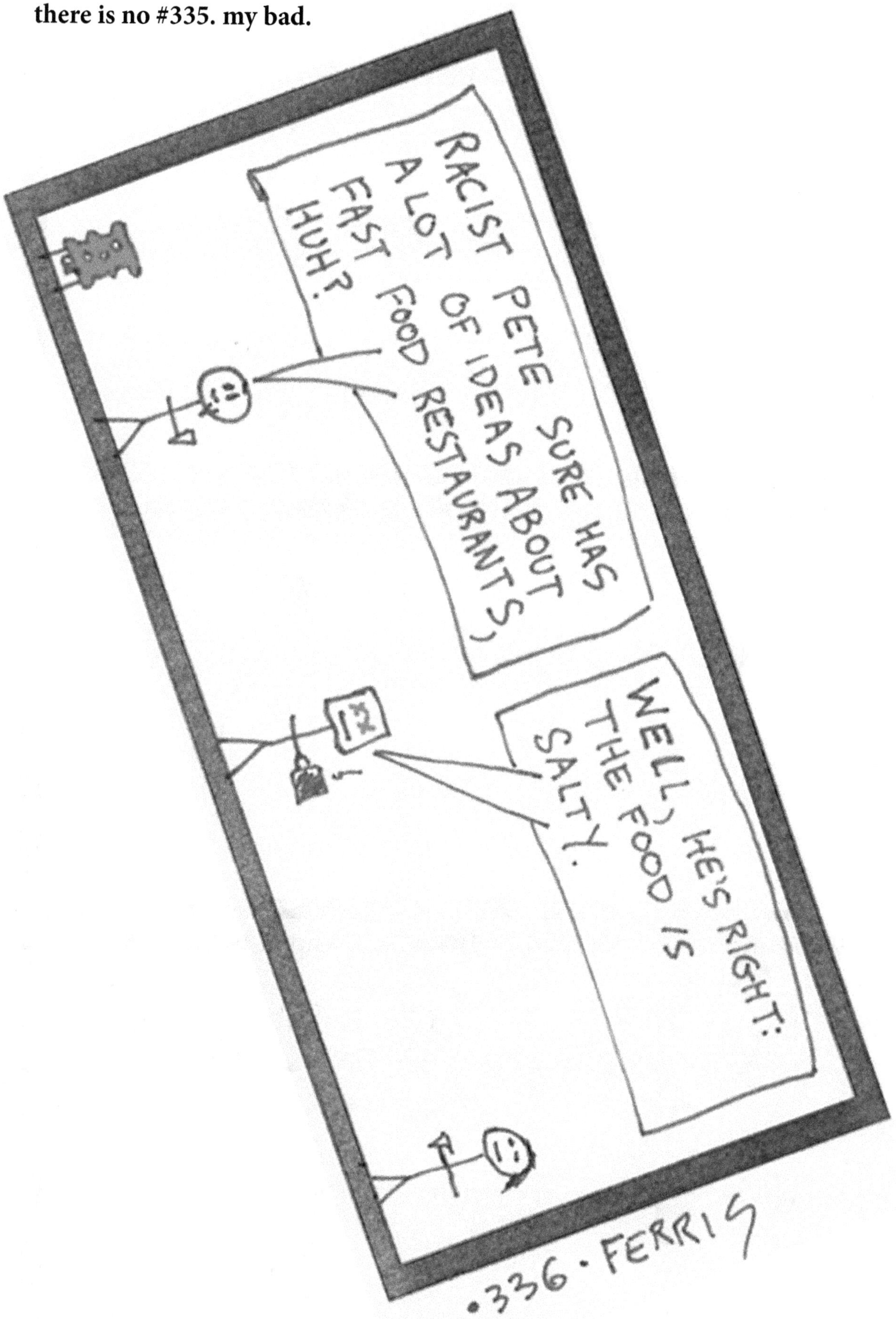
RACIST PETE SURE HAS A LOT OF IDEAS ABOUT FAST FOOD RESTAURANTS, HUH?
WELL, HE'S RIGHT: THE FOOD IS SALTY.
•336 • FERRIS

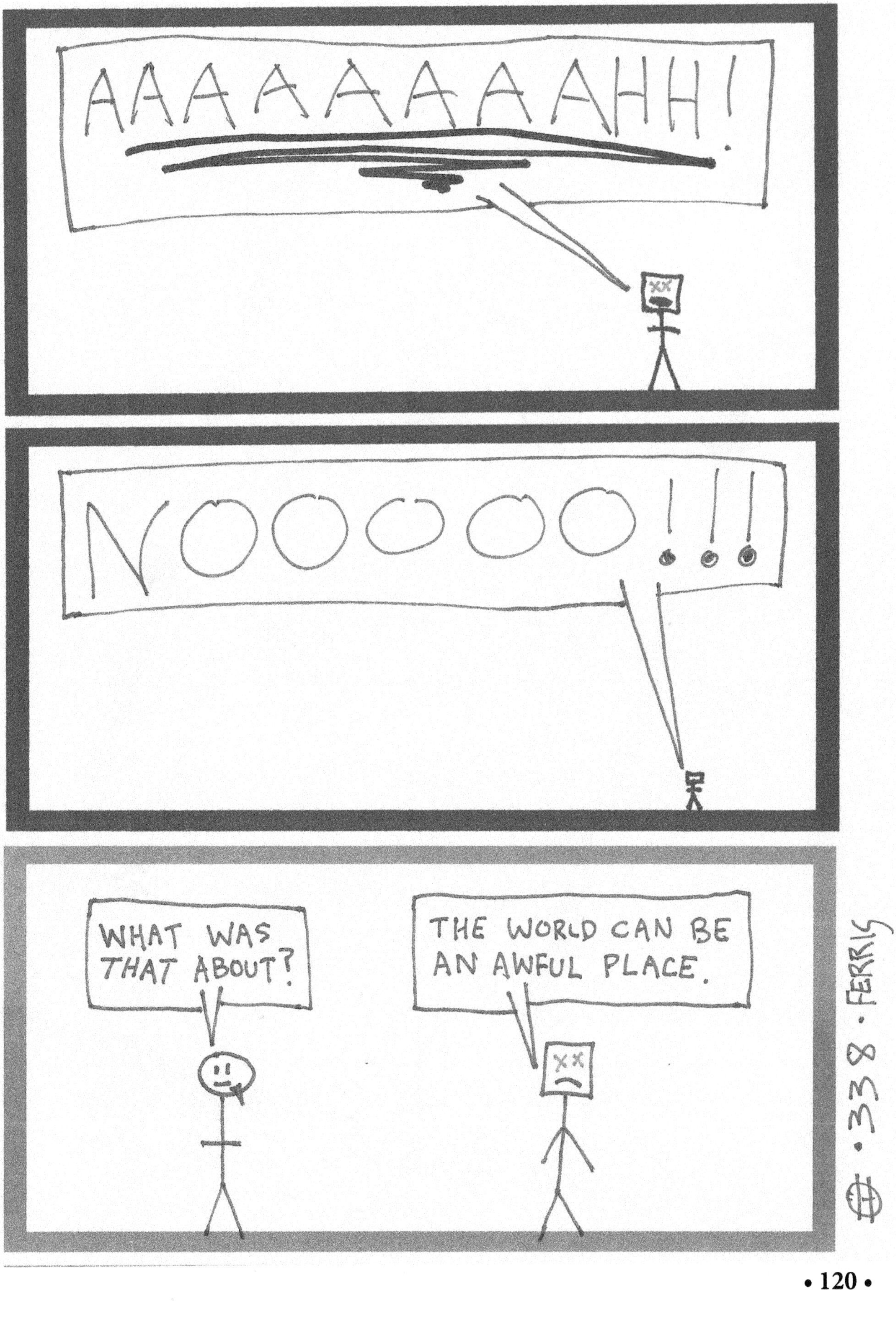
AAAAAAAAHH!
NOOOOO!!!
WHAT WAS THAT ABOUT?
THE WORLD CAN BE AN AWFUL PLACE.
·338·FERRIS

MAYBE IT WILL BE BETTER OVER THERE
MAYBE IT WILL BE BETTER OVER THERE
MAYBE IT WILL BE BETTER OVER THERE
MAYBE IT WILL BE BETTER OVER THERE
·337· FERRIS

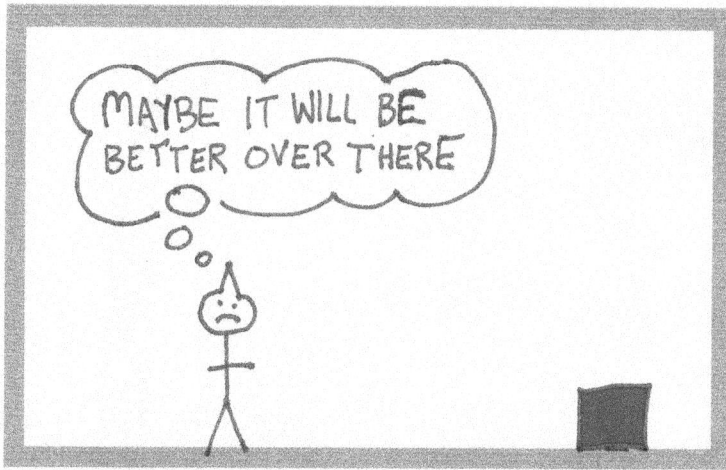

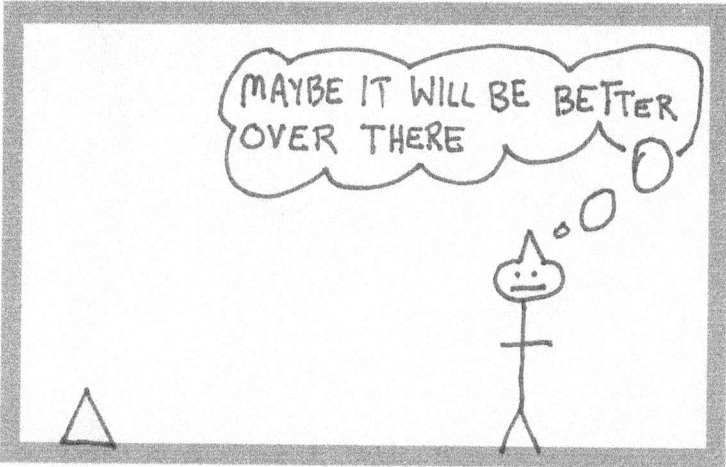

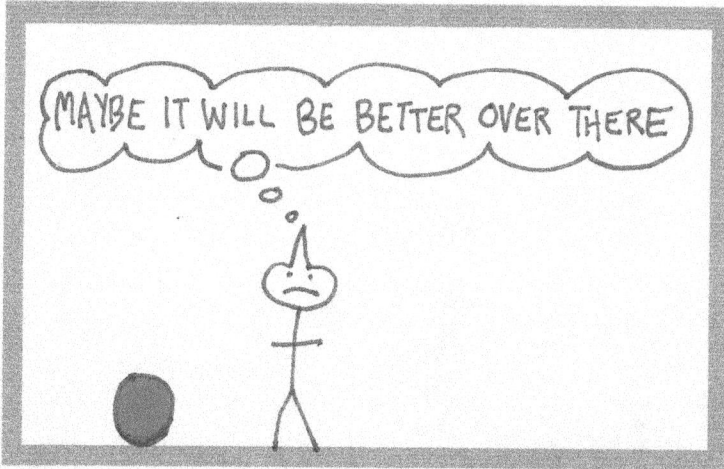

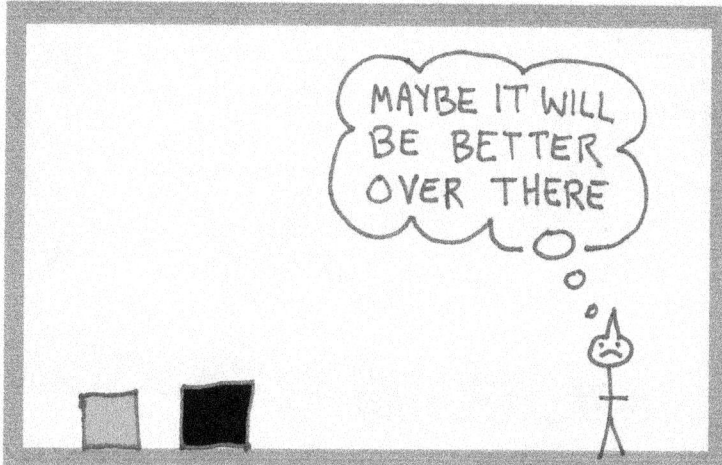

DUDE RIDING HIS BIKE IN THE MIDDLE OF THE ROAD. HE'S A DAMNED TERRORIST DISRUPTING THE SYSTEM.
I NEED TO EXERCISE WHERE PEOPLE CAN SEE ME!

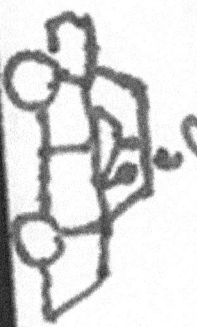

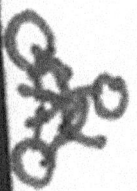

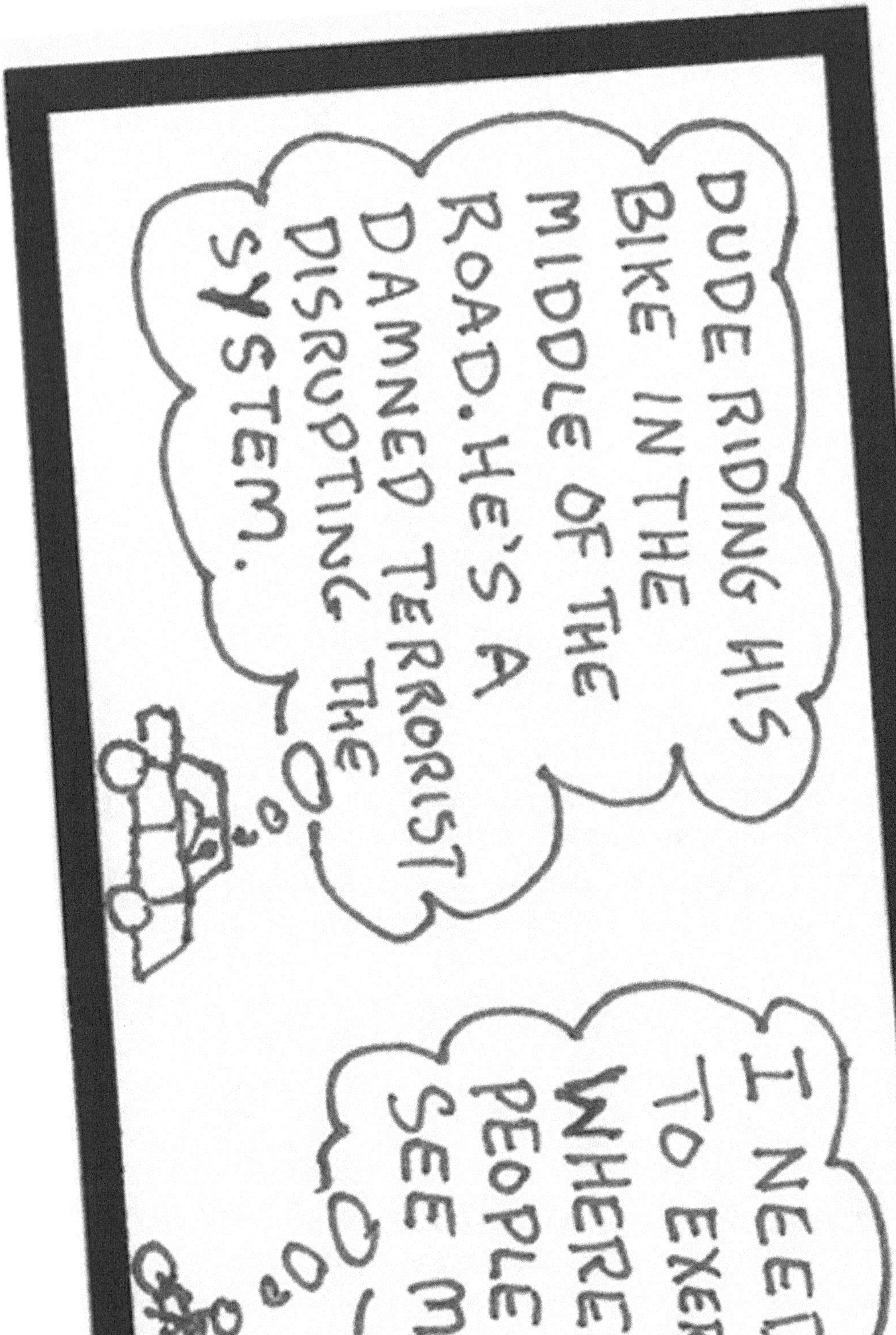

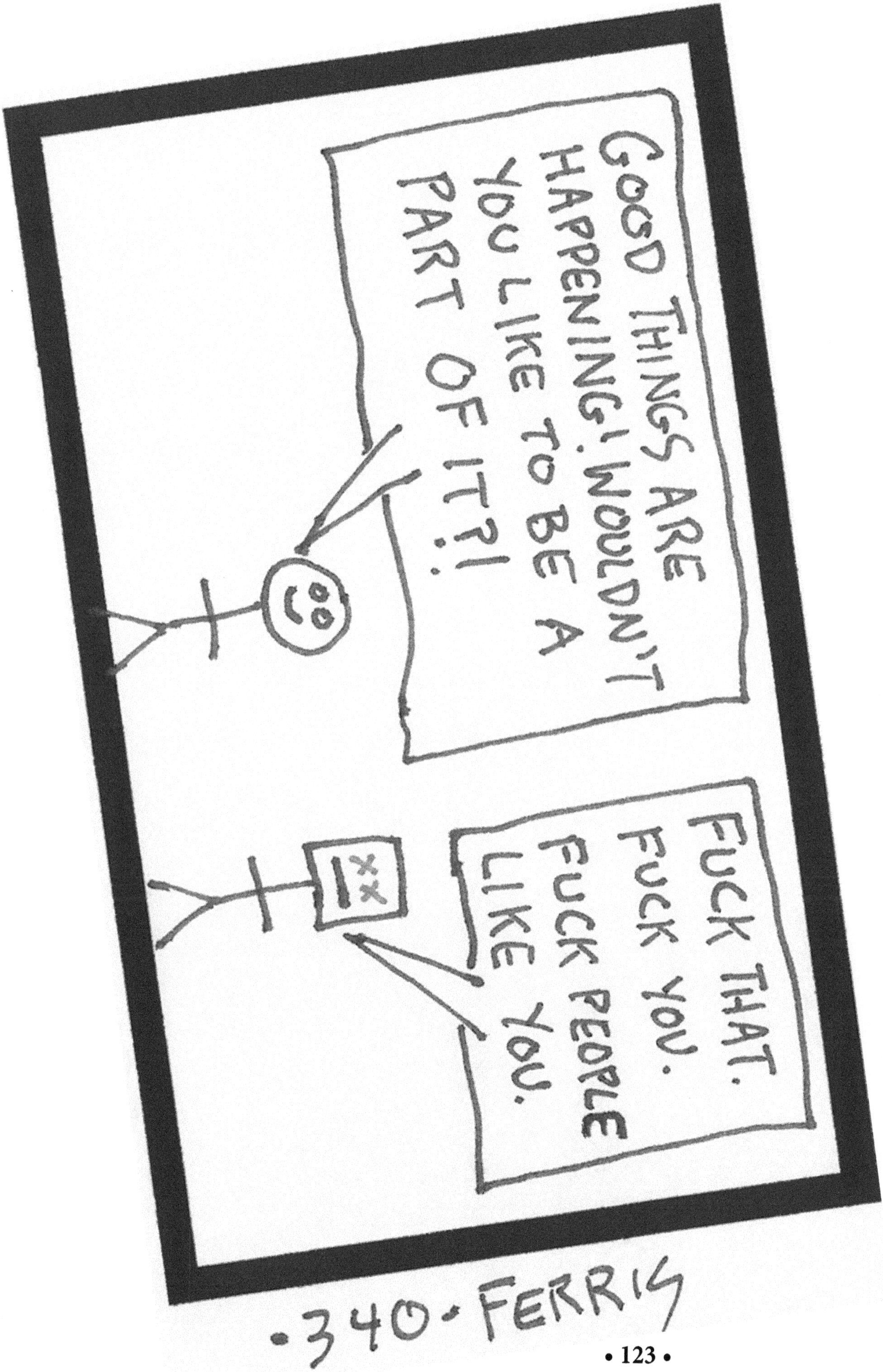
GOOD THINGS ARE HAPPENING! WOULDN'T YOU LIKE TO BE A PART OF IT?!
FUCK THAT. FUCK YOU. FUCK PEOPLE LIKE YOU.

•340• FERRIS

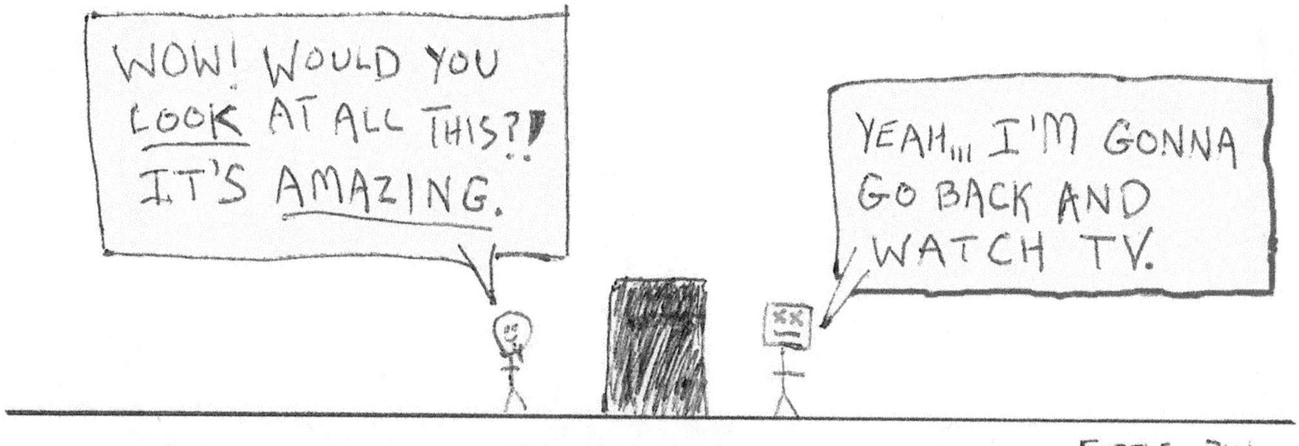
WOW! WOULD YOU LOOK AT ALL THIS?! IT'S AMAZING.
YEAH... I'M GONNA GO BACK AND WATCH TV.
FERRIS • 341

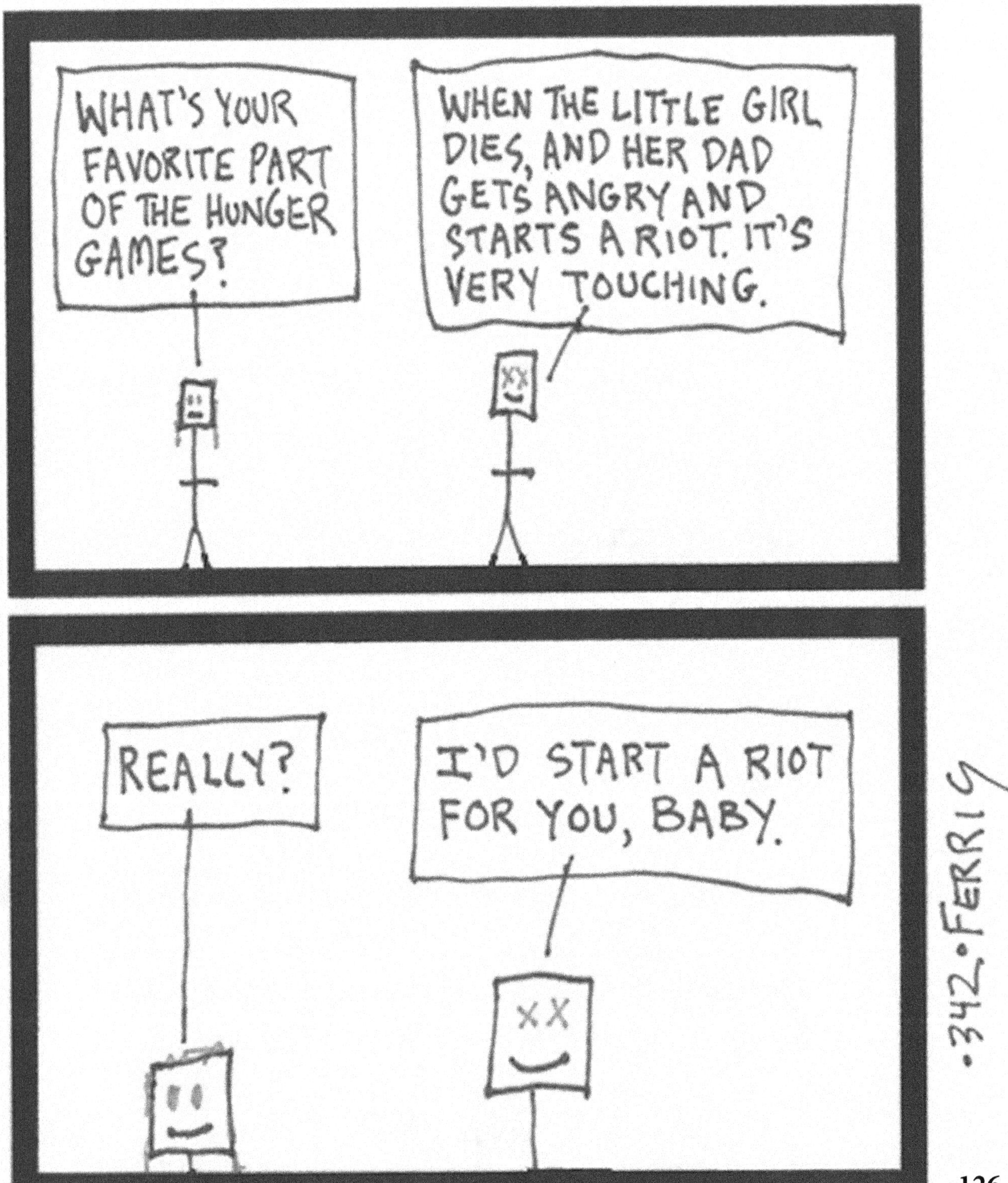
WHAT'S YOUR FAVORITE PART OF THE HUNGER GAMES?
WHEN THE LITTLE GIRL DIES, AND HER DAD GETS ANGRY AND STARTS A RIOT. IT'S VERY TOUCHING.
REALLY?
I'D START A RIOT FOR YOU, BABY.
•342•FERRIG

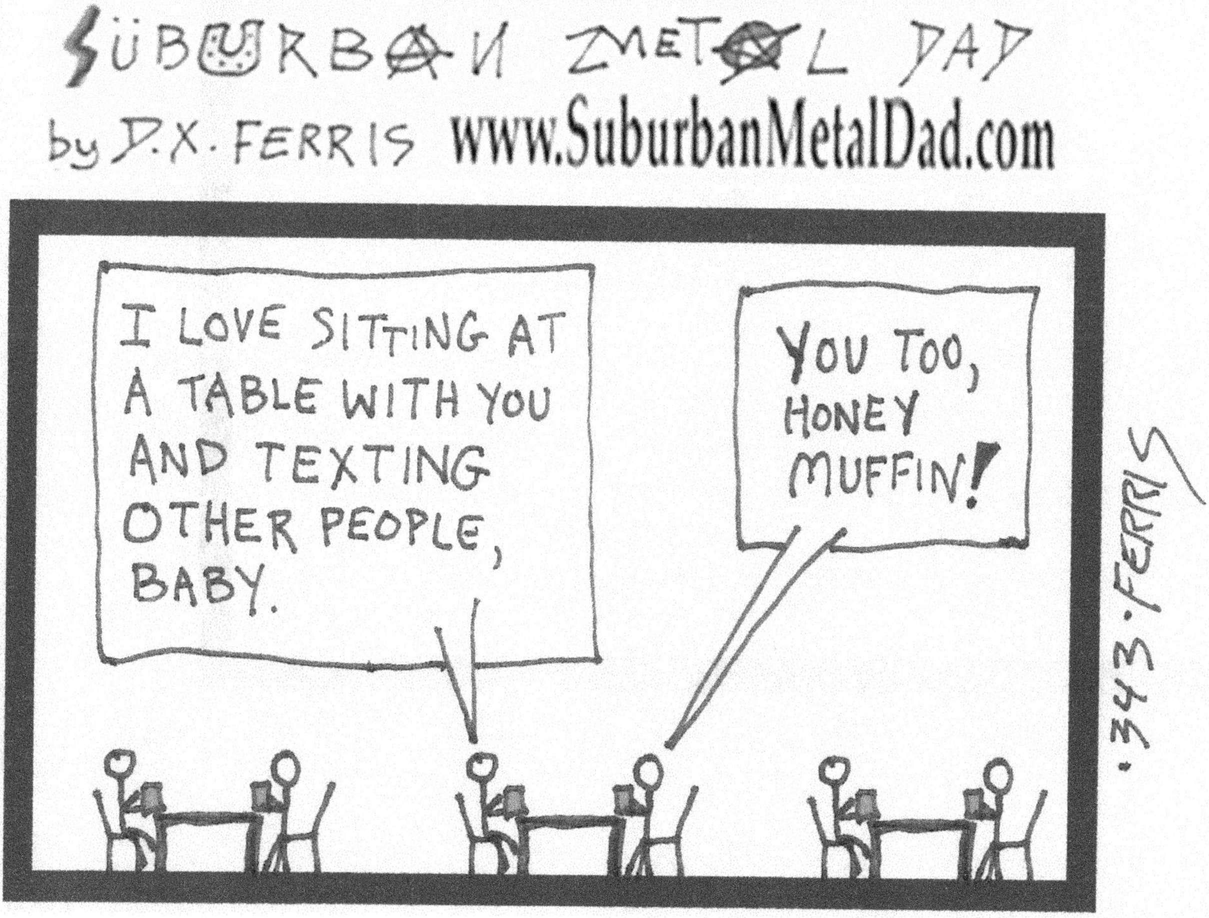
SUBURBAN METAL DAD
by D.X. FERRIS www.SuburbanMetalDad.com
I LOVE SITTING AT A TABLE WITH YOU AND TEXTING OTHER PEOPLE, BABY.
YOU TOO, HONEY MUFFIN!
·343·FERRIS

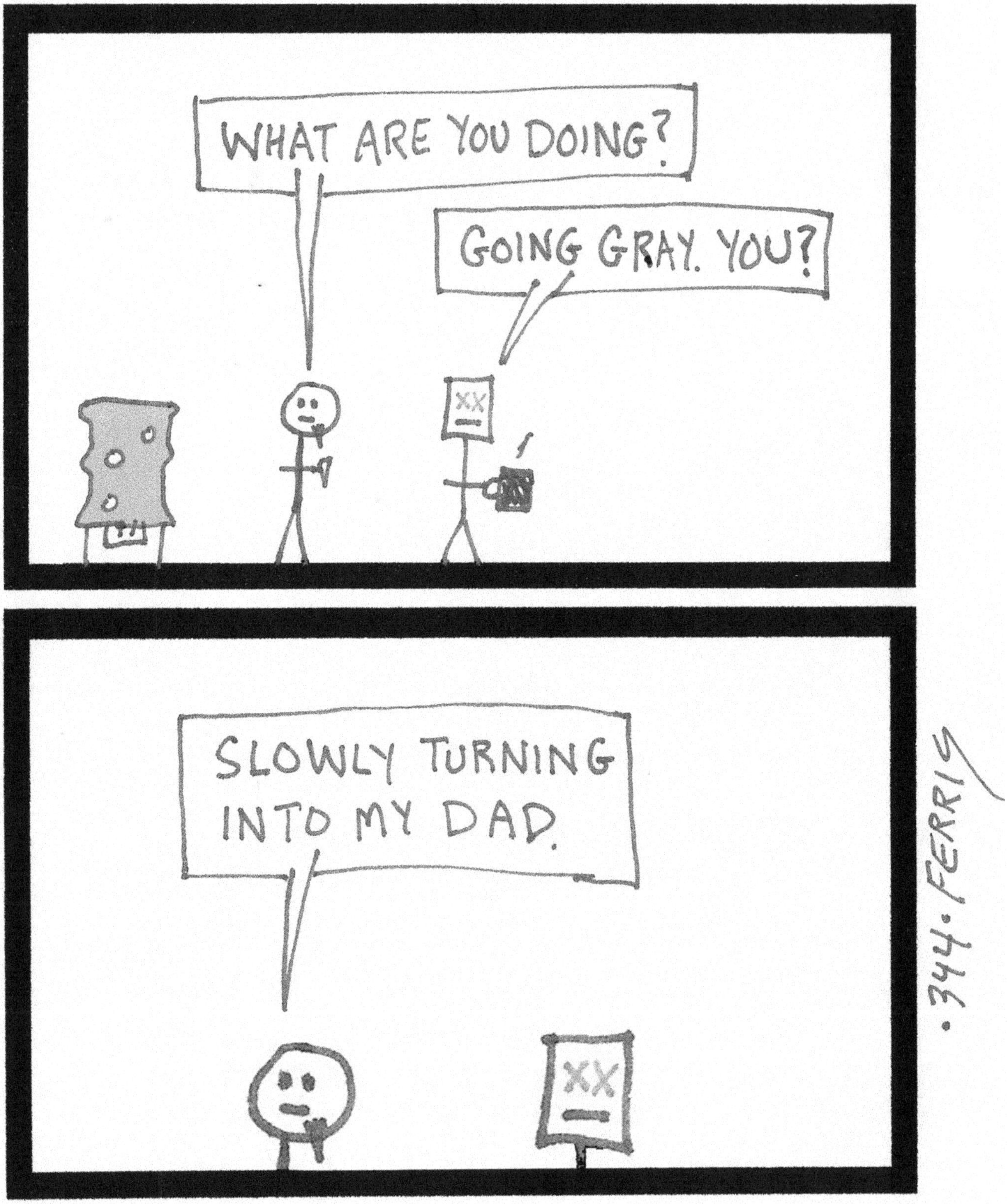
WHAT ARE YOU DOING?
GOING GRAY. YOU?
SLOWLY TURNING INTO MY DAD.
•344•FERRIS

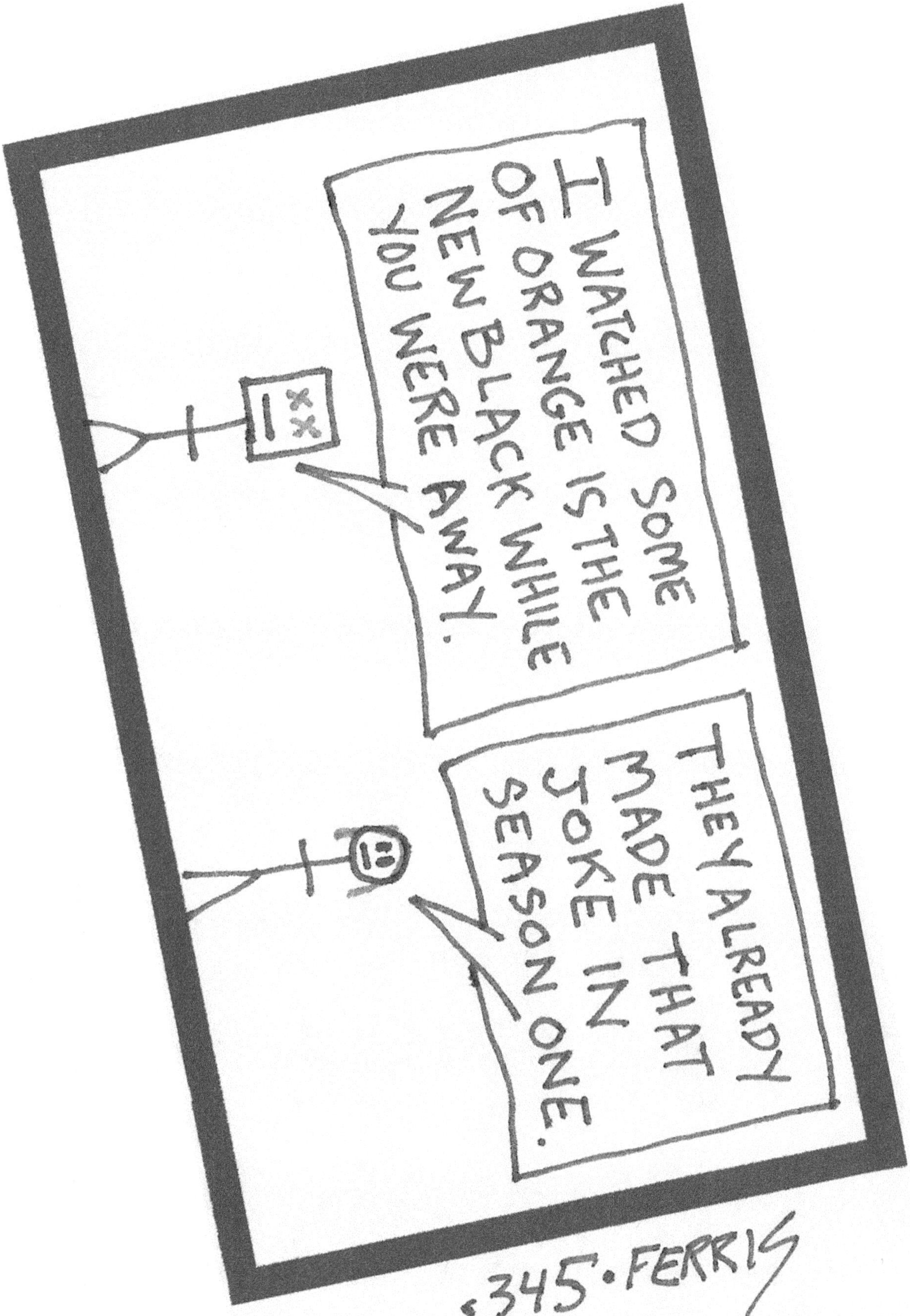
I WATCHED SOME OF ORANGE IS THE NEW BLACK WHILE YOU WERE AWAY.
THEY ALREADY MADE THAT JOKE IN SEASON ONE.
•345•FERRIS

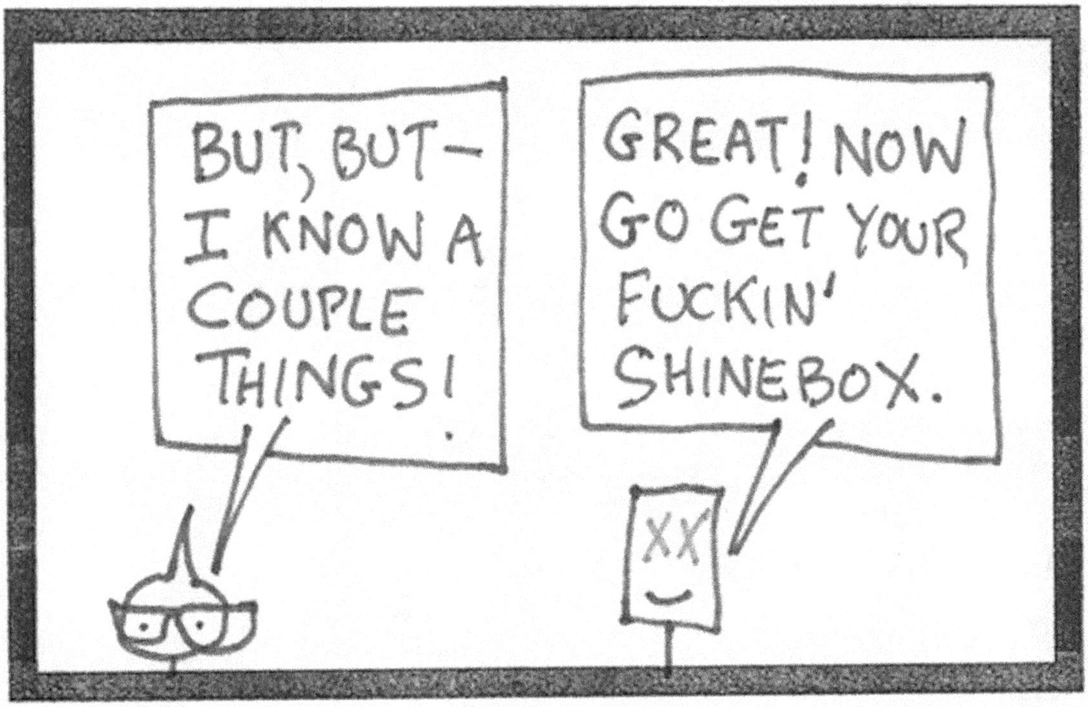
BUT, BUT- I KNOW A COUPLE THINGS!
GREAT! NOW GO GET YOUR FUCKIN' SHINEBOX.

•379•FERRIS

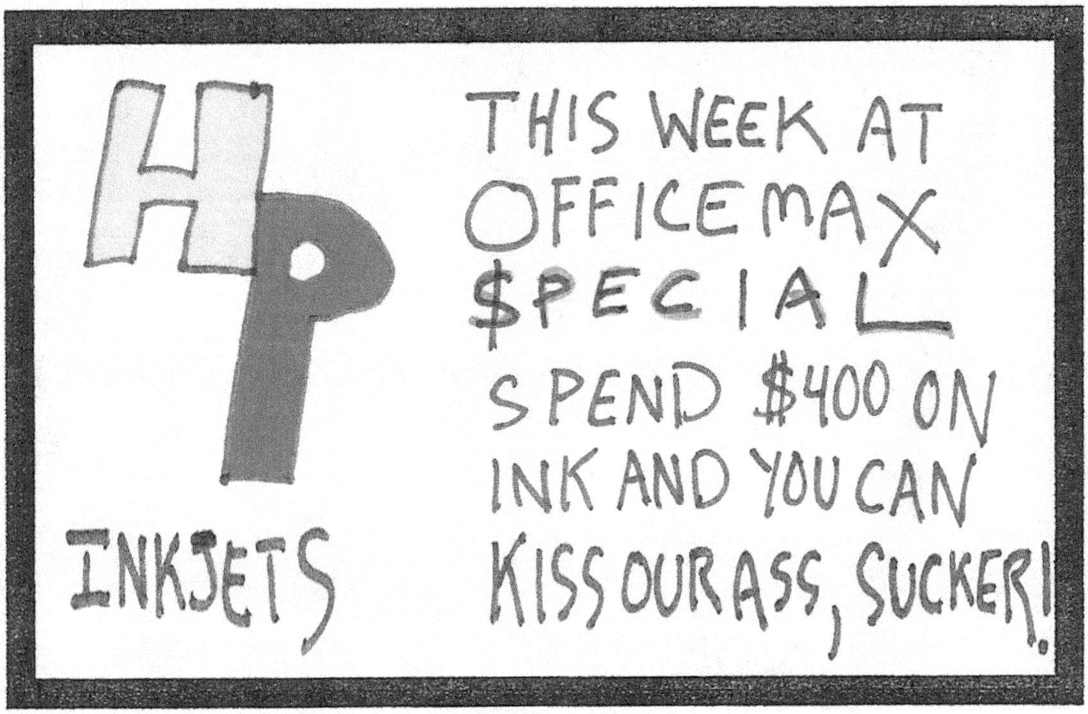
HP
INKJETS
THIS WEEK AT OFFICEMAX $PECIAL
SPEND $400 ON INK AND YOU CAN KISS OUR ASS, SUCKER!

•380•FERRIS

DO YOU NEED A CASE FOR YOUR iPAD?
I HAVE ONE. I JUST DON'T LIKE USING IT.
DO YOU LIKE HAVING AN iPAD THAT WORKS?
WHATEVER.
SHATTER
HOW'S YOUR iPAD?
BROKEN iPADS ARE THE COOLEST, OLD MAN.
·346·FERRIS

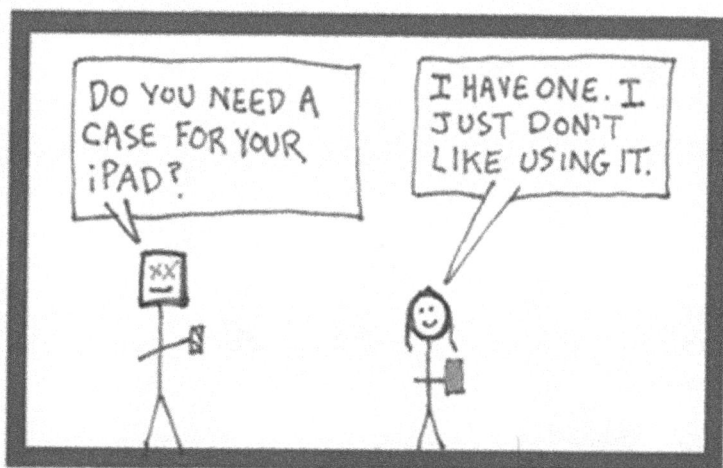

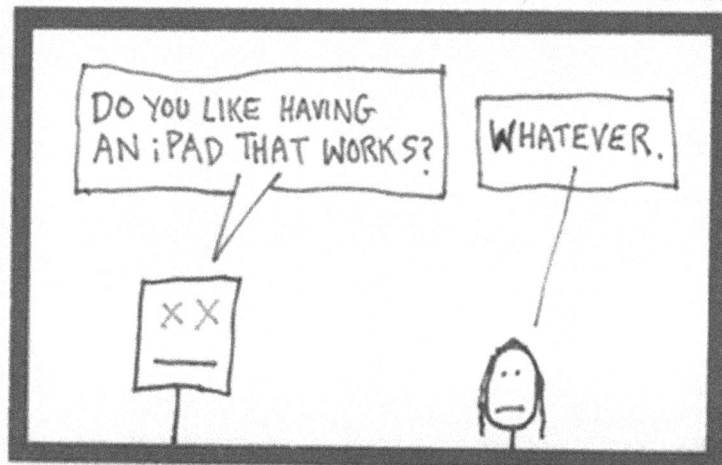

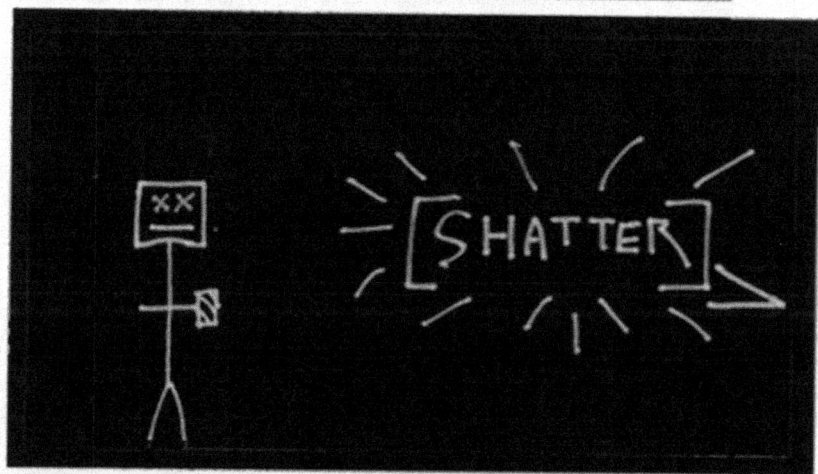

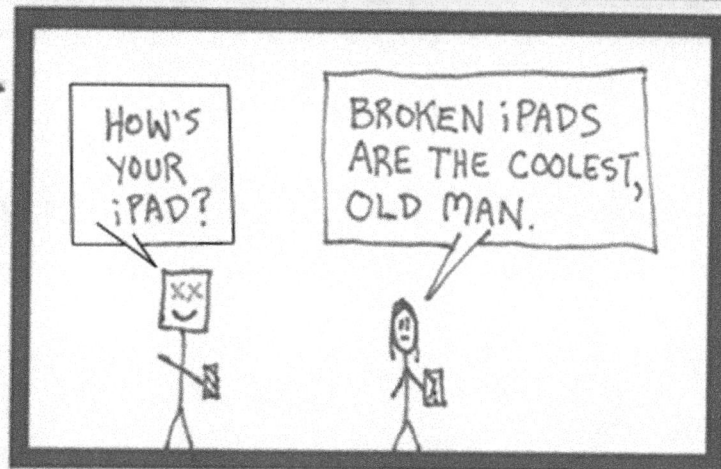

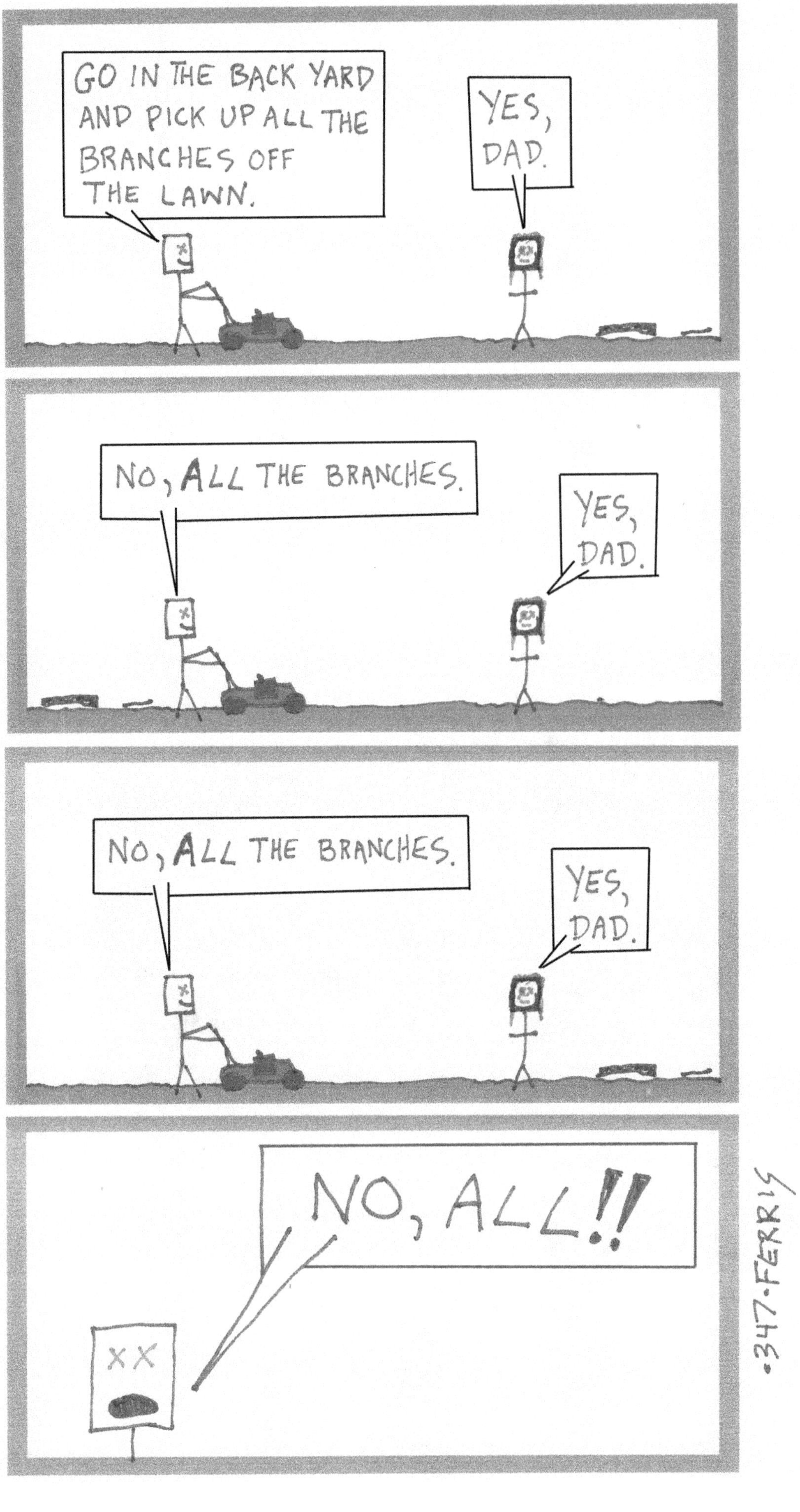
GO IN THE BACK YARD AND PICK UP ALL THE BRANCHES OFF THE LAWN.
YES, DAD.
NO, ALL THE BRANCHES.
YES, DAD.
NO, ALL THE BRANCHES.
YES, DAD.
NO, ALL!!
•347•FERRIS

SMD # 347: "SUBURBAN POP-PUNK DAD"

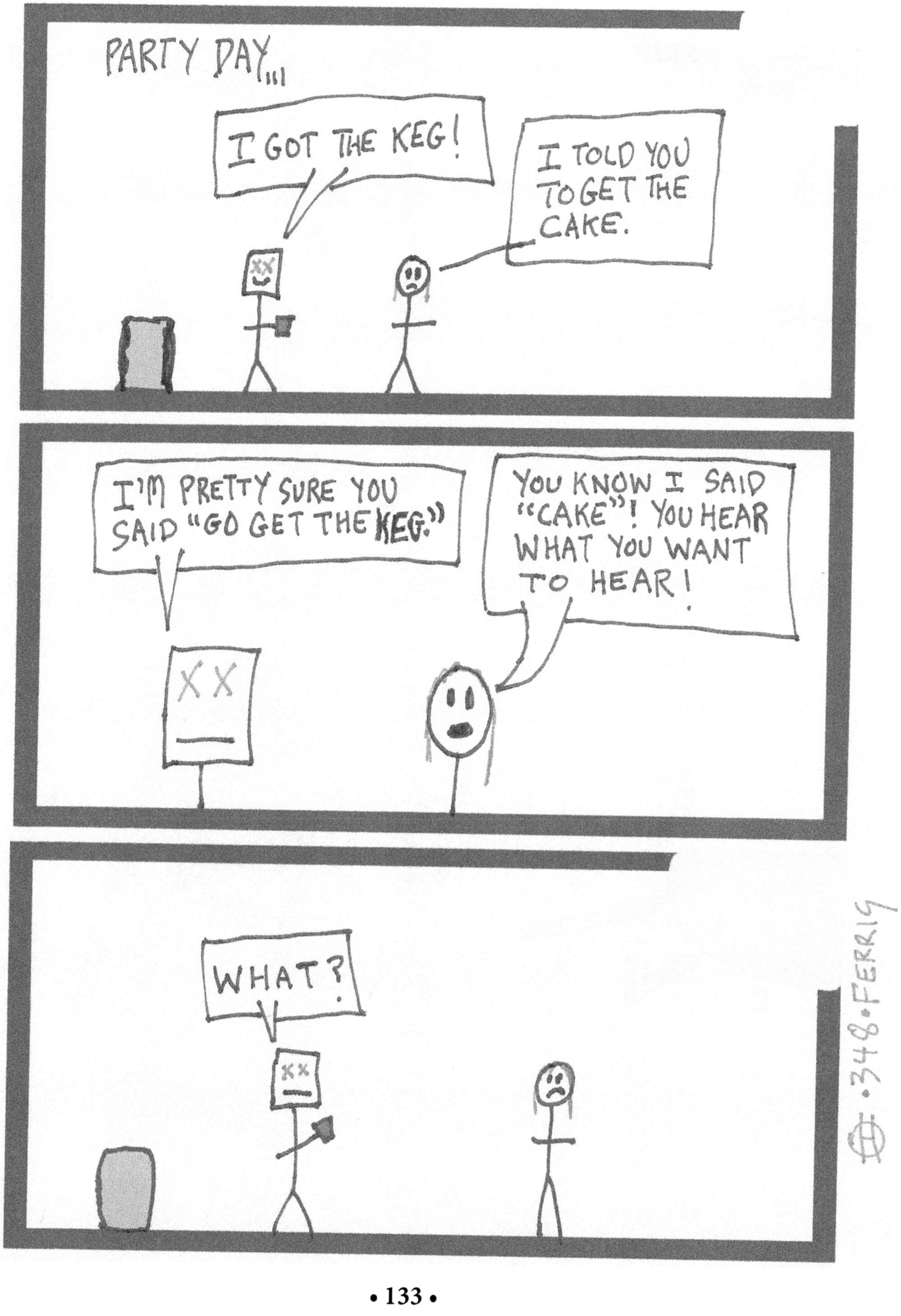
PARTY DAY...
I GOT THE KEG!
I TOLD YOU TO GET THE CAKE.
I'M PRETTY SURE YOU SAID "GO GET THE KEG."
YOU KNOW I SAID "CAKE"! YOU HEAR WHAT YOU WANT TO HEAR!
WHAT?
•348•FERRIS

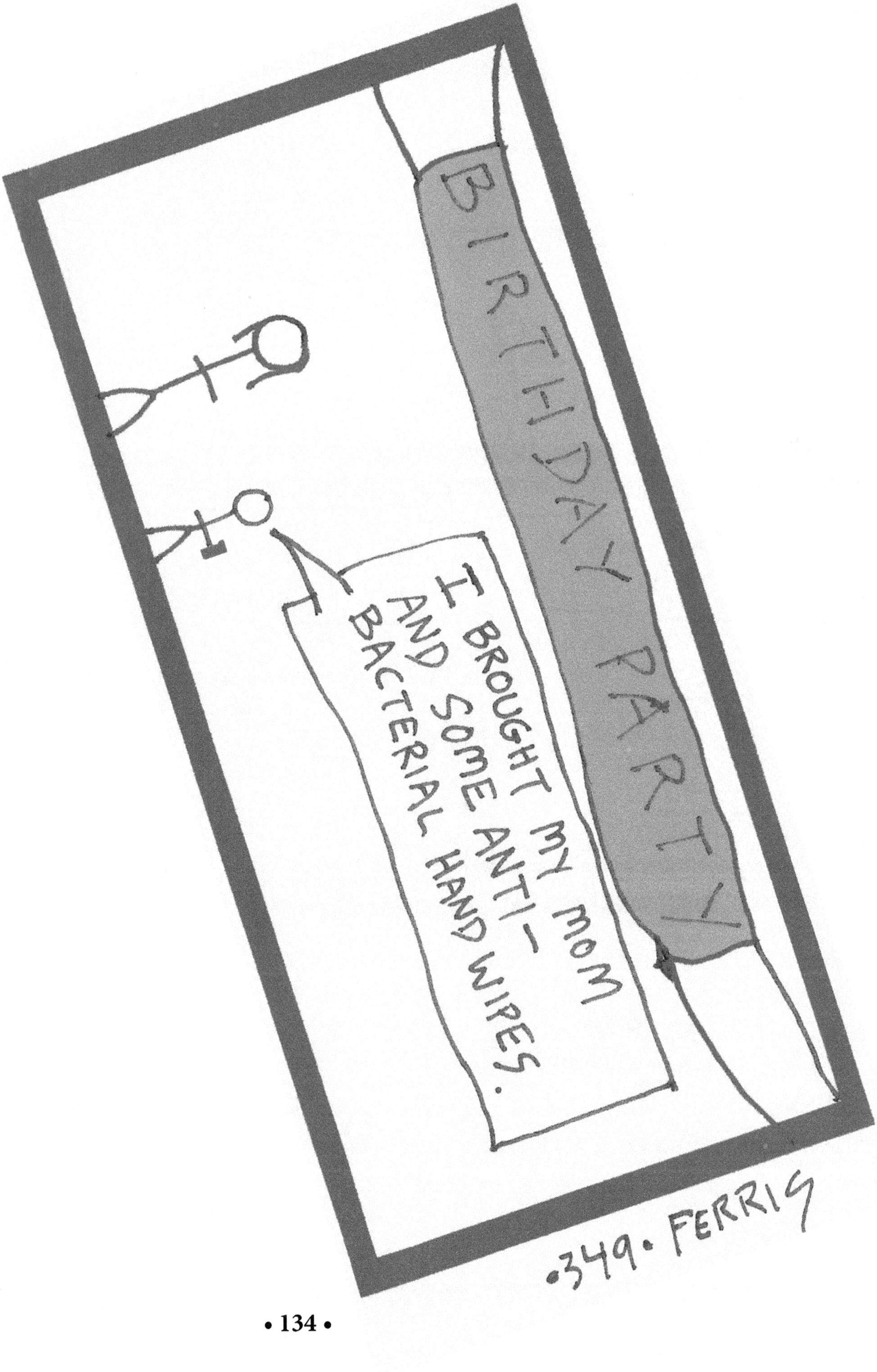
BIRTHDAY PARTY
I BROUGHT MY MOM AND SOME ANTI-BACTERIAL HAND WIPES.
•349• FERRIS

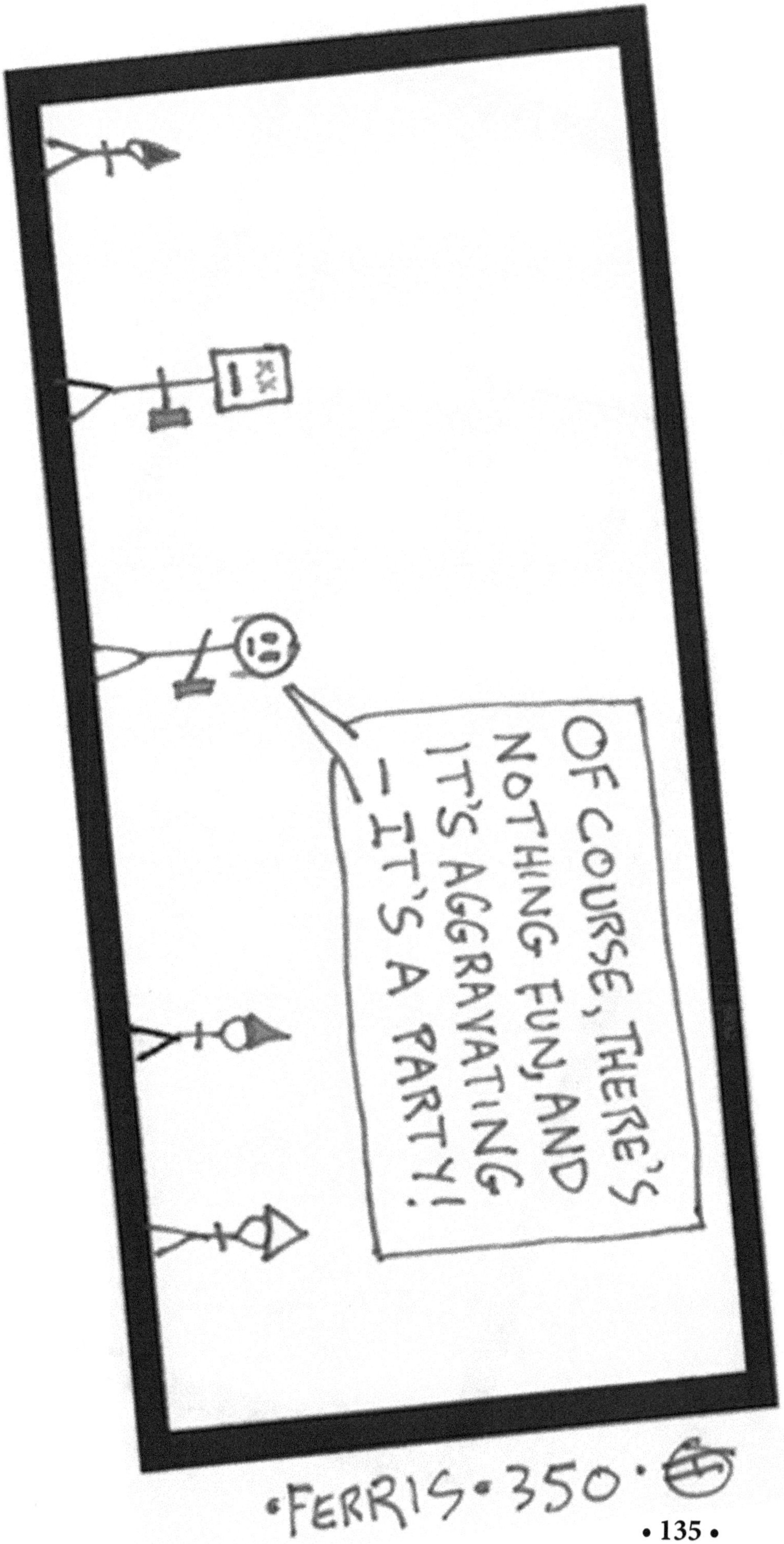
OF COURSE, THERE'S NOTHING FUN, AND IT'S AGGRAVATING — IT'S A PARTY!
•FERRIS•350•

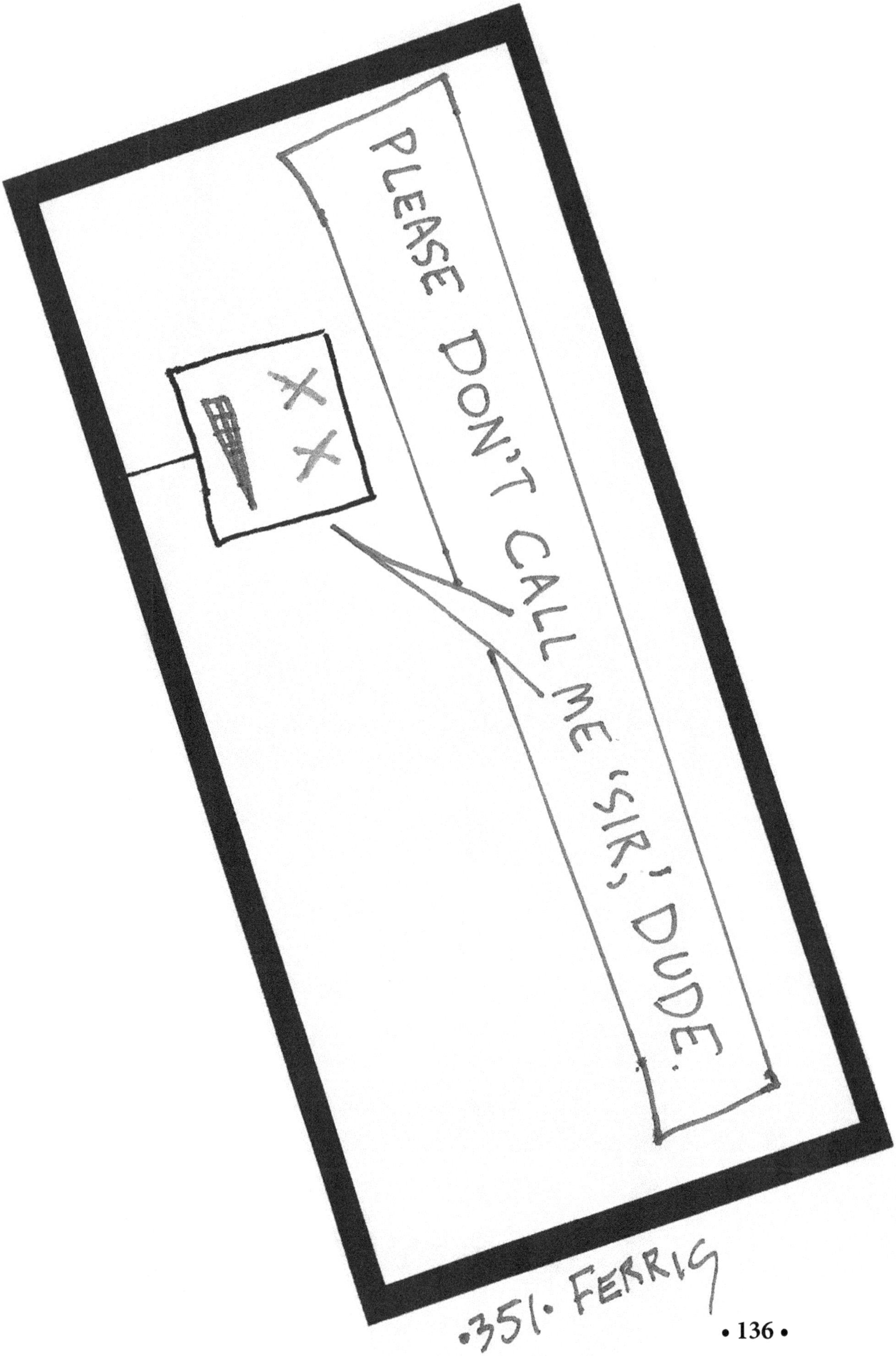
PLEASE DON'T CALL ME 'SIR,' DUDE.
·351· FERRIS

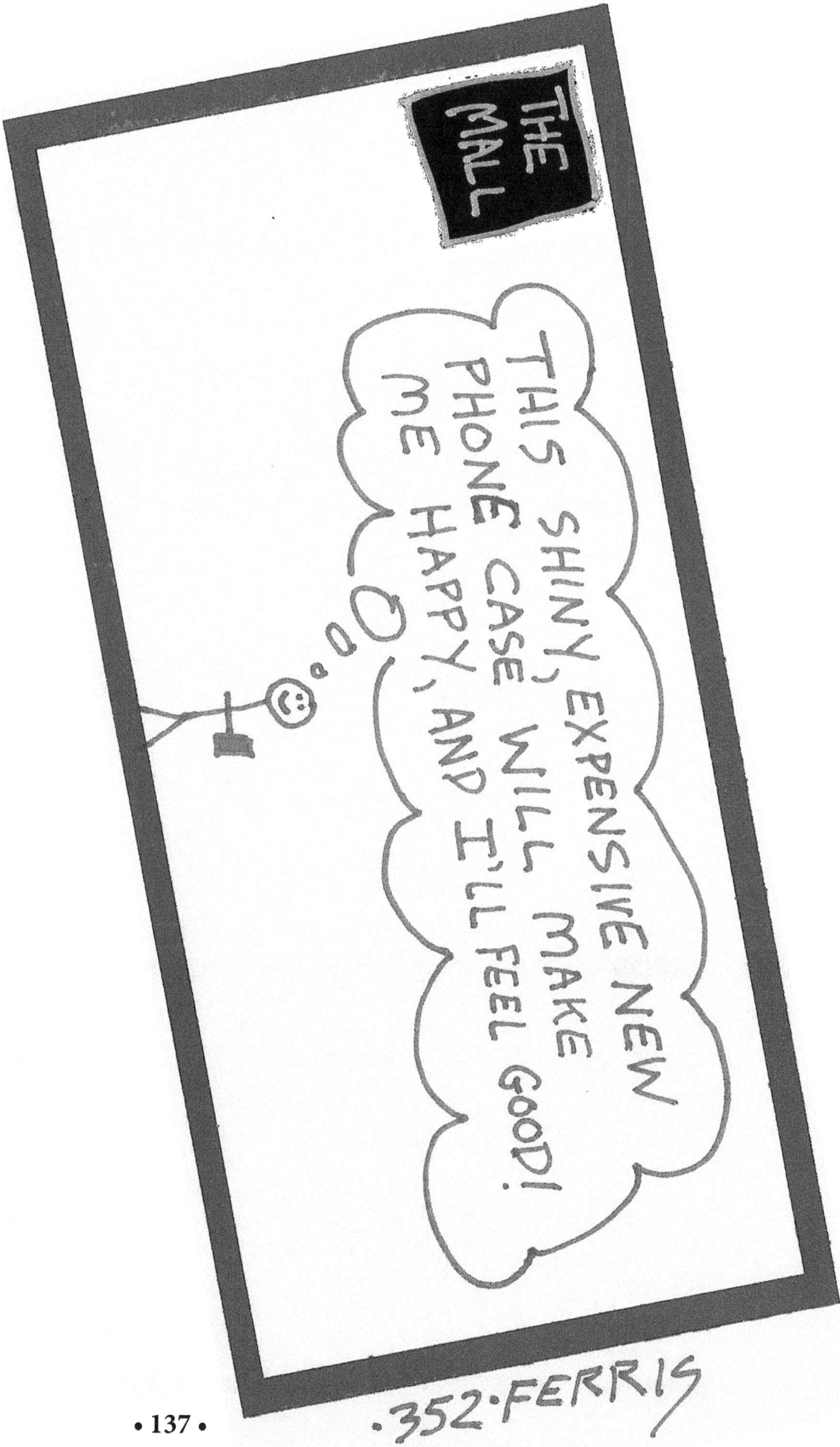
THE MALL
THIS SHINY, EXPENSIVE NEW PHONE CASE WILL MAKE ME HAPPY, AND I'LL FEEL GOOD!

·352·FERRIS

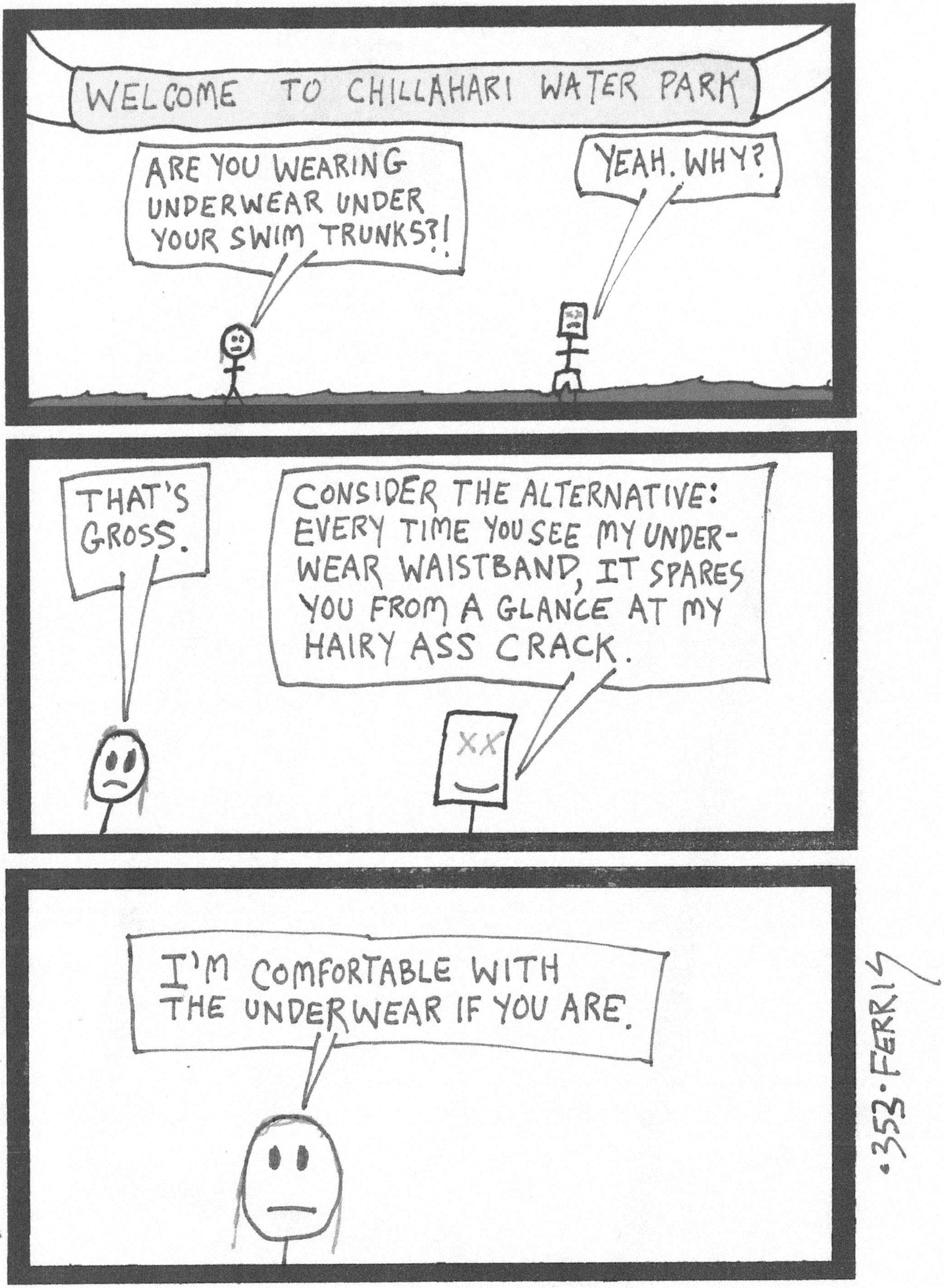
WELCOME TO CHILLAHARI WATER PARK
ARE YOU WEARING UNDERWEAR UNDER YOUR SWIM TRUNKS?!
YEAH. WHY?
THAT'S GROSS.
CONSIDER THE ALTERNATIVE: EVERY TIME YOU SEE MY UNDER-WEAR WAISTBAND, IT SPARES YOU FROM A GLANCE AT MY HAIRY ASS CRACK.
I'M COMFORTABLE WITH THE UNDERWEAR IF YOU ARE.
•353•FERRIS

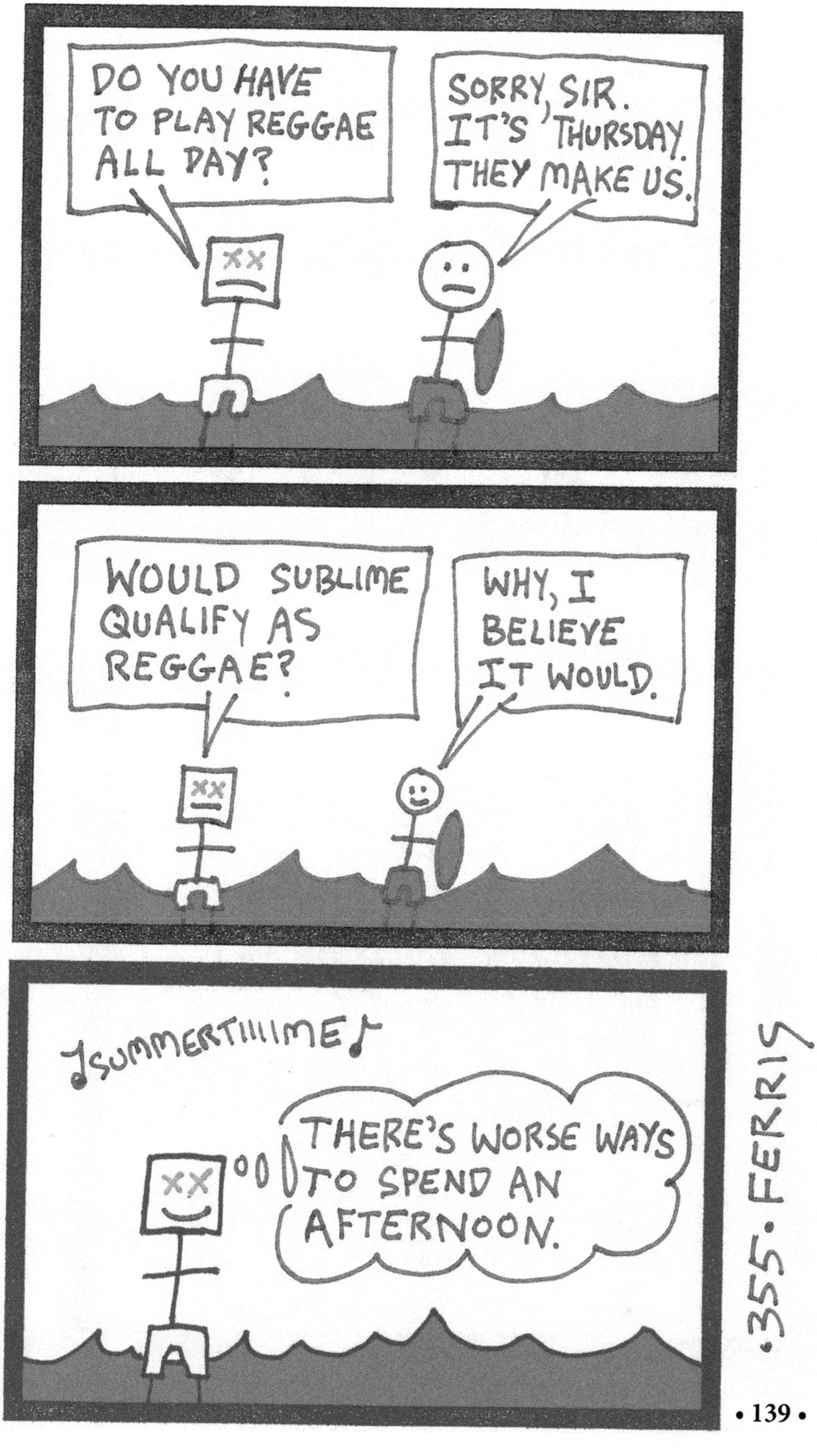
DO YOU HAVE TO PLAY REGGAE ALL DAY?
SORRY, SIR. IT'S THURSDAY. THEY MAKE US.
WOULD SUBLIME QUALIFY AS REGGAE?
WHY, I BELIEVE IT WOULD.
♪SUMMERTIIIIIME♪
THERE'S WORSE WAYS TO SPEND AN AFTERNOON.
·355· FERRIS

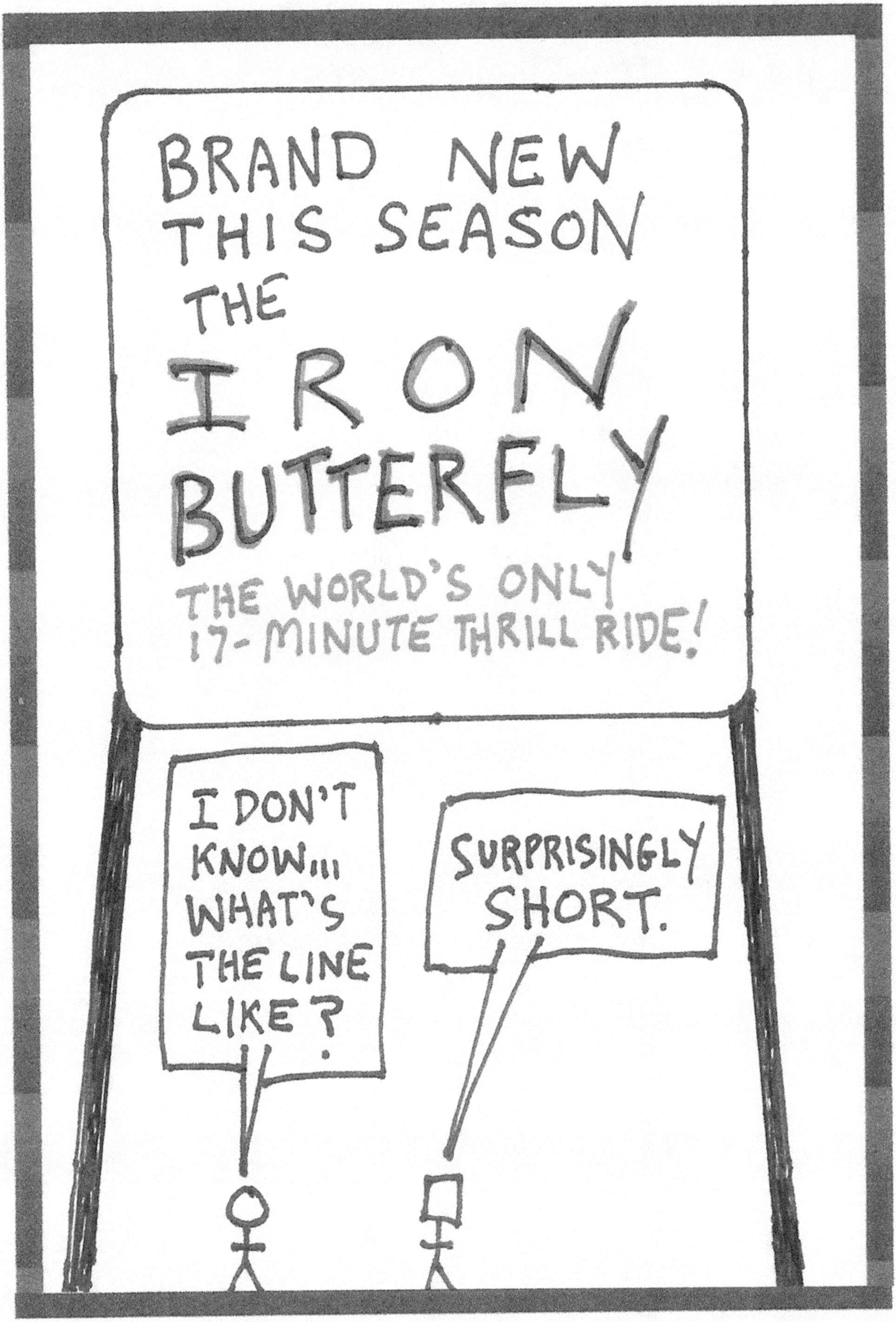
BRAND NEW THIS SEASON THE IRON BUTTERFLY
THE WORLD'S ONLY 17-MINUTE THRILL RIDE!
I DON'T KNOW... WHAT'S THE LINE LIKE?
SURPRISINGLY SHORT.
•354• FERRIS

THREE. 3. 3,3,3.
3. THREE. 3,3.
3 3 3 3.3
THREE. THREE.
3, THREE, 3
THREE, 3, THR
3,3,3,3,3
GO!
FOUR!
FUCK.
FERRIS 357

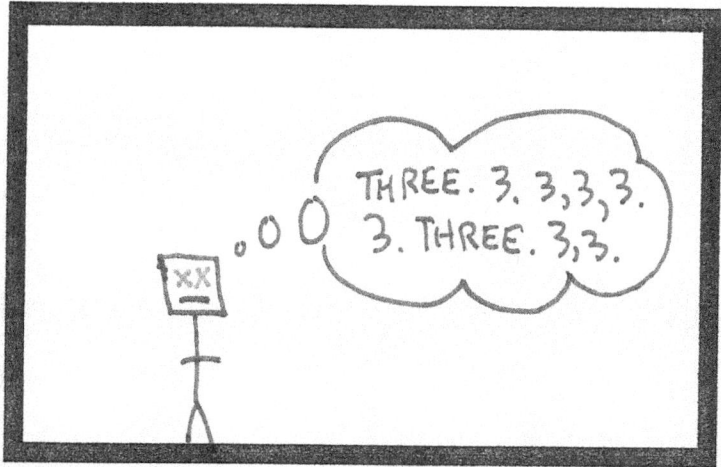

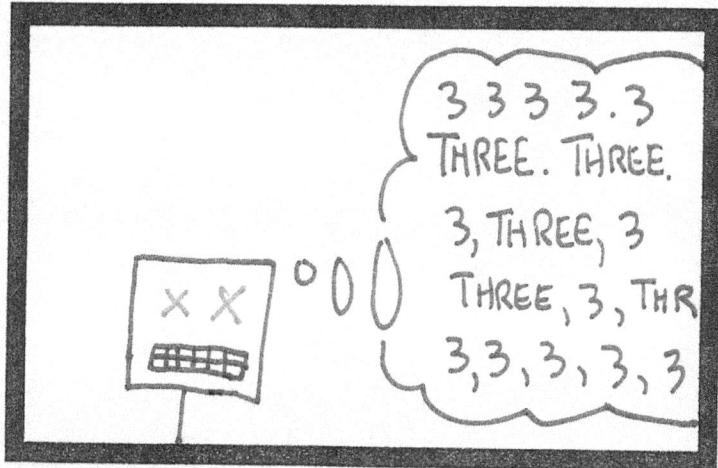

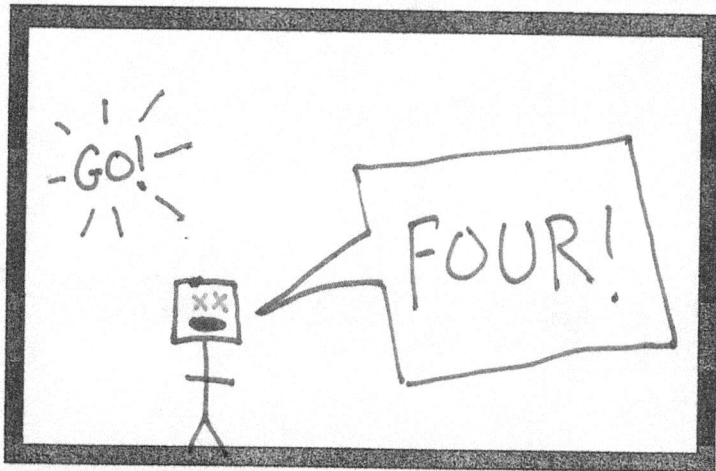

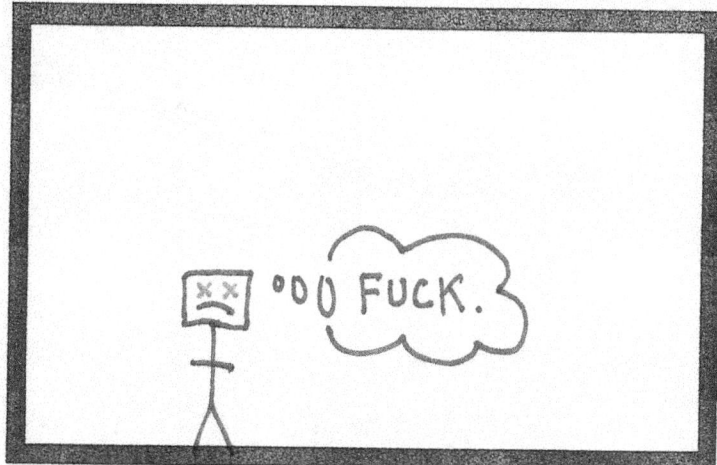

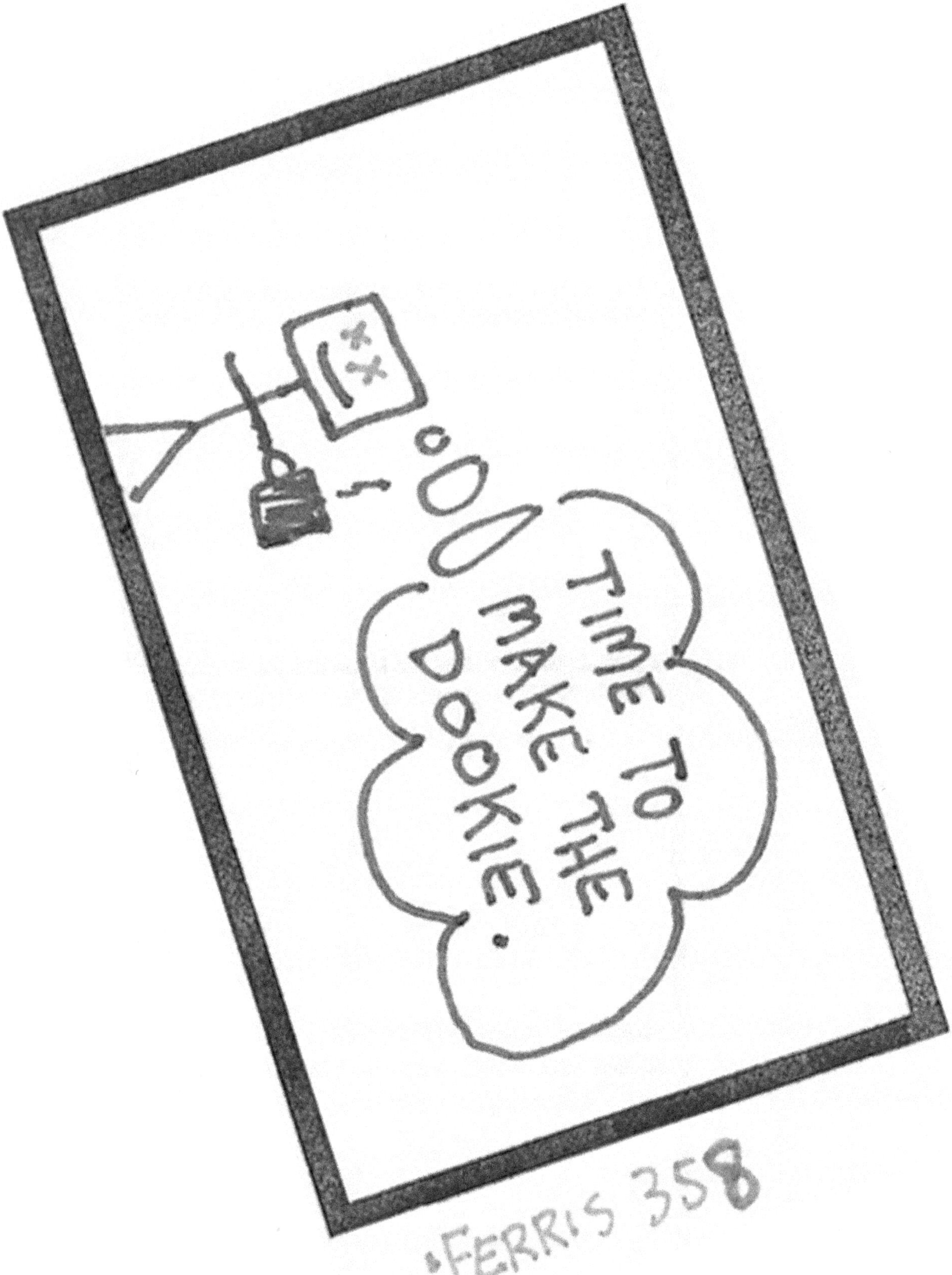
TIME TO MAKE THE DOOKIE.
FERRIS 358

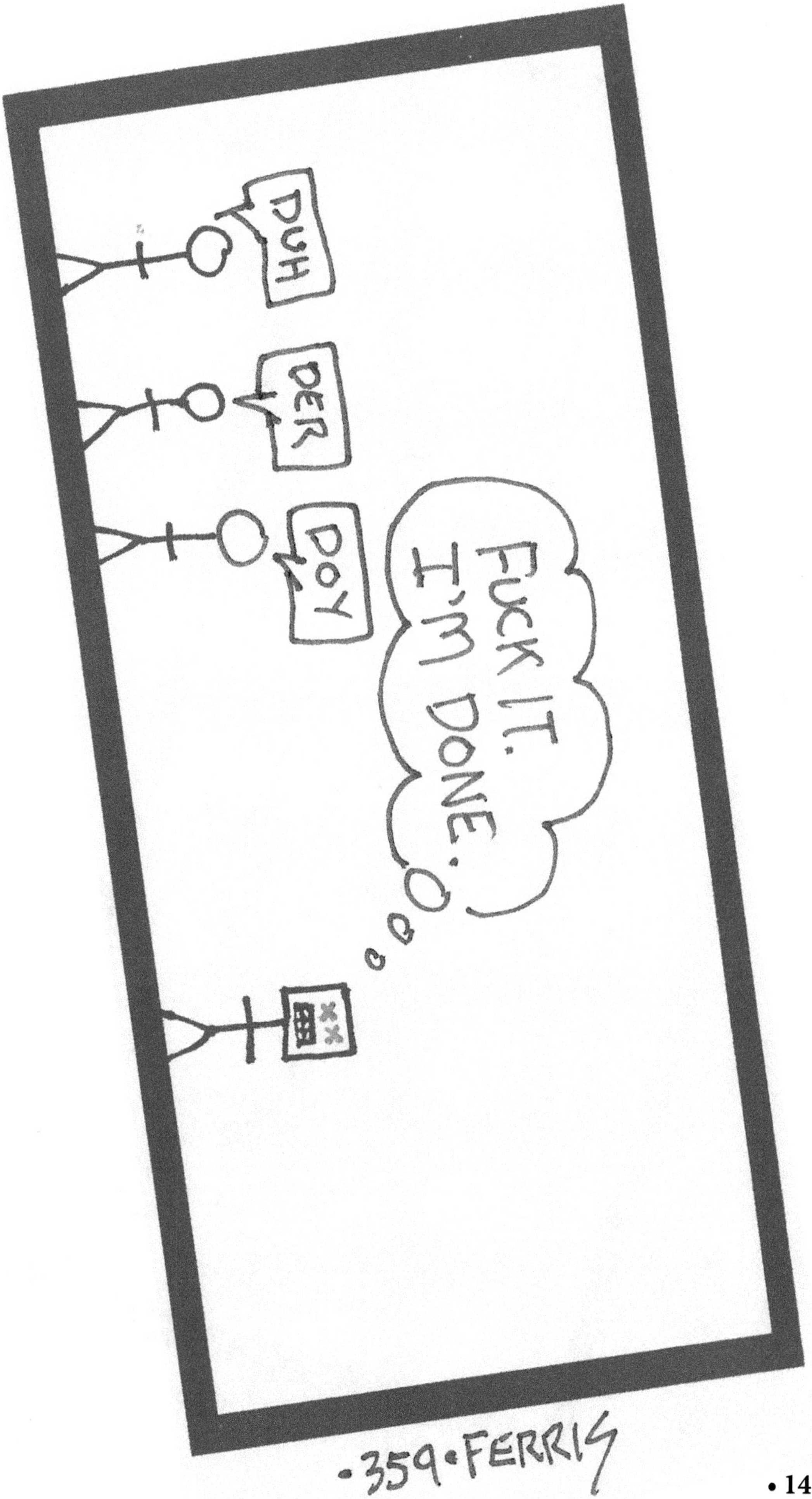
DUH
DER
DOY
FUCK IT. I'M DONE.

•359•FERRIS

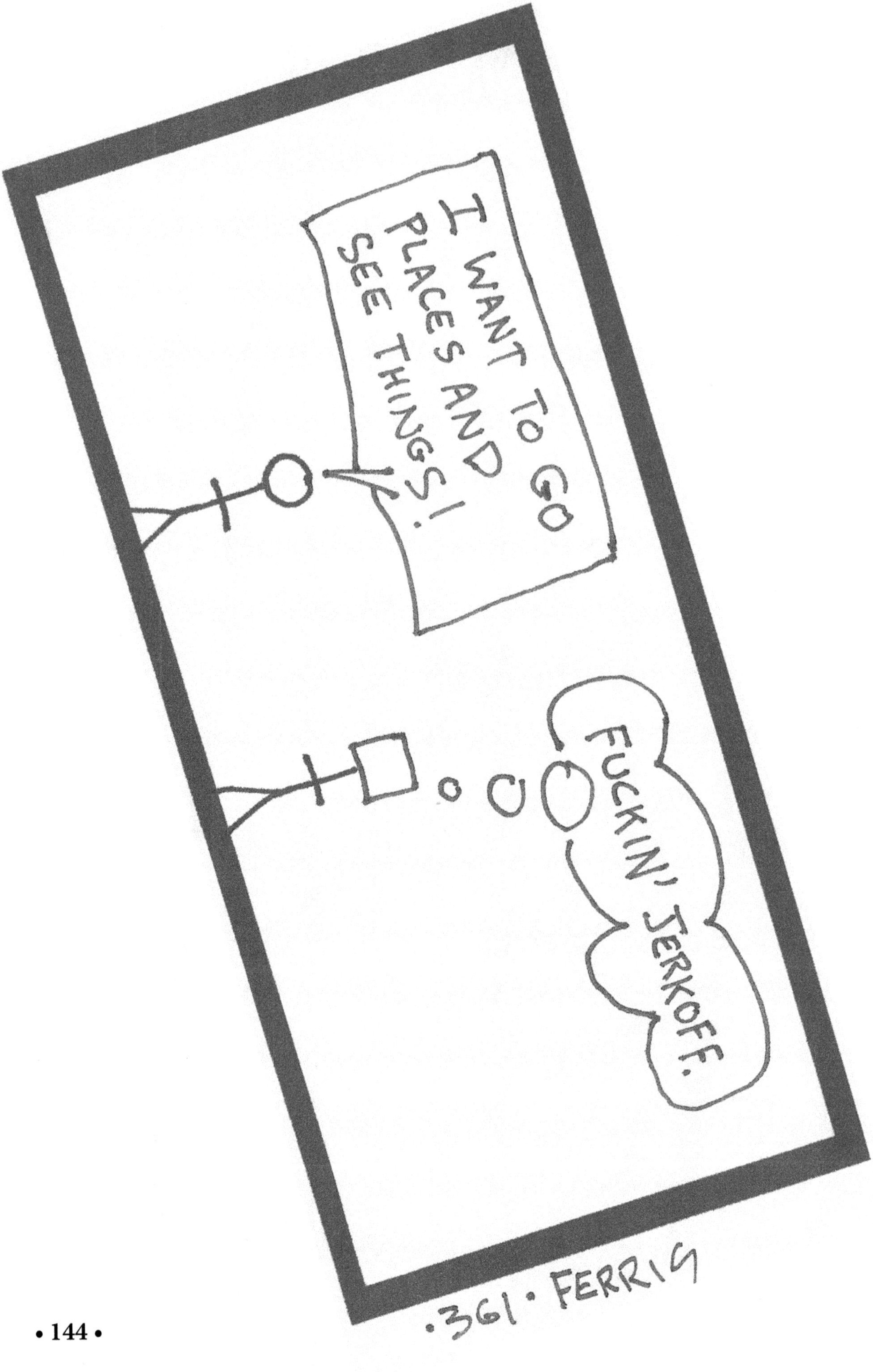
I WANT TO GO PLACES AND SEE THINGS!
FUCKIN' JERKOFF.
·361· FERRIS

MY SON LOVES TO READ, SO HE'LL PROBABLY BE A MILITARY LAWYER, LIKE HIS GRANDFATHER.
NICE. HOW OLD IS HE?
THREE.
•360•FERRIG

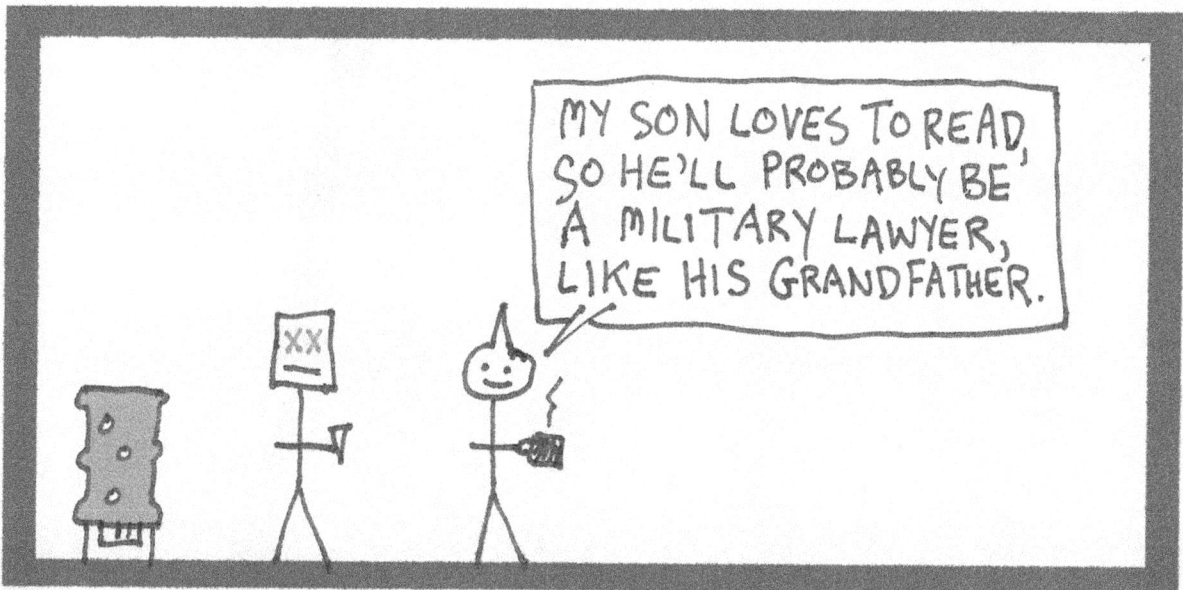

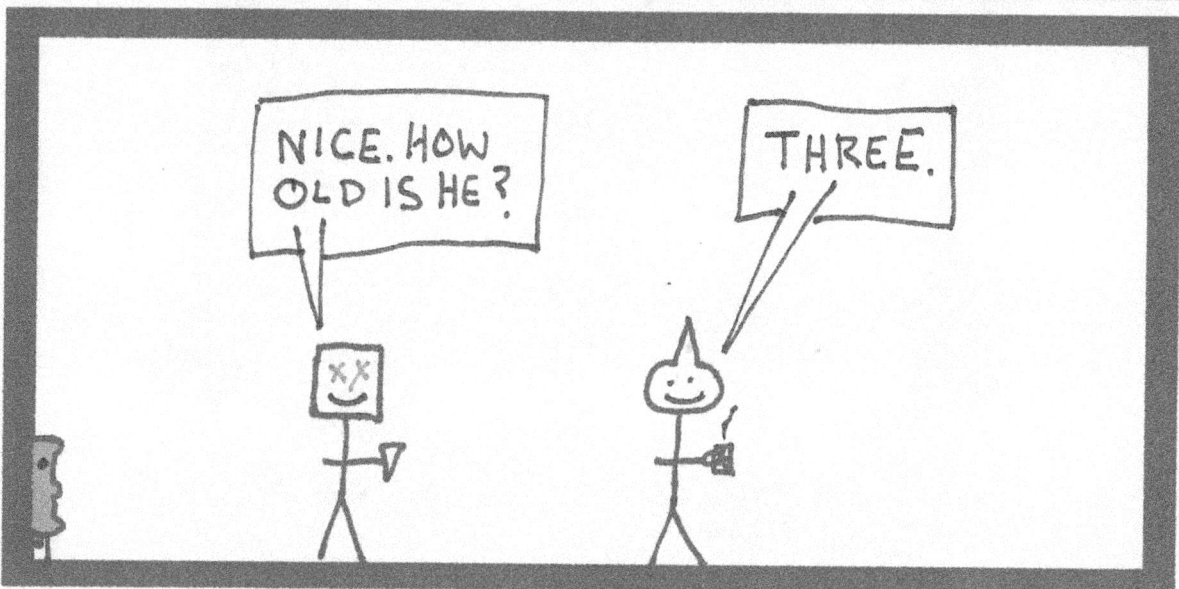

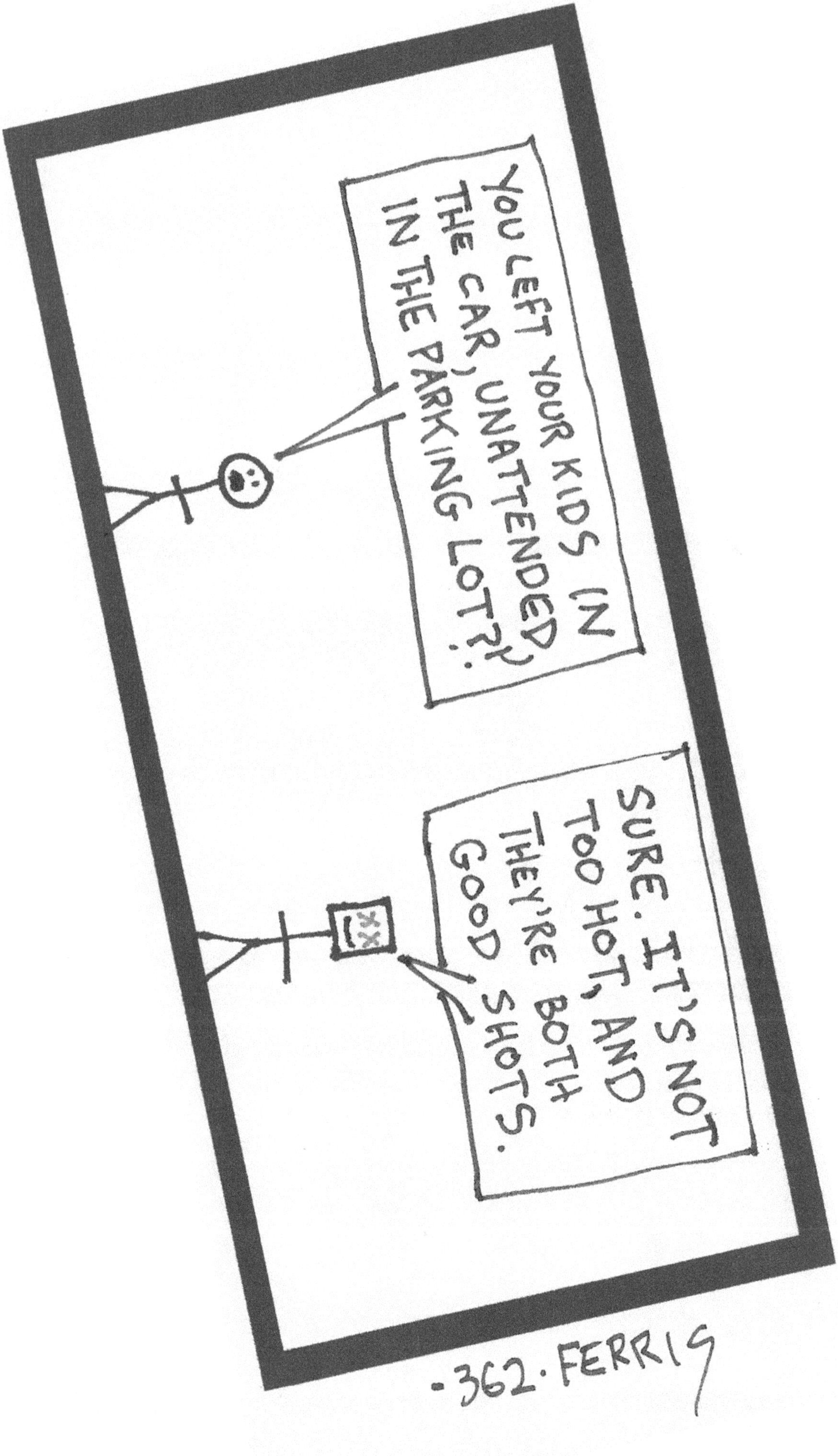
YOU LEFT YOUR KIDS IN THE CAR, UNATTENDED, IN THE PARKING LOT?!
SURE. IT'S NOT TOO HOT, AND THEY'RE BOTH GOOD SHOTS.
•362• FERRIS

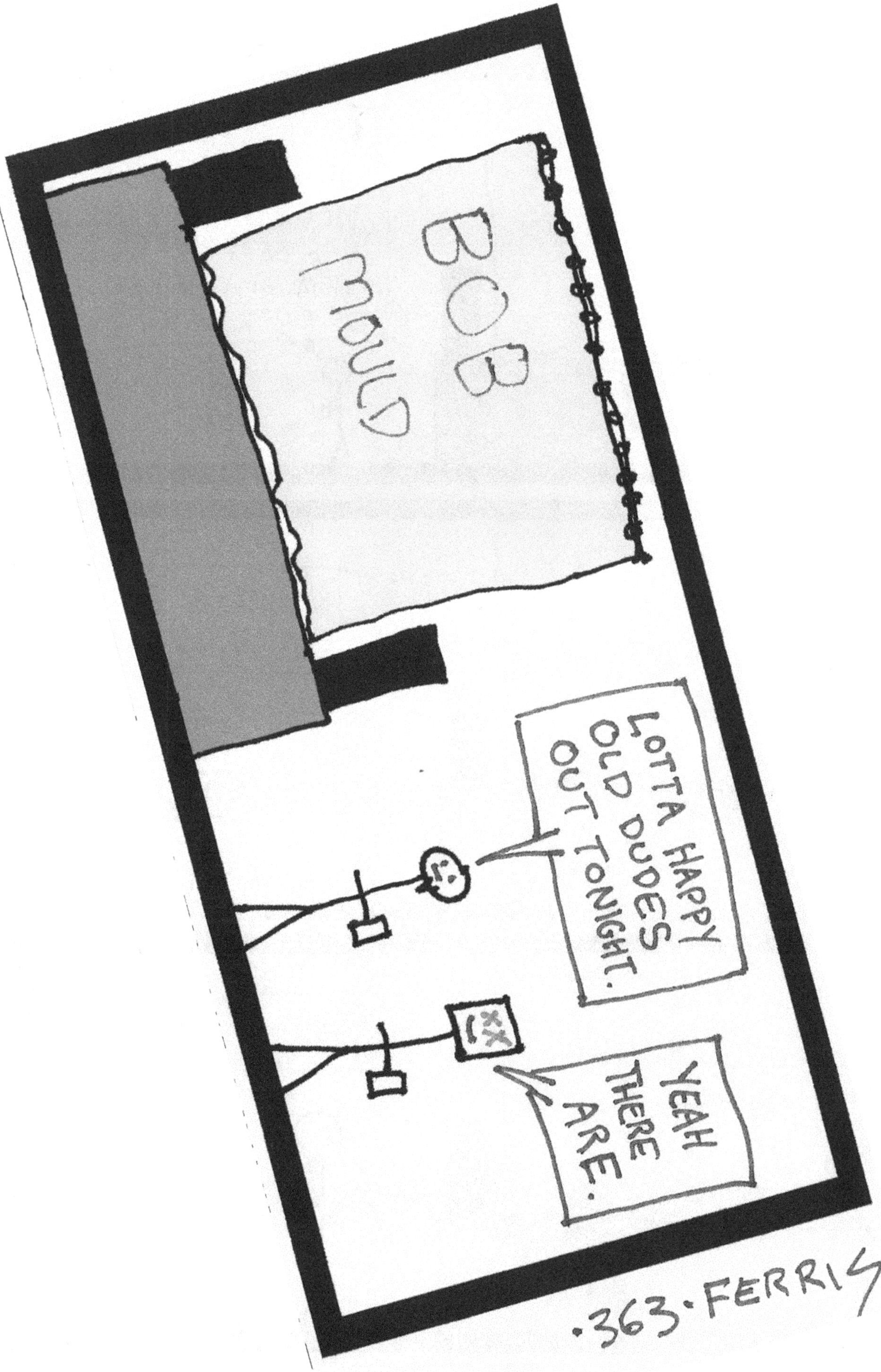
BOB MOULD
LOTTA HAPPY OLD DUDES OUT TONIGHT.
YEAH THERE ARE.
·363·FERRIS

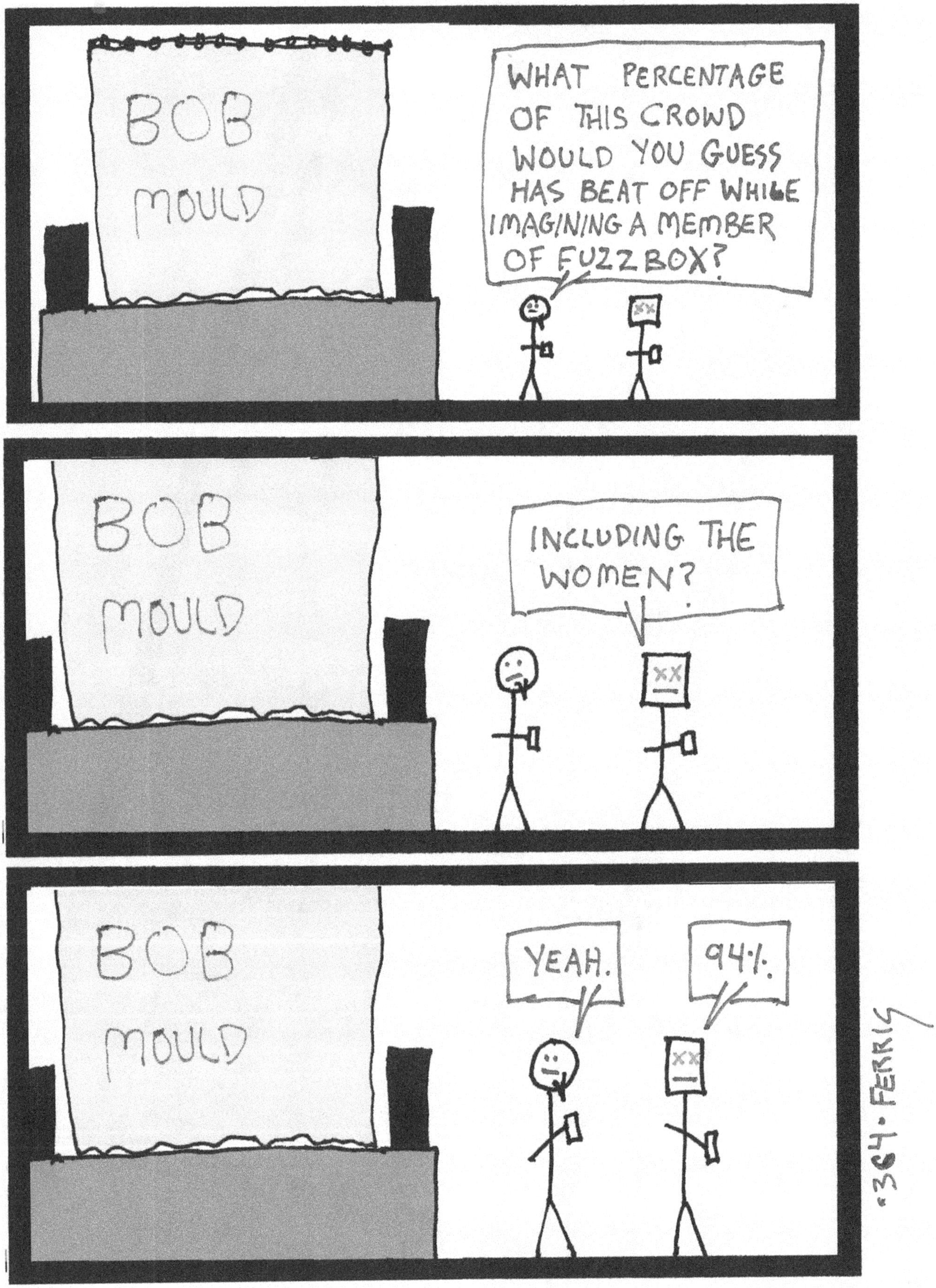
BOB MOULD
WHAT PERCENTAGE OF THIS CROWD WOULD YOU GUESS HAS BEAT OFF WHILE IMAGINING A MEMBER OF FUZZBOX?
BOB MOULD
INCLUDING THE WOMEN?
BOB MOULD
YEAH.
94%.
©364 • FERRIS

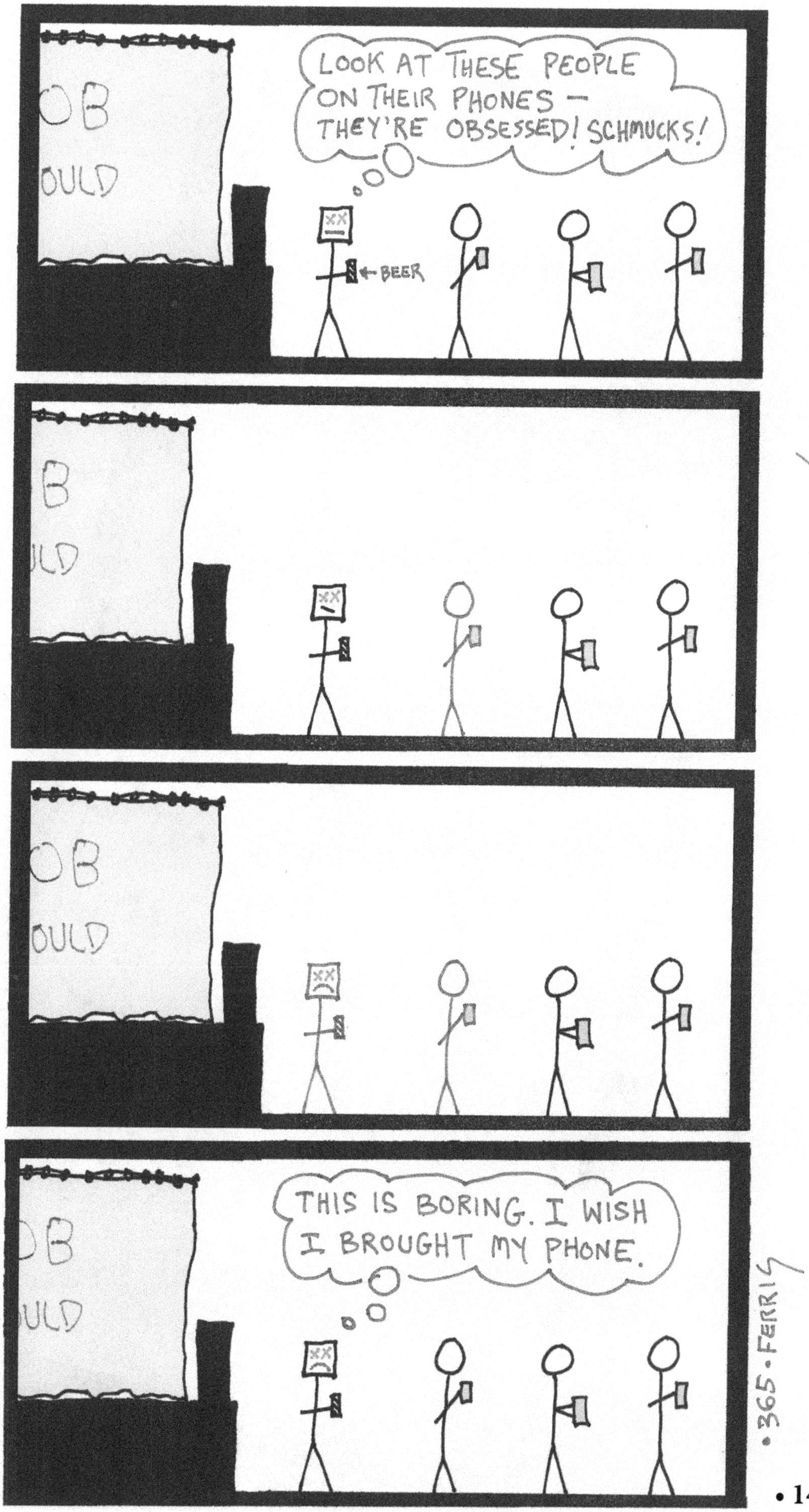
LOOK AT THESE PEOPLE ON THEIR PHONES – THEY'RE OBSESSED! SCHMUCKS!
BEER
THIS IS BORING. I WISH I BROUGHT MY PHONE.
• 365 • FERRIS

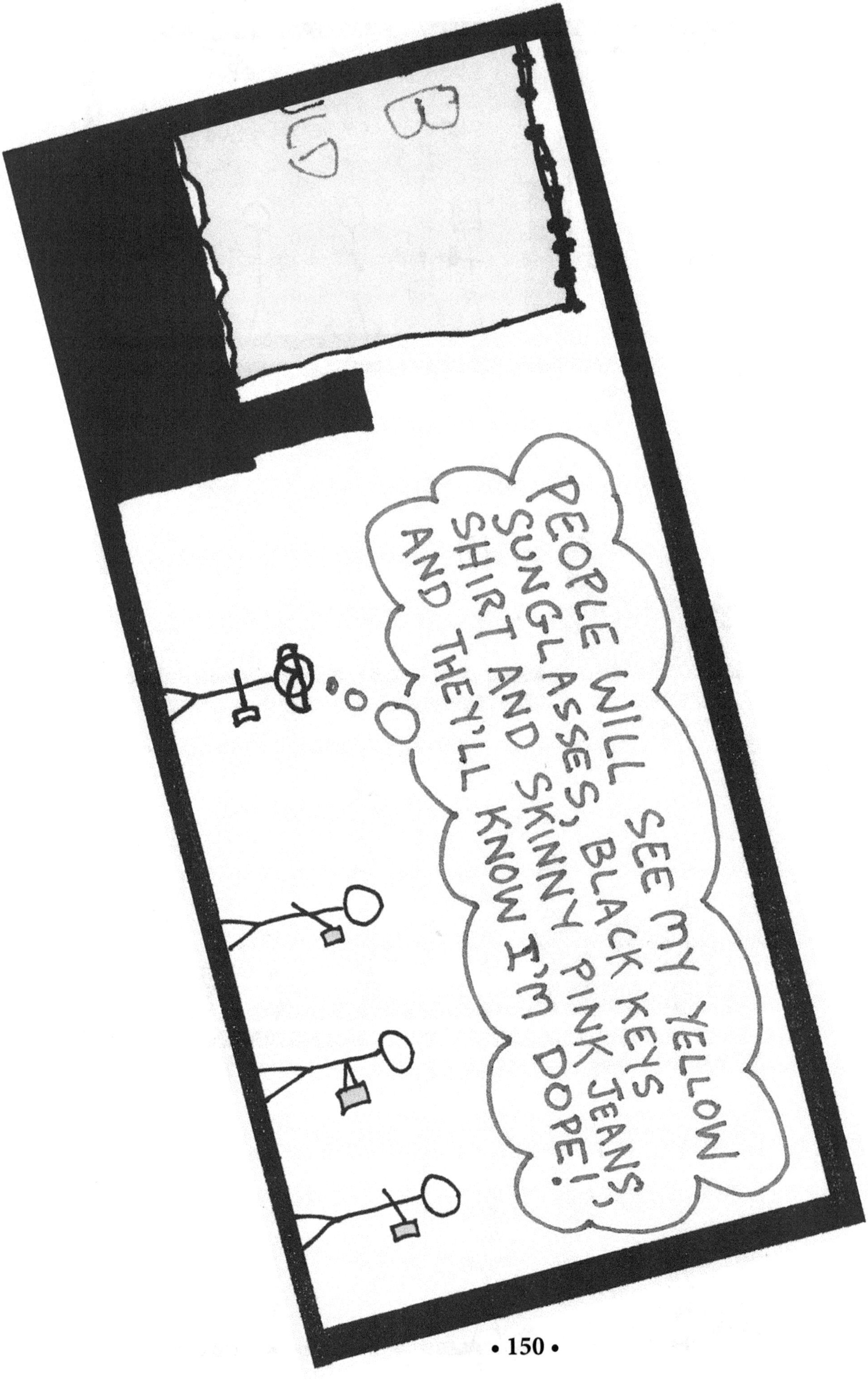
PEOPLE WILL SEE MY YELLOW SUNGLASSES, BLACK KEYS SHIRT AND SKINNY PINK JEANS, AND THEY'LL KNOW I'M DOPE!

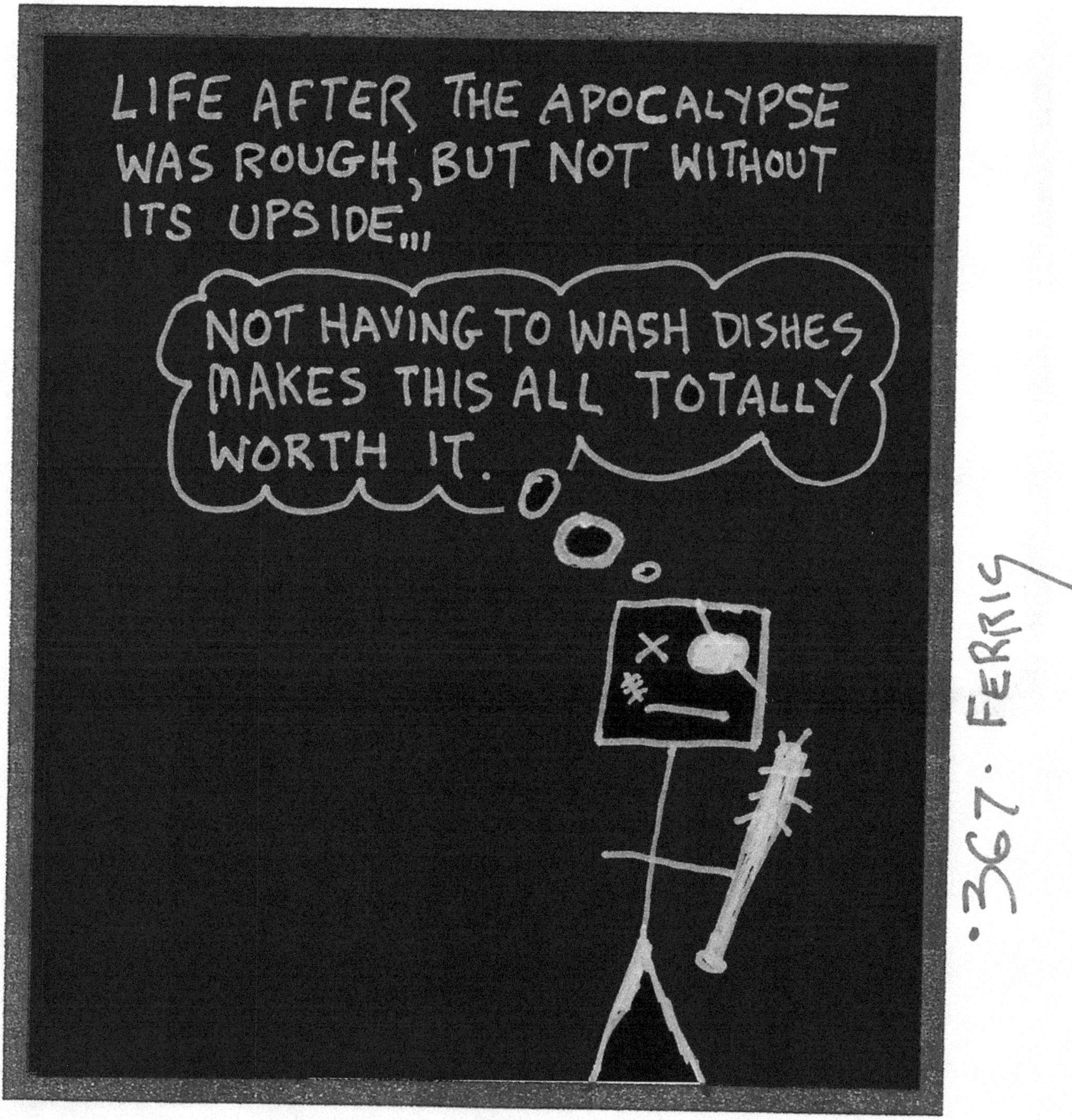
LIFE AFTER THE APOCALYPSE WAS ROUGH, BUT NOT WITHOUT ITS UPSIDE...
NOT HAVING TO WASH DISHES MAKES THIS ALL TOTALLY WORTH IT.
·367· FERRIS

# MARC'S

## IF YOU FIND THIS RESTROOM IN UNSATISFACTORY CONDITION OR UNSANITARY, PLEASE GO SHIT AT GIANT EAGLE

BORED. WORK SUCKS.
SEEK THE WARMTH OF THE SAMHAIN FIRES!!
-BAMF-
OK.
BAMF
JUST A FEW QUESTIONS, THEN. FIRST, DO YOU WANT A PARADISE?
NO.
GOOD. GOOD. NEXT, DO YOU WANT A SACRIFICE?
YEA— WAIT, IS THAT A TRICK QUESTION?
·368·FERRIS

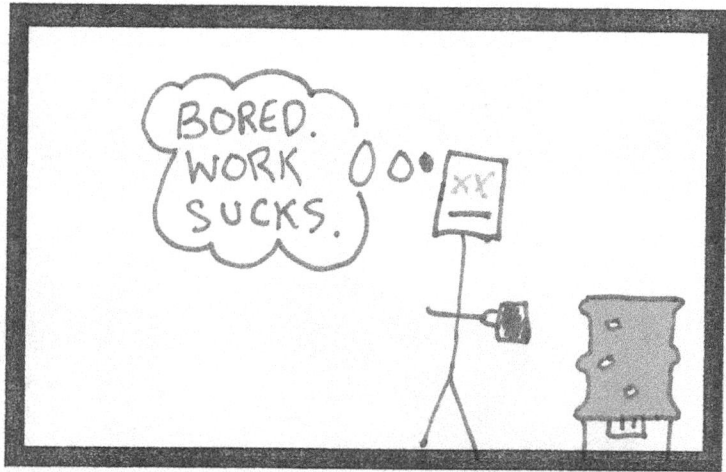

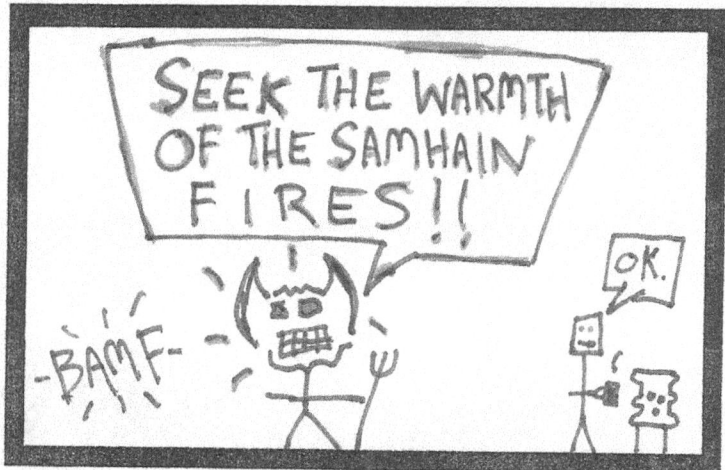

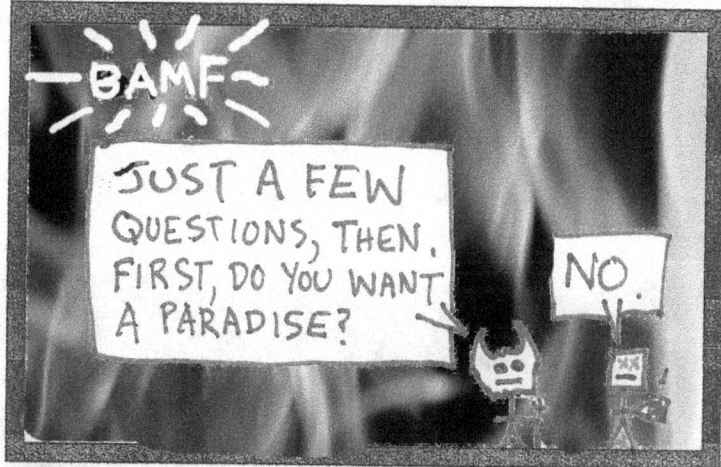

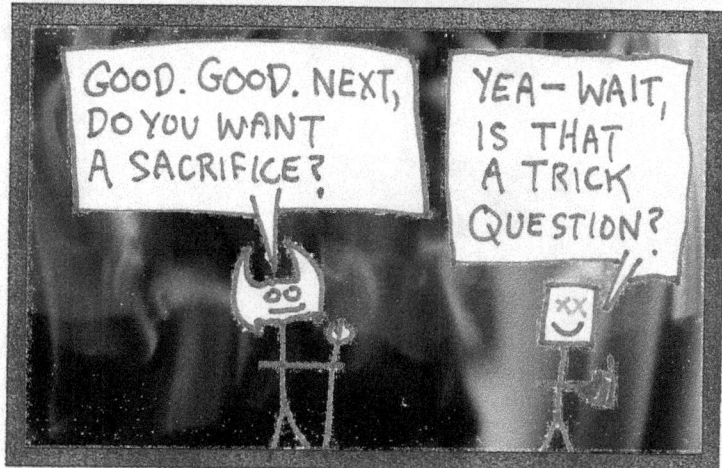

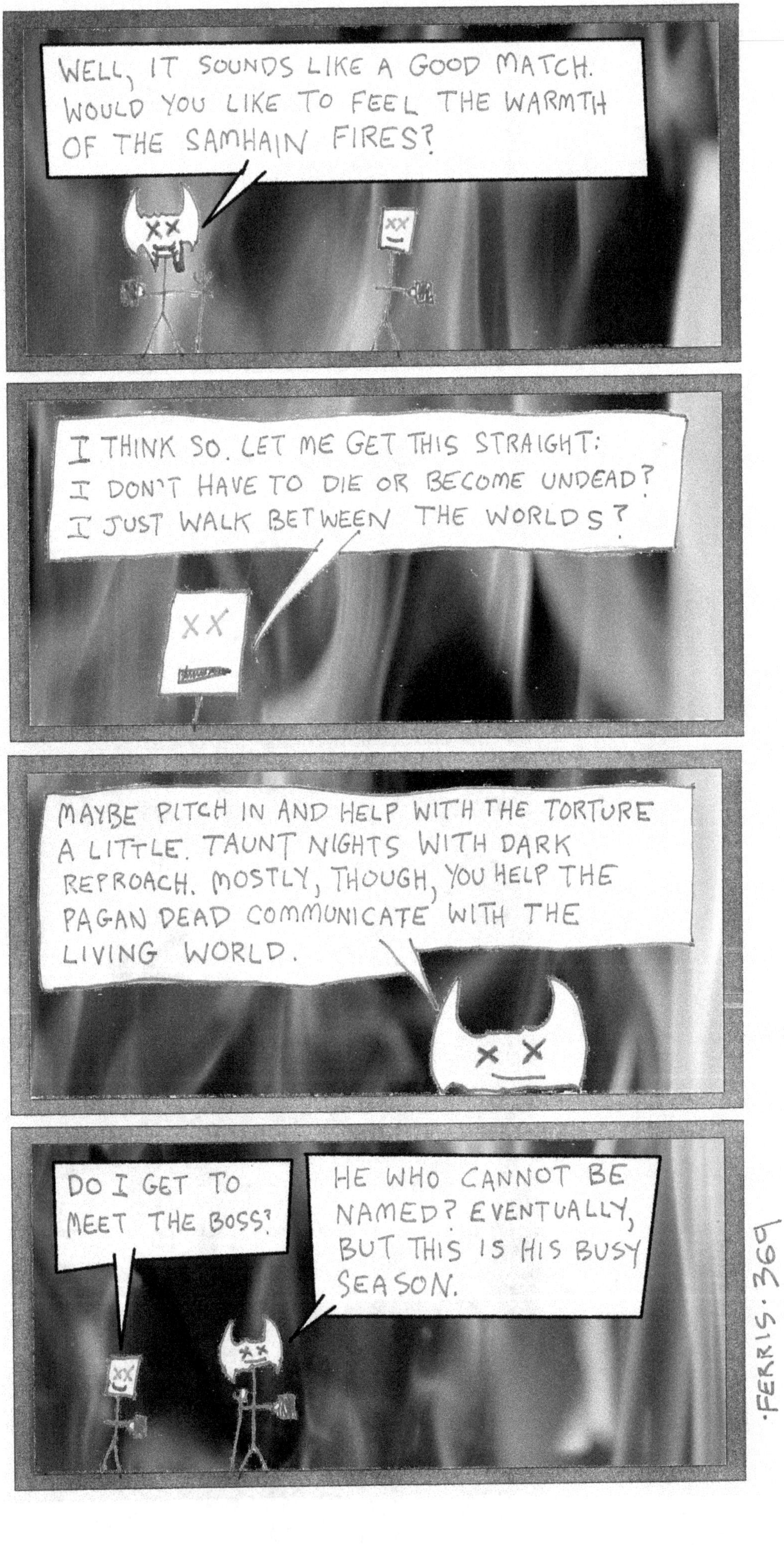
WELL, IT SOUNDS LIKE A GOOD MATCH. WOULD YOU LIKE TO FEEL THE WARMTH OF THE SAMHAIN FIRES?
I THINK SO. LET ME GET THIS STRAIGHT: I DON'T HAVE TO DIE OR BECOME UNDEAD? I JUST WALK BETWEEN THE WORLDS?
MAYBE PITCH IN AND HELP WITH THE TORTURE A LITTLE. TAUNT NIGHTS WITH DARK REPROACH. MOSTLY, THOUGH, YOU HELP THE PAGAN DEAD COMMUNICATE WITH THE LIVING WORLD.
DO I GET TO MEET THE BOSS?
HE WHO CANNOT BE NAMED? EVENTUALLY, BUT THIS IS HIS BUSY SEASON.
FERRIS · 369

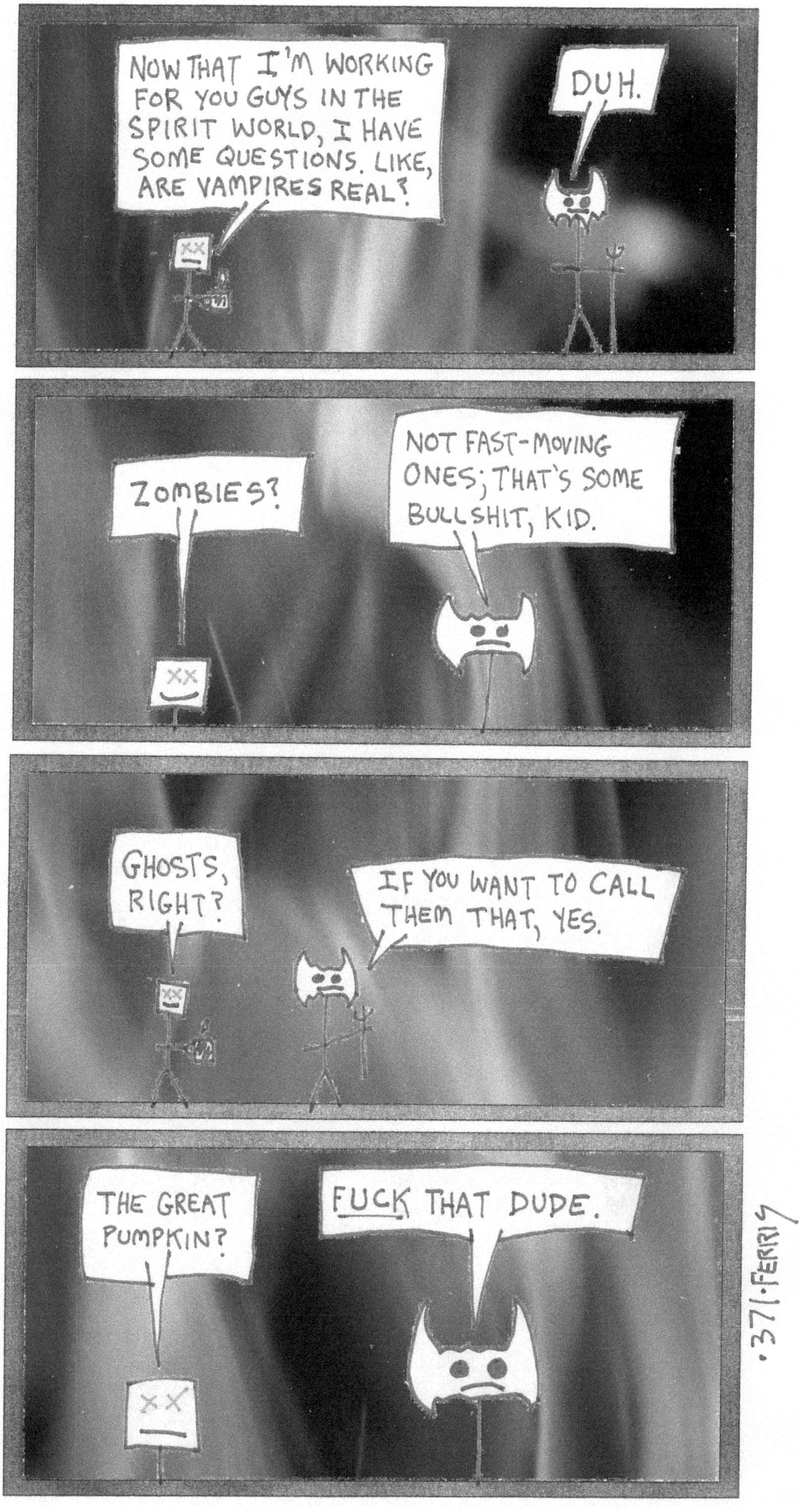
NOW THAT I'M WORKING FOR YOU GUYS IN THE SPIRIT WORLD, I HAVE SOME QUESTIONS. LIKE, ARE VAMPIRES REAL?
DUH.
ZOMBIES?
NOT FAST-MOVING ONES; THAT'S SOME BULLSHIT, KID.
GHOSTS, RIGHT?
IF YOU WANT TO CALL THEM THAT, YES.
THE GREAT PUMPKIN?
FUCK THAT DUDE.
·371·FERRIS

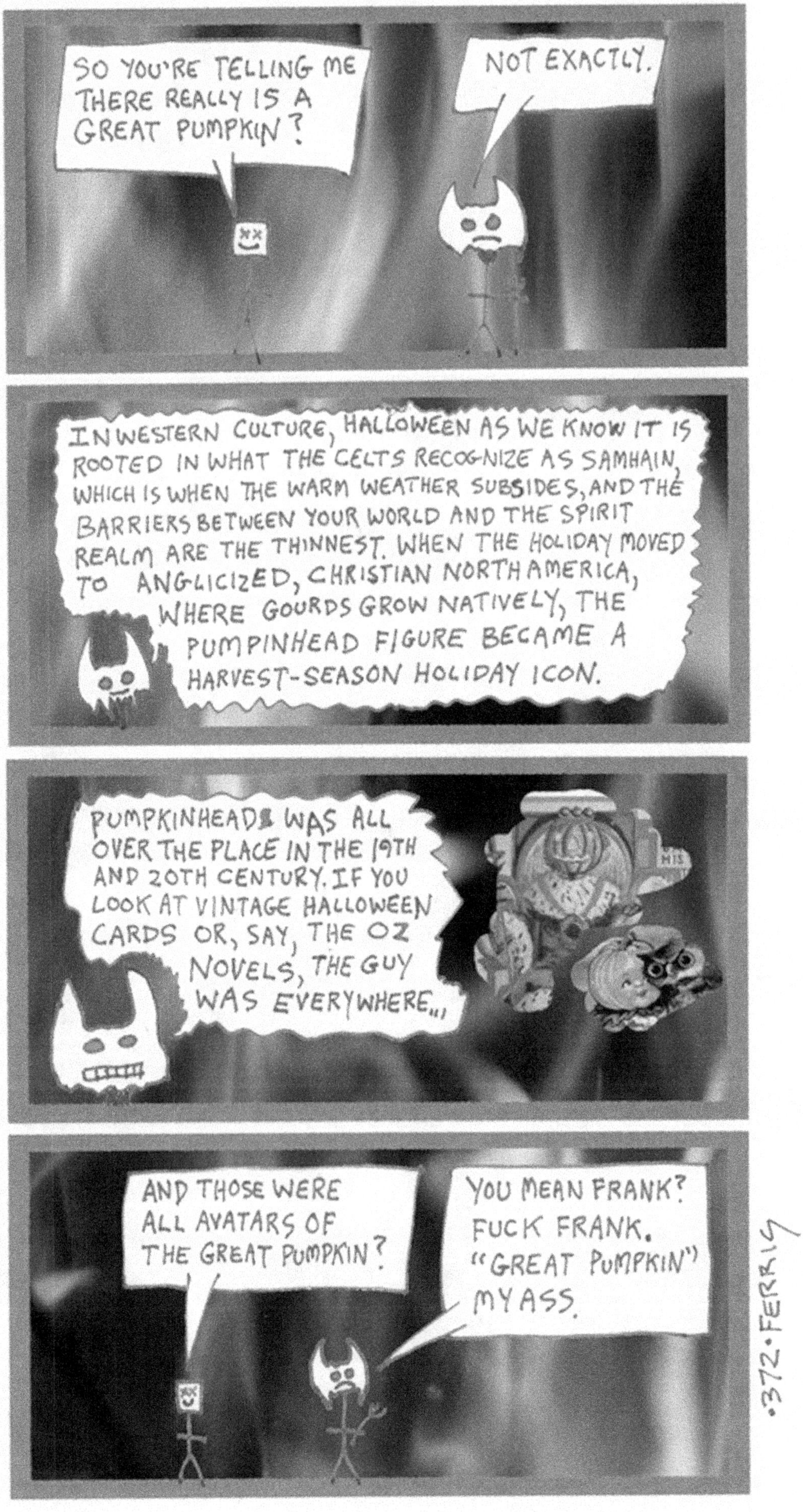
SO YOU'RE TELLING ME THERE REALLY IS A GREAT PUMPKIN?
NOT EXACTLY.
IN WESTERN CULTURE, HALLOWEEN AS WE KNOW IT IS ROOTED IN WHAT THE CELTS RECOGNIZE AS SAMHAIN, WHICH IS WHEN THE WARM WEATHER SUBSIDES, AND THE BARRIERS BETWEEN YOUR WORLD AND THE SPIRIT REALM ARE THE THINNEST. WHEN THE HOLIDAY MOVED TO ANGLICIZED, CHRISTIAN NORTH AMERICA, WHERE GOURDS GROW NATIVELY, THE PUMPINHEAD FIGURE BECAME A HARVEST-SEASON HOLIDAY ICON.
PUMPKINHEADS WAS ALL OVER THE PLACE IN THE 19TH AND 20TH CENTURY. IF YOU LOOK AT VINTAGE HALLOWEEN CARDS OR, SAY, THE OZ NOVELS, THE GUY WAS EVERYWHERE...
AND THOSE WERE ALL AVATARS OF THE GREAT PUMPKIN?
YOU MEAN FRANK? FUCK FRANK. "GREAT PUMPKIN" MY ASS.
•372•FERRIS

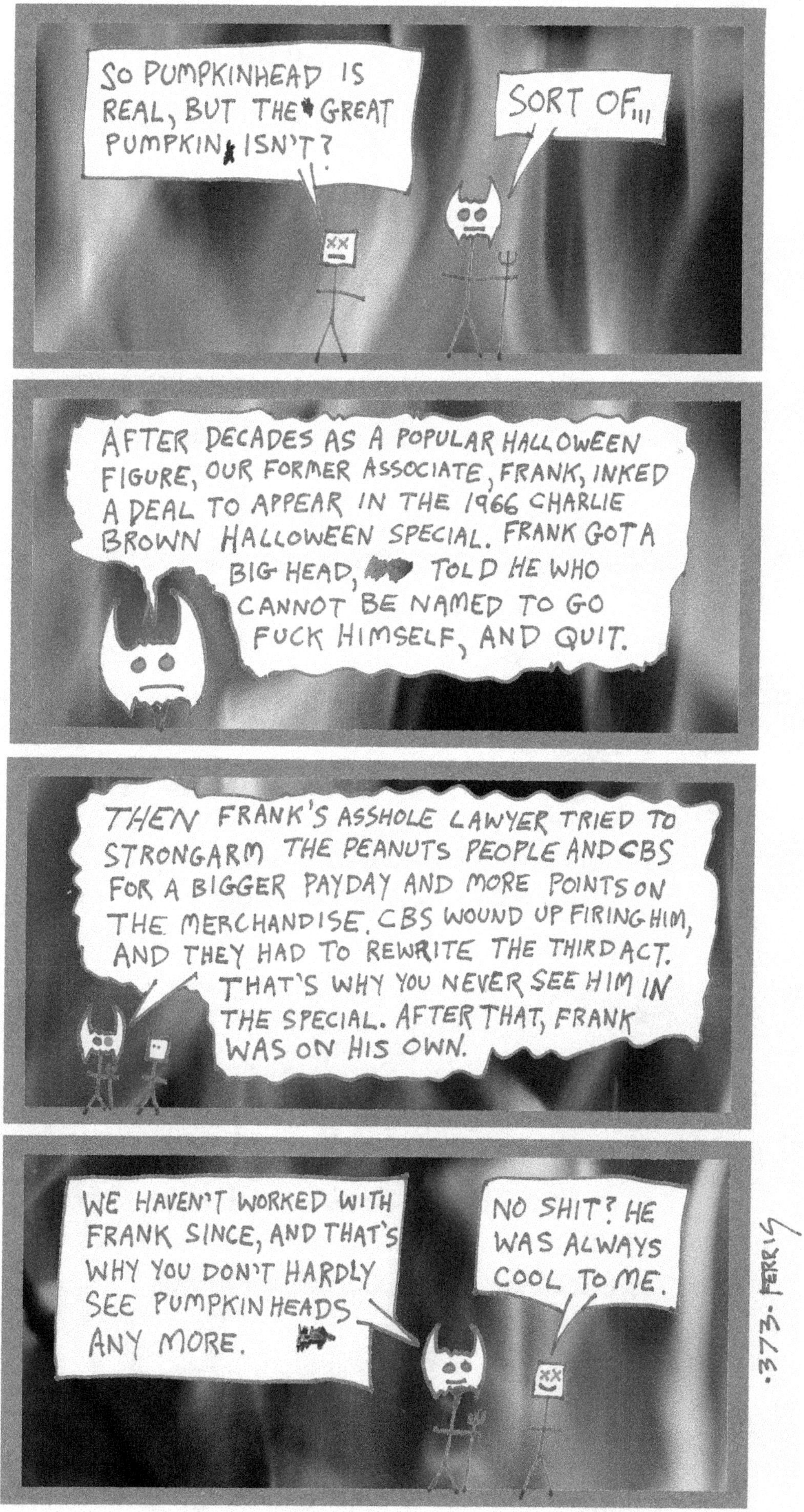
SO PUMPKINHEAD IS REAL, BUT THE GREAT PUMPKIN ISN'T?
SORT OF...
AFTER DECADES AS A POPULAR HALLOWEEN FIGURE, OUR FORMER ASSOCIATE, FRANK, INKED A DEAL TO APPEAR IN THE 1966 CHARLIE BROWN HALLOWEEN SPECIAL. FRANK GOT A BIG HEAD, TOLD HE WHO CANNOT BE NAMED TO GO FUCK HIMSELF, AND QUIT.
THEN FRANK'S ASSHOLE LAWYER TRIED TO STRONGARM THE PEANUTS PEOPLE AND CBS FOR A BIGGER PAYDAY AND MORE POINTS ON THE MERCHANDISE. CBS WOUND UP FIRING HIM, AND THEY HAD TO REWRITE THE THIRD ACT. THAT'S WHY YOU NEVER SEE HIM IN THE SPECIAL. AFTER THAT, FRANK WAS ON HIS OWN.
WE HAVEN'T WORKED WITH FRANK SINCE, AND THAT'S WHY YOU DON'T HARDLY SEE PUMPKIN HEADS ANY MORE.
NO SHIT? HE WAS ALWAYS COOL TO ME.
·373· FERRIS

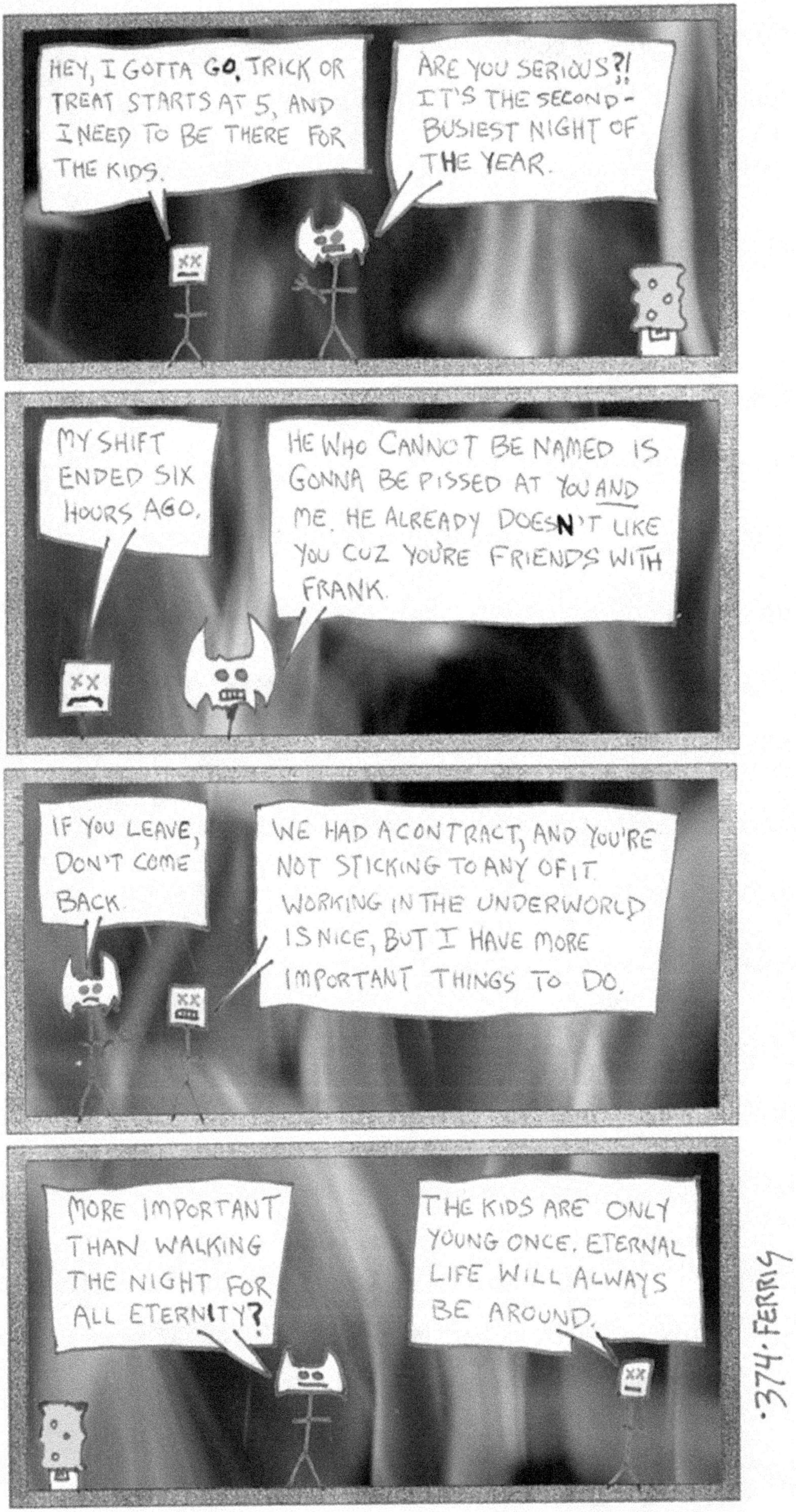
HEY, I GOTTA GO. TRICK OR TREAT STARTS AT 5, AND I NEED TO BE THERE FOR THE KIDS.
ARE YOU SERIOUS?! IT'S THE SECOND-BUSIEST NIGHT OF THE YEAR.
MY SHIFT ENDED SIX HOURS AGO.
HE WHO CANNOT BE NAMED IS GONNA BE PISSED AT YOU AND ME. HE ALREADY DOESN'T LIKE YOU CUZ YOU'RE FRIENDS WITH FRANK.
IF YOU LEAVE, DON'T COME BACK.
WE HAD A CONTRACT, AND YOU'RE NOT STICKING TO ANY OF IT.
WORKING IN THE UNDERWORLD IS NICE, BUT I HAVE MORE IMPORTANT THINGS TO DO.
MORE IMPORTANT THAN WALKING THE NIGHT FOR ALL ETERNITY?
THE KIDS ARE ONLY YOUNG ONCE. ETERNAL LIFE WILL ALWAYS BE AROUND.
·374·FERRIS

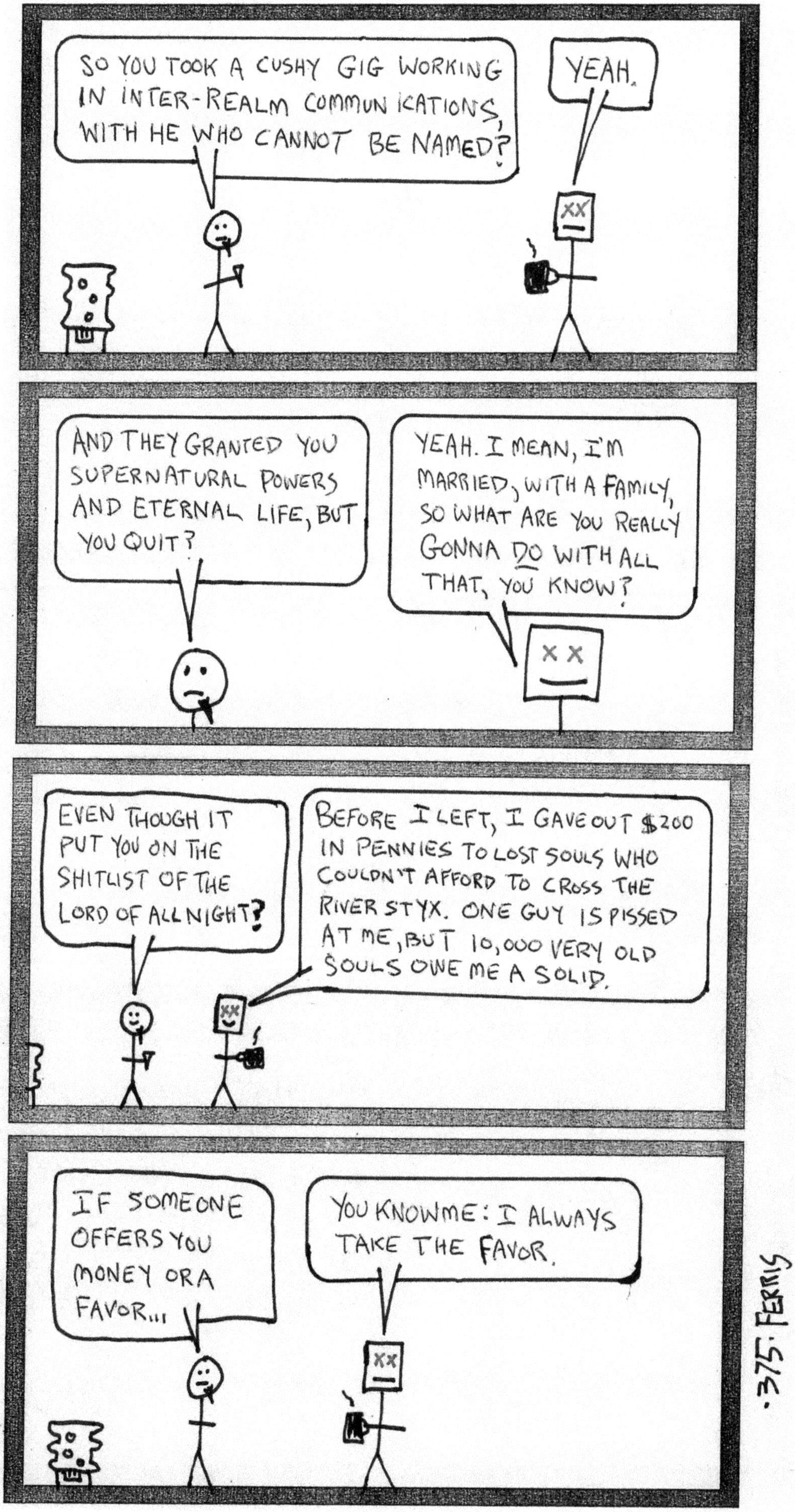
SO YOU TOOK A CUSHY GIG WORKING IN INTER-REALM COMMUNICATIONS, WITH HE WHO CANNOT BE NAMED?
YEAH.
AND THEY GRANTED YOU SUPERNATURAL POWERS AND ETERNAL LIFE, BUT YOU QUIT?
YEAH. I MEAN, I'M MARRIED, WITH A FAMILY, SO WHAT ARE YOU REALLY GONNA DO WITH ALL THAT, YOU KNOW?
EVEN THOUGH IT PUT YOU ON THE SHITLIST OF THE LORD OF ALL NIGHT?
BEFORE I LEFT, I GAVE OUT $200 IN PENNIES TO LOST SOULS WHO COULDN'T AFFORD TO CROSS THE RIVER STYX. ONE GUY IS PISSED AT ME, BUT 10,000 VERY OLD SOULS OWE ME A SOLID.
IF SOMEONE OFFERS YOU MONEY OR A FAVOR...
YOU KNOW ME: I ALWAYS TAKE THE FAVOR.
·375· FERRIS

"FROSTY THE SNOWMAN / WAS A JOLLY, HAPPY SOUL / WITH A FUCKED UP EYE / AND A BLOOD SHOT NOSE / HE WAS OUT TO MACK A HO."
IS NOTHING SACRED TO YOU?
I'M NOT THE ONE PLAYING CHRISTMAS SONGS OVER A PUBLIC ADDRESS SYSTEM THE FIRST WEEK OF NOVEMBER. THEY STARTED IT. I'M GONNA FINISH IT.
376 · FERRIS

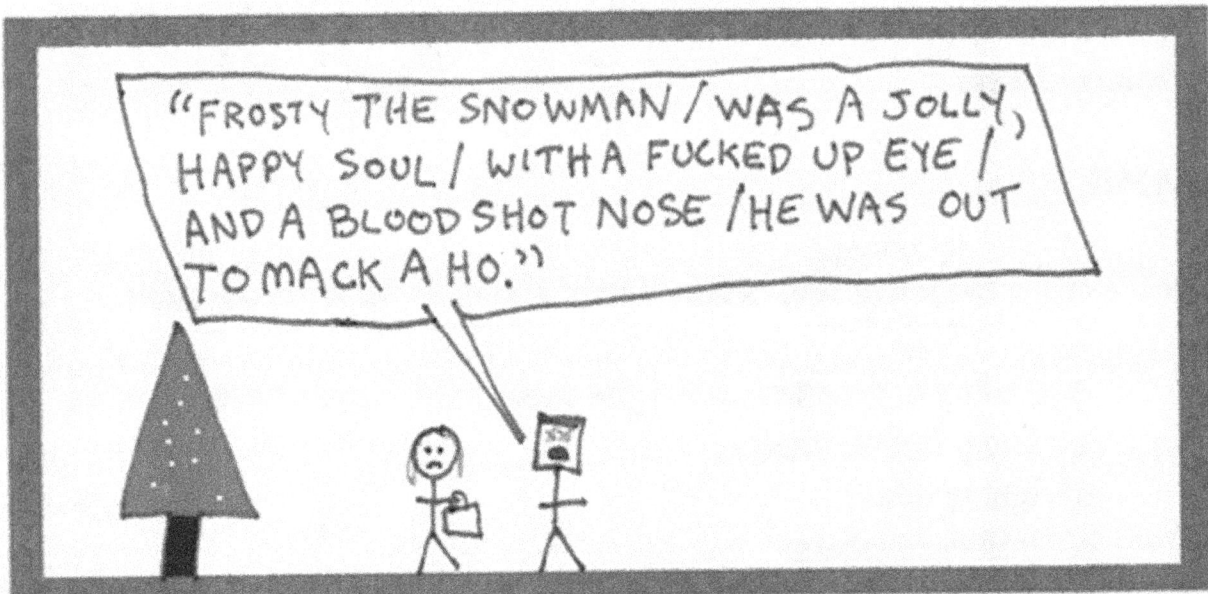

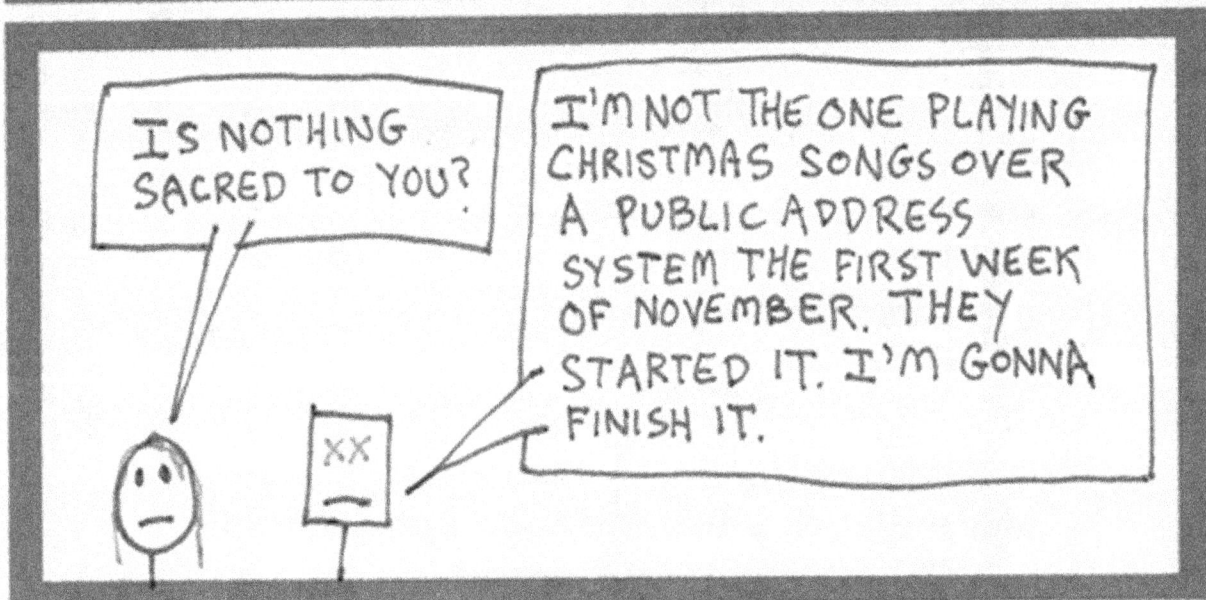

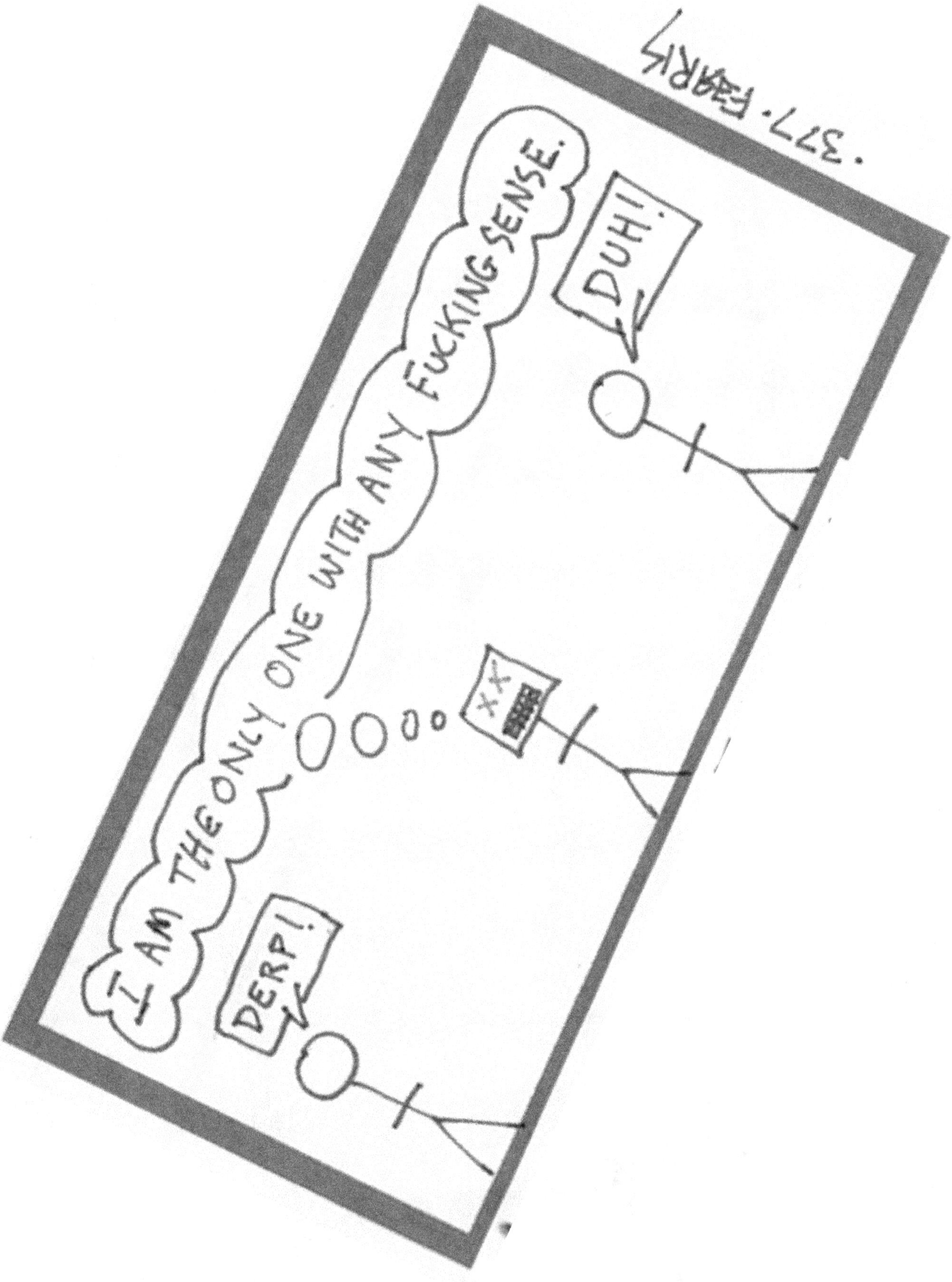
I AM THE ONLY ONE WITH ANY FUCKING SENSE.
DERP!
DUH!
· 377 · FARRIS

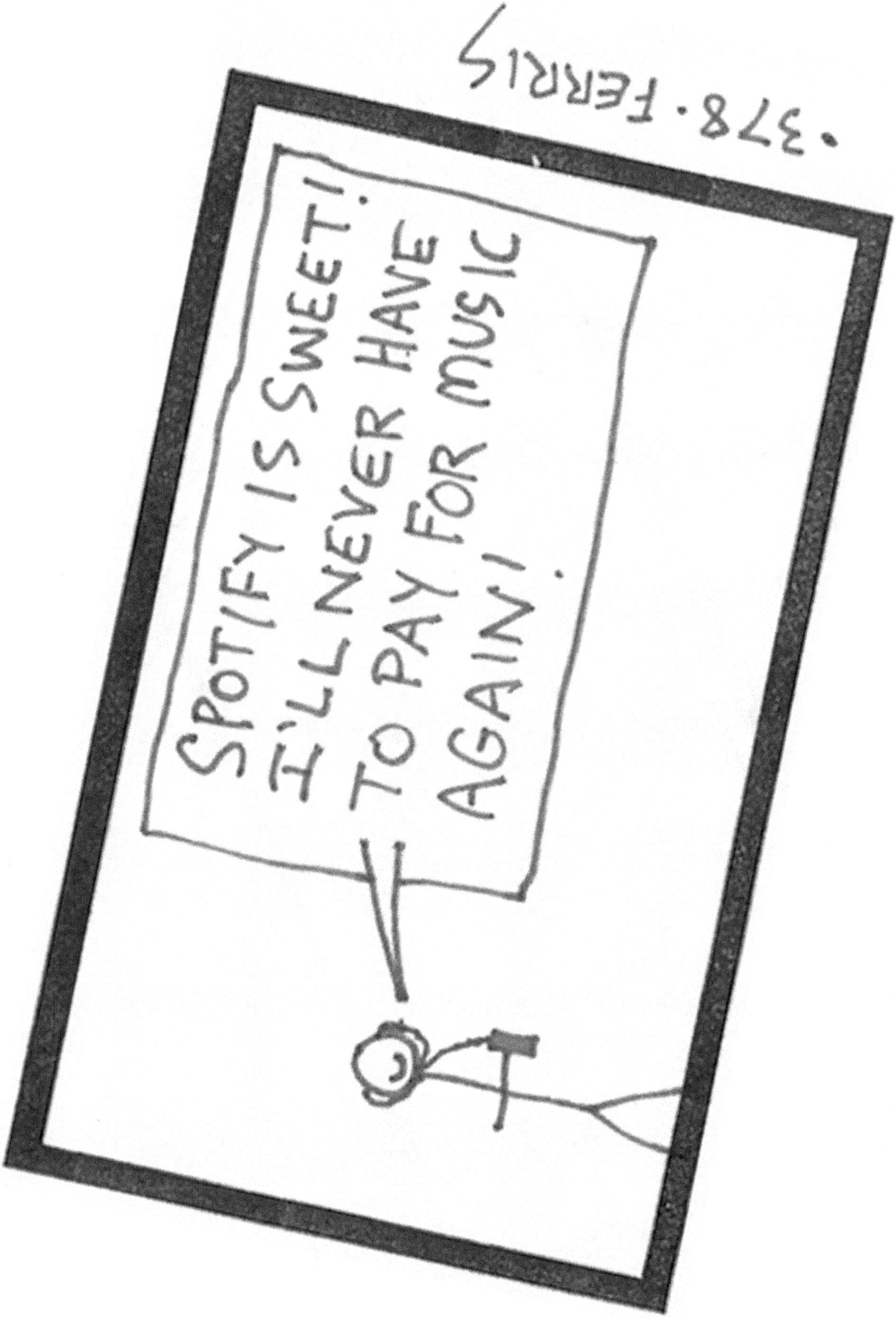
·378·FERRIS
SPOTIFY IS SWEET! I'LL NEVER HAVE TO PAY FOR MUSIC AGAIN!

zZzZ
BEEP BEEP BEEP BEEP
FUCK IT.
-CLICK-
28 HOURS LATER...
...AND THAT WAS THE BEST MORNING OF MY LIFE.
FERRIS 381

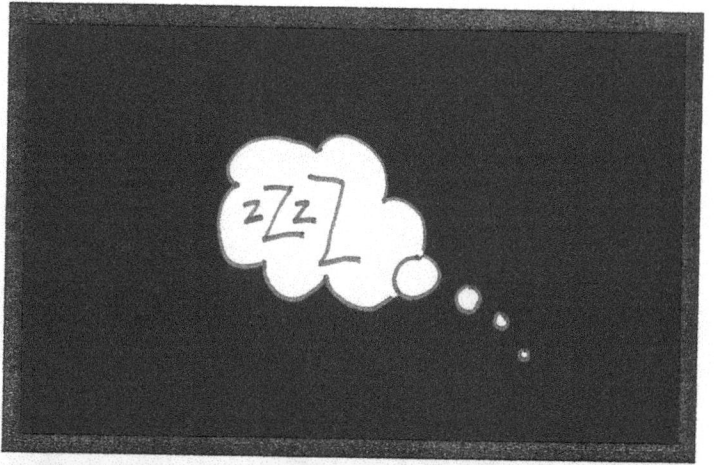

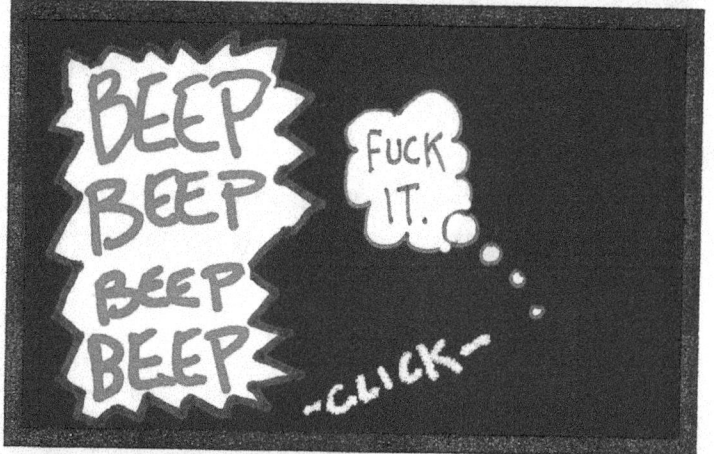

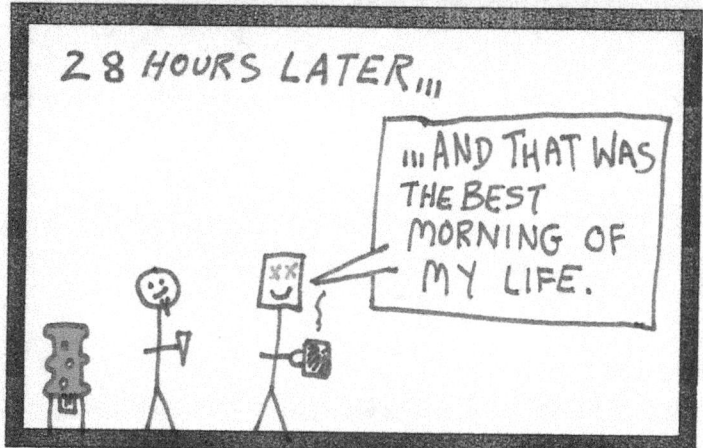

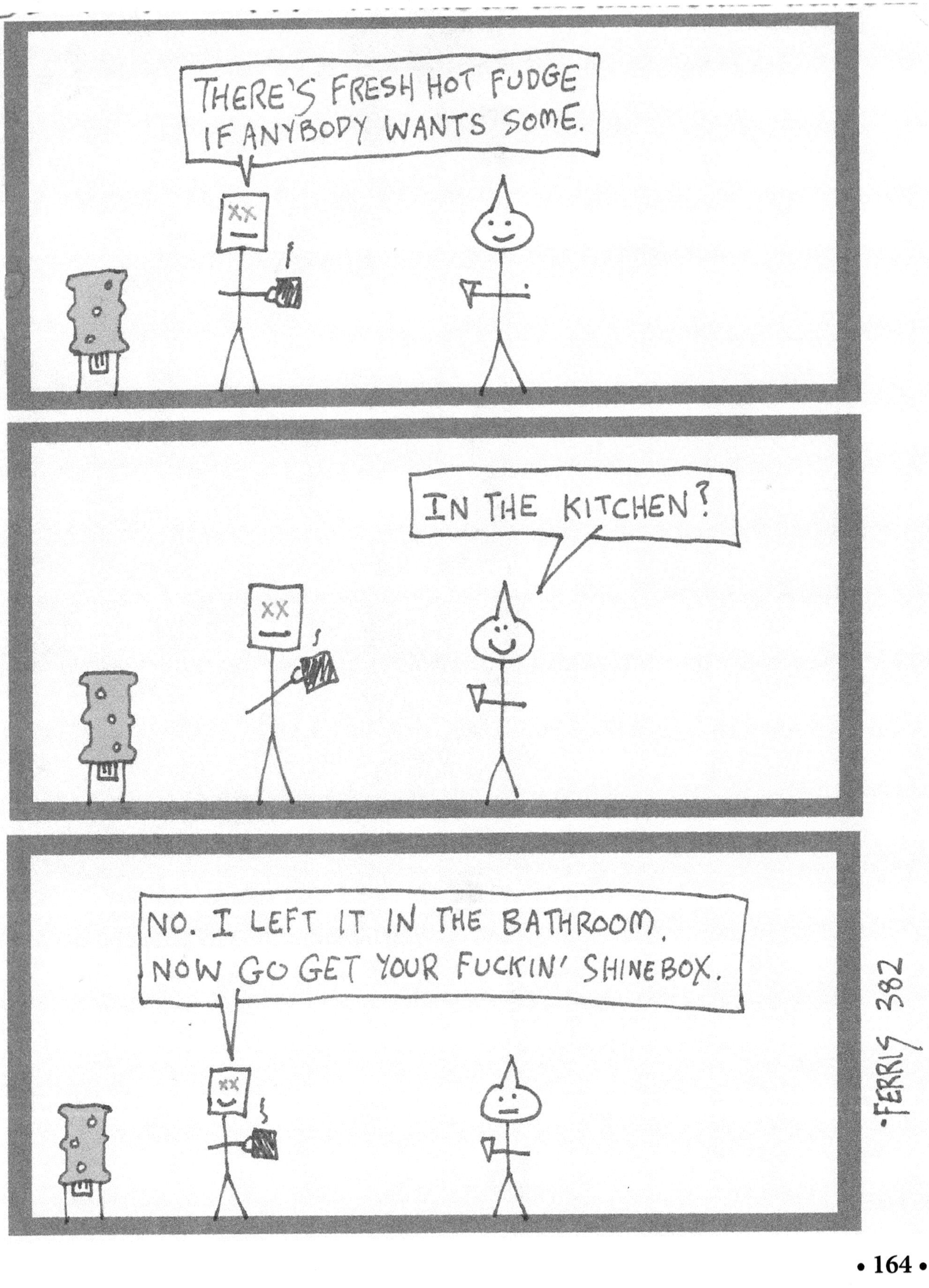
THERE'S FRESH HOT FUDGE IF ANYBODY WANTS SOME.
IN THE KITCHEN?
NO. I LEFT IT IN THE BATHROOM. NOW GO GET YOUR FUCKIN' SHINEBOX.
-FERRIS 382

# "DOYLE RULES," or, "LAST GOOD DAY."

## A TRUE STORY FROM THE ADVENTURES OF METAL DAD.

### DATELINE: OCTOBER 2014

The Great Pumpkin came early this year. He left a guitar pick. In my car. The pick was used by legendary Misfits guitarist Doyle Wolfgang von Frankenstein.

That's the short version.

You probably shouldn't bother reading this post. It's long and unnecessary, but it's a story.

It's about a bunch of stuff that I care about, but pretty much only matters to me and people like me.

And then I use a bunch of coincidental extraneous elements to connect it all. Everybody has weird metaphysical stuff going on in their head that only makes sense to them. And they use it to validate their way of life.

I hate people like that, especially when they write blog posts. But I do it too. So quit reading now. Long story short, I have a guitar pick, and it makes me happy.

Anyhow, I've been to three shows this week. Which I never do. Maybe never have done before. Two of them were Monday night.

The temperature dropped this week. Fall is here. For me, it's Misfits season. I listen to Misfits-related music all through the fall, like it's dark, early Christmas music. Forget evergreens; I like it when leaves drop off trees, leaving them barren and skeletal. Samhain is real, whether or not you're attuned to it.

Former Hüsker Dü frontman Bob Mould was playing Monday, and his set was chock-full of iconic HD tunes. The set list for this tour included one of my favorite songs, period: "Real World." So I felt like I needed to see that. It was a good show. Totally worth it. I never saw the guy before, and I own more of his product than I've bought. So after nearly 30 years, I figured the guy deserved some of my cash.

The same night, on the other town, Doyle was playing. Doyle Wolfgang von Frankenstein is the iconic ex-guitarist of the horror-themed punk group the Misfits, which might be the best band ever (assuming you like that kind of thing). His latest band is called Doyle; his previous one was rad too.

Let's skip the details: I love the Misfits. They're fun, and they've done more than any other band to keep my interest in music alive over the last decade. The band is like a big ball of all kinds of stuff I liked when I was five, plus everything I picked up since: monsters, dark stuff, and hardcore punk rock. Misfits Fiends dress, look, and/or think a certain way. A certain kind of person cares about this stuff.

**IMAGE SUBSTANTIALLY ALTERED FOR PURPOSES OF SATIRE**

But not that many people. You learn how few people are dedicated Fiends when a secondary player from a convoluted underground mythos plays Cleveland on a rainy Monday night.

I trusted the GPS, which is always a bad move, especially in Ohio. And I lingered after Bob Mould, made some small talk with friends. And I knew the socializing would come back, bite me in the ass, and cost me some valuable time. But we're alive on the planet, and we're part of society, and good people in your life are a gift. So you go with it.

The clock strikes 11:25 or whatever, and I made it across town, and I arrive at the Foundry, a respectable club the size of a big shoe box. I pull into a parking spot directly across from the club. This kind of VIP parking only happens in movies. Cleveland can be something of a wasteland, but it usually works to your benefit.

Parked on street, I can see and hear the band from my car. I'm late. They're playing "Last Caress," an ecstatically morbid song Metallica covered in 1988, which pretty much broke the Misfits from the underground into mass pop-cult consciousness. Go, go, go.

Roll in thru the door, and nobody's even collecting a cover. Take a few ginger steps in, and nobody asks me for $17 DOS. A couple more steps. Nobody's asking for money. One more step, still unchallenged, and "Last Caress" is almost over. No time to waste; proceed directly to the pit.

It's a small pit. Seconds later, I'm standing zero feet away from Doyle, who stands like 6'8", a hulk, all chiseled muscle. Not for nothing did he add the "Frankenstein" to his stage name. His face is painted white, he has bolts on his neck, and I'm pretty sure they're real.

It's a good show. Not croweded I'd guess under 100 in attendance. Certainly not 50 in the pit. In front of the stage, the crowd isn't three Fiends thick. Thankfully, not much crowd surfing, cuz there's not enough people.

So the show is awesome. It's Doyle's birthday. The band and crew sprayed him with ropy white silly string. He blasted the crowd with some, too. I got hit. He slimed me.

Then the show is over.

We savvy concert goers know this is the best — and safest — time to look for guitar picks. A horde of scavengers whip out their phones, put 'em on flashlight mode, and scan the sticky, blackened floor.

I don't see any picks. What I do find is a black hat, knocked in the corner, by a giant black speaker cabinet, all hidden in a black shadow, in a dark club.

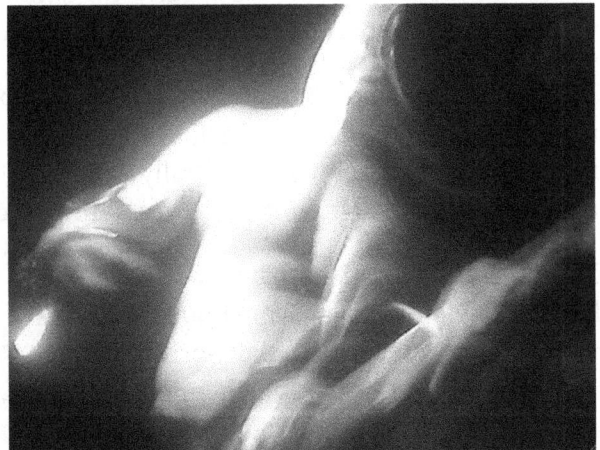

*Doyle, the ivory ghost. Shitty flip-phone pic by me.*

Losing your hat sucks. I figure maybe somebody's missing it. I pick it up and put it on the amp, on the chance maybe whoever will notice it and be reunited.

And as I resume my unproductive quest for a pick, a girl zooms over to where the hat was, scoops up a pick, and walks off, smiling. Fuck. I was right there. If I would have been paying attention, it would have been mine. If I would have looked, it would have been mine. But I didn't. Now I don't get no pick. I try to take some solace in the fact I helped someone else find a pick, and she's seems happier than I would have been.

But still, it woulda been nice.

And then it's midnight, the show's over, time to go.

I'm almost out the door, and I pass the merch table. Before I step through the doorway, I loop back around and check out the Doyle merch. I'm feeling good. I just saw one of the true hardcore icons. People talk about "intimate club shows," and it's usually bullshit… you, a thousand people, and a band that can't fill a theater any more. But this was it: The dude from one of my favorite bands, playing some of my favorite songs, and it's all been free. Nobody ever did collect my cover charge.

So I scan the merch table and buy a CD. I have a free digital promo copy. But I don't own a real disc. I don't collect much stuff, but I do have a couple boxes full of Misfits-related swag.

I do the math, and I figure the purchase of one compact disc should put some money in the band's collective pocket. I can live without the CD. But it's Doyle. And he has earned my money. So I buy it.

Then I go home.

On the way, I listen to the CD. I'm glad I got it. Doyle plays monstrous riffs that sound exactly like the Frankenstein monster stomping down a dusty castle hallway. Frontman Alex "Wolfman" Story is

*My Fits collection's in an oblong box.*

an offbeat lyricist and vocalist, but that's a good thing, and the songs grow on you. It was a good purchase. Definitely the most fun Misfits-related release since American Psycho, and much more consistent than Famous Monsters (which has its moments). The show is over, but the disc keeps the good feels coming.

Next day, I think about overlooking that guitar pick. I check my shitty flip-phone and look at the picture I took from the pit. It's blurry, and Doyle looks like a real ghost, which is kinda cool in its own way. I shoulda taken another — but it was a good time, and I don't want to be the douche playing with his phone for the whole show. And the band was working, so show some respect, right? I do have a couple souvenirs from the gig, but nothing stellar. All in all, adequate, though.

Two days later, I'm driving around, running errands, heading to work. Still listening to the Doyle disc. Still regretting not getting a better picture. Bummed that I missed half the set. I keep thinking it woulda been nice to get that pick. So I keep telling myself: I helped someone else get one. That's a good thing. I had fun, I enhanced someone else's experience. It's a win.

Stop at home. I park the car. I reach for something, and I happen to glance down at the mat, by the gas pedals.

Sitting there, on the rubber mat, is a black guitar pick. With a square white Frankenstein head on it.

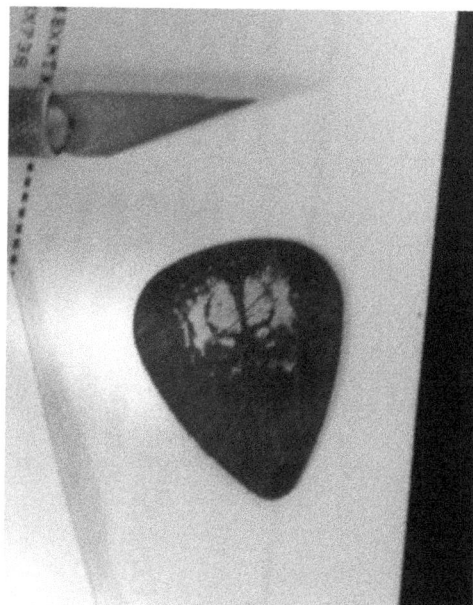

I grab it and flip it over. It says DOYLE. Out of nowhere. Magically. It just appeared. A used, worn, scraped guitar pick, from the oversized hand of Doyle Wolfgang von Frankenstein.

OK, maybe not magically. Obviously, as I was pacing the sticky nightclub floor, looking for a keepsake, a pick stuck to my shoe. And it stayed there for a couple hundred feet, through the very short walk out of the club, across the street, and into my car. You can read it that way if you want to.

Me, I say it was magic. In fact, I figure it was from the Great Pumpkin himself. (I say "himself" because Linus says the Great Pumpkin is a guy.)

If we could do all the math and account for every variable, the universe would probably be completely predictable. But we usually can't. And when all the probabilities scale up, and sychronous patterns emerge, that might as well be magic. I think so, anyway. In my experience, life has a lot of unmappable, non-linear action going on.

Here's how it works, more often than not: You want something to happen. You focus all your effort and energy into pushing in a single direction. And it doesn't happen. Then something taps you on the shoulder, and some kind of similar result is happening over in another corner, apparently randomly.

I like to think if you commit to doing the right thing, something good is going to shake loose, eventually. It might not be exactly what you wanted, but life almost never delivers exactly what you want.

Unless you want a Doyle guitar pick.

— Ferris

*THIS* STORY IS OVER; THAT SAID...

TO BE CONTINUED.

# SUBURBAN METAL DAD: THE SHIRT

*BECAUSE YOU'RE AWESOME. AND PEOPLE NEED TO KNOW.*

**MAKES A GREAT GIFT. NOT SOME CHEAP-ASS SHIRT EITHER.**

**$19.99 (XXL/XXXL $23.99) INCLUDES SHIPPING WHILE THE DEAL LASTS.**

**PAYPAL, PLEASE. HIT ME UP: DXFERRIS@YAHOO.COM / @DXFERRIS**

**FRONT**

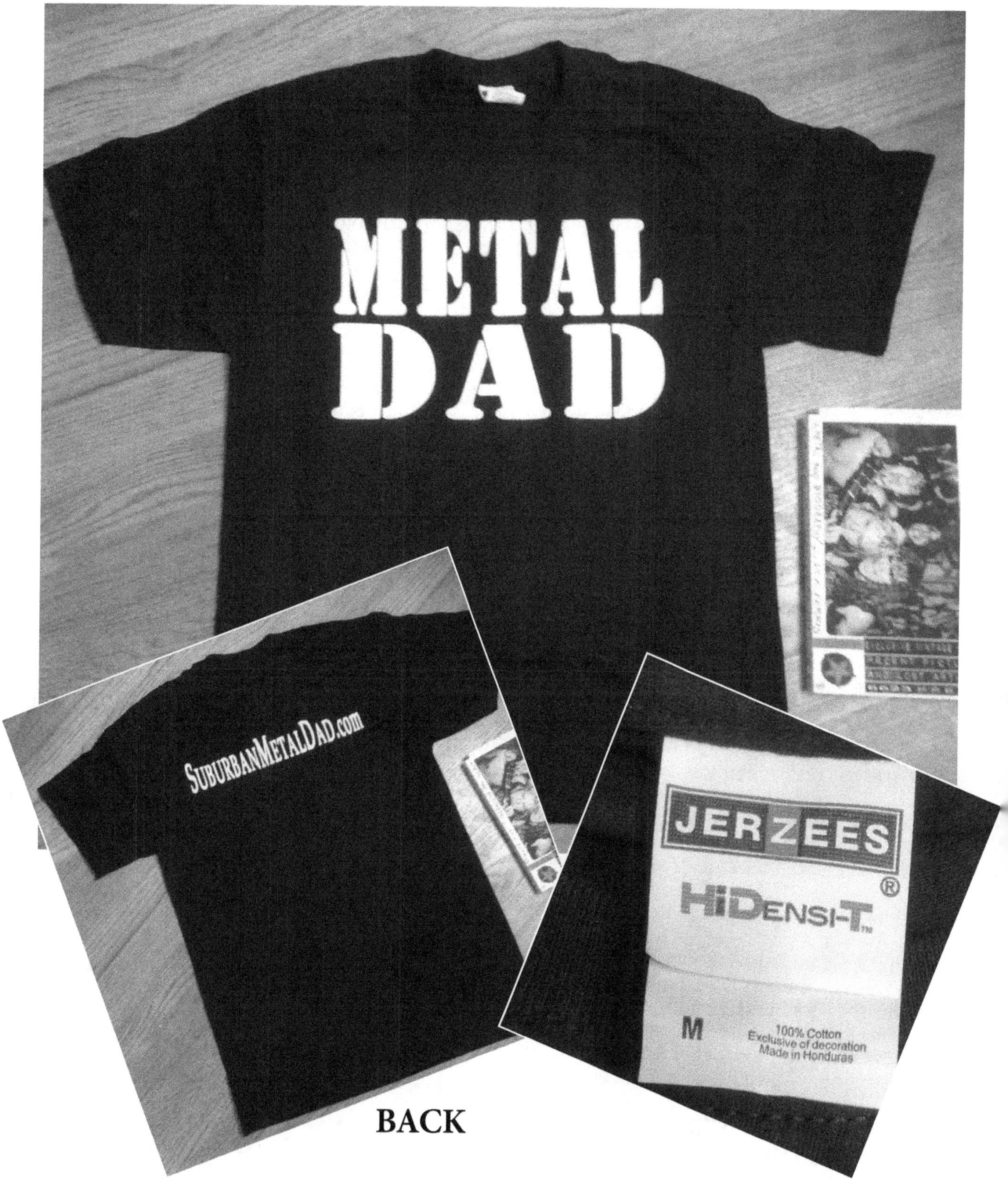
METAL
DAD
SuburbanMetalDad.com
JERZEES
HiDENSI-T
M
100% Cotton
Exclusive of decoration
Made in Honduras

**BACK**

# THANK YOU.

**MATT "WARLOCK" WARDLAW**, who encouraged this shit and gave it the first light at AddictedToVinyl.com, his dope-assed music & entertainment website.

**JEFF "JEFITO" GILES**, who continues to both tolerate and promote my bullshit via Popdose, his otherwise-respectable website, which is a distinct source for your daily doses of pop-culture news and views and doesn't run all the same godawful human-centipeded content you see retyped on every other site.

**GREG KROL, STEVE HALPIN, IAN PLAKIAS, JOSE GALVAN**, and all the regular readers & metal dads.

**THE GONNA GEEK / GALACTIC[A] WATERCOOLER FAMILY**, all o' yinz; if I start naming names, I'm gonna leave out somebody, and all y'all deserve better. So don't take it personal. Much love.

**THE WEBCOMICS ALLIANCE** (podcast and website): Dawn Griffin (Zorphbert and Fred webcomic, Abby's Adventures books), Byron Wilkins (1977 the Comic), Robin Dempsey (LeyLines), Chris Flick (Capes & Babes), Drezz Rodriguez (El Cuervo), Ken Drab (Rick the Stick). It's been awhile since we talked. But I work slow.

**Joanna Wilson, Dominic Caruso, and 1701 Press. Jason Bracelin, Mike Olszewski, Annie Zaleski & Michael Gallucci — you have seen the horror.** Aaron Burgess. Dan LeRoy. Jason Pettigrew. Michelle Gorey. Metal Sucks, Axl Rosenberg & Vince Neilstein. Carlos Ramirez. Sean Munger. Mike Shea. Greg Renoff. Christian Zyp, Eric Newby & Newbsradio. Mike Joseph. Howard Smith. Keith from The Vinyl Exam. James Greene Jr. Michael Nirenberg. Godless & Chuck & the Metal Sucks Podcast. Sage & Storm at Strange Famous. Kyle Antivenin. Erick J. Pressman. Gary Suarez. Jim Utz. John Beers. Grunge & Jax of Grand Buffet. Mark Avsec. Donnie Iris. Steven Blush. David Konow.

Donna Lee Stone. James Pietrzak. Bill Bennett. Audrey Sepesy. CM Fecek.

**RIP.** Sumner Ferris. Vera Lehane. Dave Moran. Lorna Ferris. Nora Ferris. Gertrude (Kozel) Roskovensky. Vincent Roskovensky. Lori Martin. Minet. Jeff Hanneman. Amy Winehouse. Ronald & Anna Mae (Kozel) Nypaver — thank you forever for the Mego dolls. Chyna. John Hughes. J. Budd Grebb — you were right.

Charles Schultz. Roger Waters. Bill Waterson. Berkley Breathed. R.L. Stine. Delia Ephron. Kevin Smith. Brian Koppelman. Matt Wagner. Bernie Mierault. Chris Claremont. Alan Moore. Frank Miller. Bryan Lee O'Malley. Randall Munroe. David Simon. Tom Kapinos. Ben B'Affleck. Dan Harmon. Justin Roiland. Ed Brubaker, Christopher Markus, Stephen McFeely, Anthony Russo, Joe Russo, Philip J Silvera, James Young, and Aaron Toney. Everybody involved with Civil War, The Flash and Daredevil. (Arrow is really good too.) John C. Kelley & Jon Bernthal (Is the Punisher the ultimate Metal Dad?). Dice (hourback). Jay Mohrs & Barry Katz. W. Kamau Bell & Kevin Avery. Neil Gaiman. John Romita Jr. George Pérez. Marv Wolfman. Len Wein. Will Hunting. Mike Judge. Paulsen & Krenn. And Jovial Rob Stine, possibly the funniest person who ever walked the planet. I don't know any of these cats, but they've entertained & inspired & educated me endlessly. So gratitude.

Diamond Dallas Page and Rob at **DDP Yoga**. It works. Changed my life. Thanks twice, gentlemen.

Vince Bloom. Lucas Bloom. Tracy Bloom. Tom Morrissey. Randy Harper. Tony Erba. Joe Minadeo. Gerard Dominick. Dave Ignizio & Square Records. Don Foose. Brad Warner. Dean B. Trew. Bart. Christy Carathers Carmody. J, Sumner, Sam & Max Ferris. Ken Ertel. Joanna Abel & 3rd Street Belly Dance. Alan Natali. All Forsythes, including but not limted to Ronald, Cheryl, Woog, Anne, Athena, Arwen, Astrid, and Neil. LA Smith. Jim "Seamus" Lakely. Marjorie Blackthorn, MFA. Urban Eats. Everybody else who ever put me on.

**RACHEL, RYLEY, SYDNEY.**
**YOU ARE THE BEST. LOVE IS LIKE A ROCK.**

# ABOUT THE ARTISTE.

**D.X. Ferris** is an Ohio Society of Professional Journalists Reporter of the Year, so he should know better. He wrote the first English-language book about Slayer, which is part of Bloomsbury Academic's prestigious 33 1/3 series. Comic strips, metal, and super heroes are the three things that have held his interest since he was old enough to crap.

At least 50% of what is wrong with him is rooted in attending 9.38 years of Catholic School, where his parents believed he would receive a better education than he would have at the California Area School District, though they were totally and tragically wrong about that shit.

Ferris has worked for the A.V. Club, Metal Sucks, Rolling Stone, Alternative Press, the Village Voice, Decibel, Cleveland Scene, and other outlets. His Heavy Metal Game of Thrones Reviews have run on several sites — look for #GameOfThronesHeavyMetalReview. (He has a theory about the books that would have blown your fucking mind before season 6.) His Pentagrammarian.com / @Pentagrammarian collects thoughts on grammar, usage, ethics, writing, and the business thereof. He's working on some other stuff. Big stuff. Good stuff. Secret, evil stuff.

He teaches.

His spec script is an episode of Maron where Marc makes friends with Danzig.

He has thunder in his head. He is metal-thrashin' mad.

Follow his bullshit online…

He's always on Twitter:
@**SlayerBook** for metal.
@**Pentagrammarian** for notes on grammar, usage, writing good, and the business thereof.
@**dxferris** for a barrage of random information about TV, movies, Batman, martial arts, comics, and gum.
Link to it all via **www.CheckOutMyButt.com**.

Photo by 'Wing or Shark Taco. The goat had it comin'.

He's not much of a Facebook person, though you can find him at **Facebook.com/SlayerBook**. But don't take it personal if he takes a month to confirm your friend request.

Visit Ferris' Slayer Book(s) Blog here: **Slayerbook.Tumblr.com**. He posts Slayer updates, news, author podcast appearances, interviews, merchandise, images, musings musical favorites, and other metal-related goodness. He's really not into music much lately, though; compression drives him nuts.

**This book was made with assistance from Marvin Gaye's Trouble Man soundtrack, John Carpenter's Escape From New York soundtrack, and Beastie Boys instrumentals.**

**Read Suburban Metal Dad every Monday and Friday at Popdose (.com & @Popdose).**

66 & 2/3: A series of creator-owned books about music that rules.

Cool paperbacks and cooler e-books.

By 6623 Press.

#1: *Slayer, The Jeff & Dave Years: A Metal Band Biography...*
    by D.X. Ferris

#2: *For Whom the Cowbell Tolls: 25 Years of* Paul's Boutique
    by Dan LeRoy and Peter Relic

More to come.

Available from Amazon and select retailers.

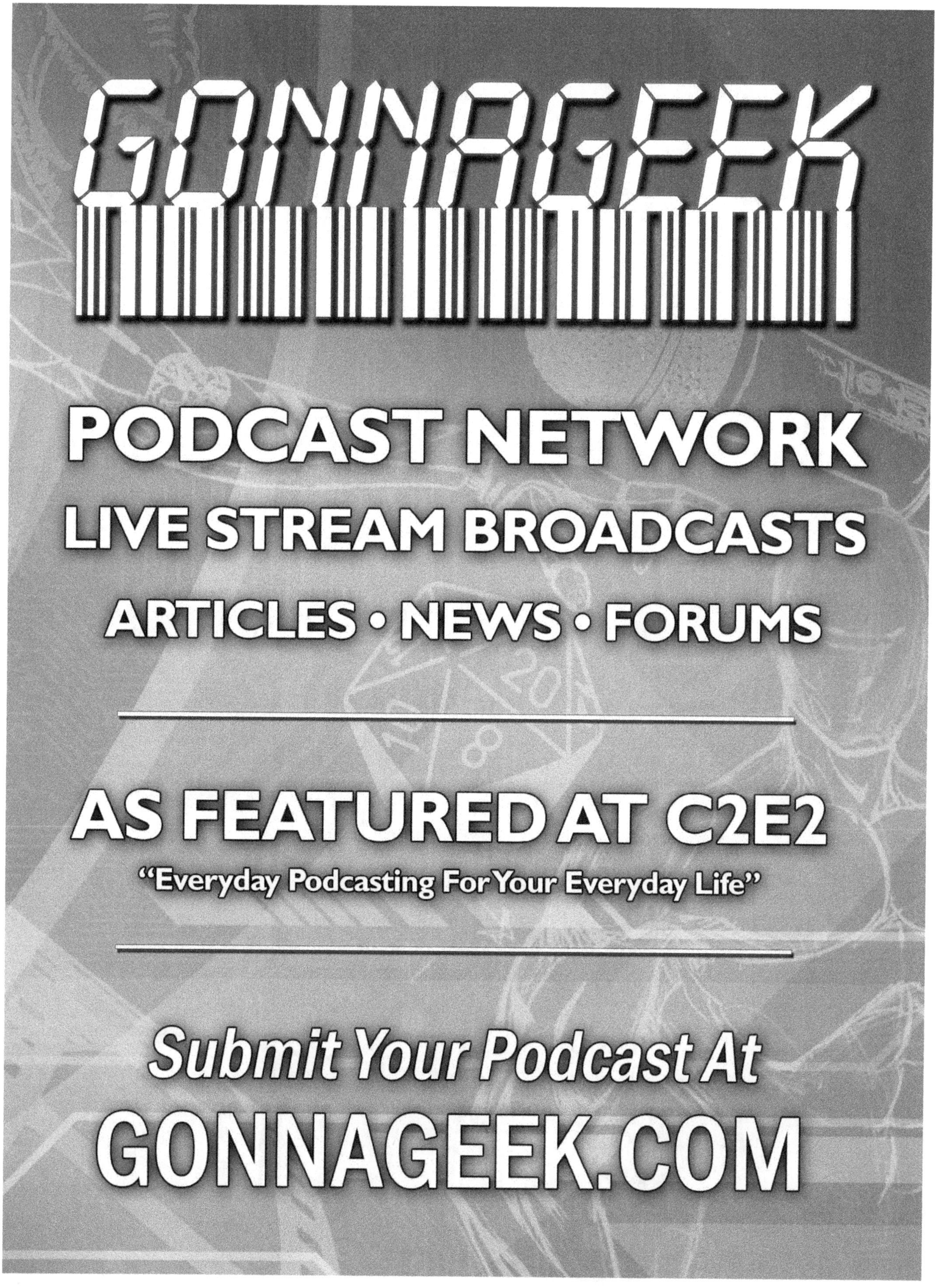
GONNAGEEK
PODCAST NETWORK
LIVE STREAM BROADCASTS
ARTICLES • NEWS • FORUMS
AS FEATURED AT C2E2
"Everyday Podcasting For Your Everyday Life"
Submit Your Podcast At
GONNAGEEK.COM

## HIDDEN TRACK:
## SMD DEMOS, CIRCA LATE 2010.

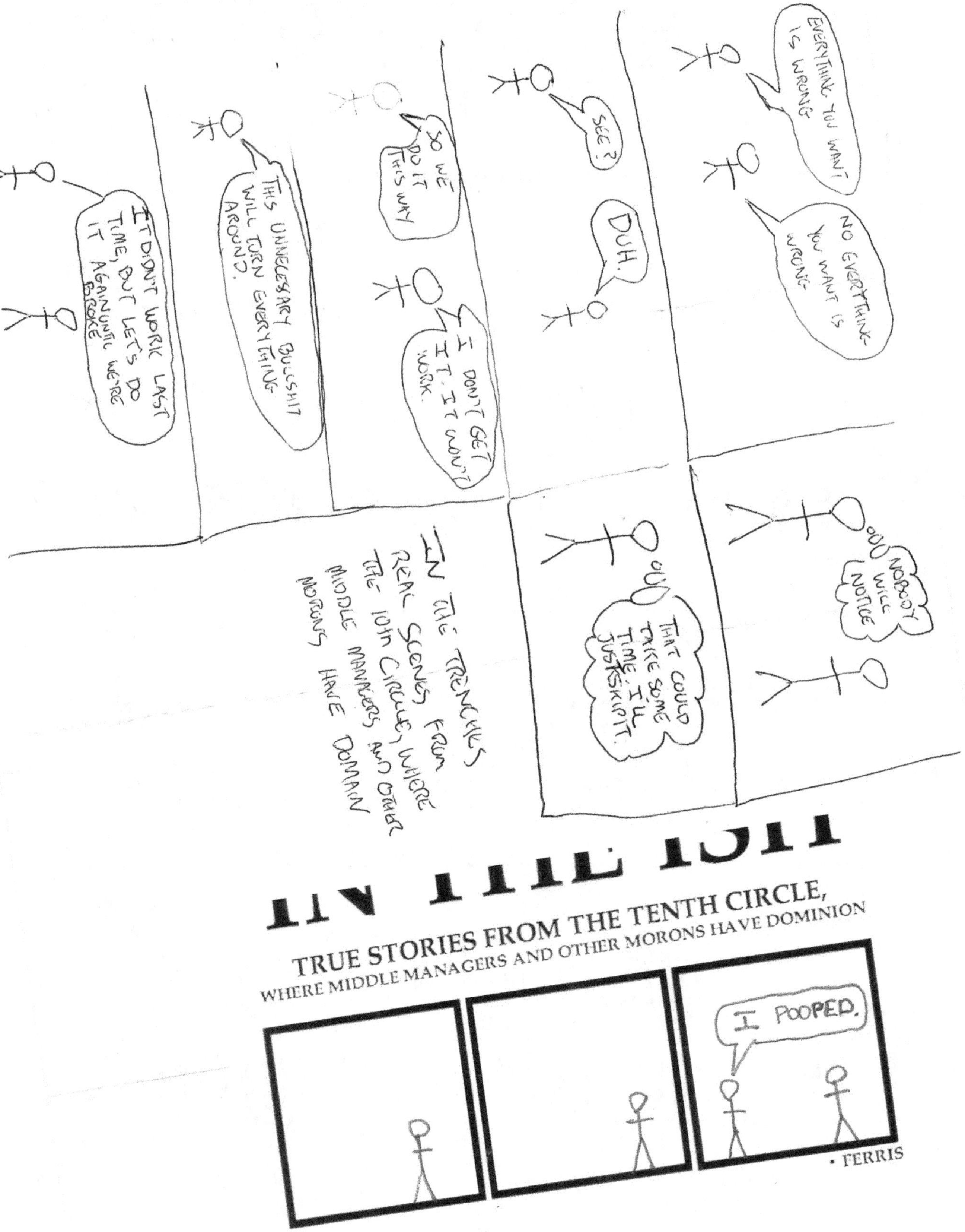
EVERYTHING YOU WANT IS WRONG
NO EVERYTHING YOU WANT IS WRONG
SEE?
DUH.
SO WE DO IT THIS WAY
I DON'T GET IT. IT WON'T WORK.
THIS UNNECESSARY BULLSHIT WILL TURN EVERYTHING AROUND?
IT DIDN'T WORK LAST TIME, BUT LET'S DO IT AGAIN UNTIL WE'RE BROKE
NOBODY WILL NOTICE
THAT COULD TAKE SOME TIME. I'LL JUST SKIP IT.
IN THE TRENCHES REAL SCENES FROM THE 10th CIRCLE, WHERE MIDDLE MANAGERS AND OTHER MORONS HAVE DOMAIN
TRUE STORIES FROM THE TENTH CIRCLE,
WHERE MIDDLE MANAGERS AND OTHER MORONS HAVE DOMINION
I POOPED.
• FERRIS

# *For Whom the Cowbell Tolls: 25 Years of* Paul's Boutique

## by Peter Relic and Dan LeRoy, author of *33 1/3: Beastie Boys'* Paul's Boutique

**Think you know everything possible about the Beastie Boys classic album Paul's Boutique? Think again. To commemorate the album's 25th birthday, author Dan LeRoy and journalist Peter Relic joined forces to "drop the new science and kick the new knowledge" about this legendary 1989 release. This all-new book is crammed with deep research and fresh information. These cats found legit diamonds that even the *Beasties* didn't know about.**

"If you are a music fan, Dan LeRoy's obsessive work covering the Beastie Boys' most fascinating and complicated album, *Paul's Boutique*, is essential reading."

**— Brian Coleman, author of *Check the Technique* and *Rakim Told Me***

NOW WITH MORE COWBELL
For Whom the Cowbell Tolls
25 Years of Paul's Boutique
By Dan LeRoy and Peter Relic
6623
Press
THE EXPANDED PAPERBACK EDITION OF FOR WHOM THE COWBELL TOLLS FEATURES EXCLUSIVE CONTENT, INCLUDING PHOTOS FROM THE PAUL'S BOUTIQUE SESSIONS BY BEASTIE BOYS PRODUCER MARIO CALDATO JR. AND A FOREWORD BY HIP-HOP ICON SAGE FRANCIS.
SFR

$14.99 paperback, available at Amazon and www.StrangeFamousRecords.com
$5.99 e-book runs on any tablet, phone or PC with free Kindle software, online exclusively at Amazon.com

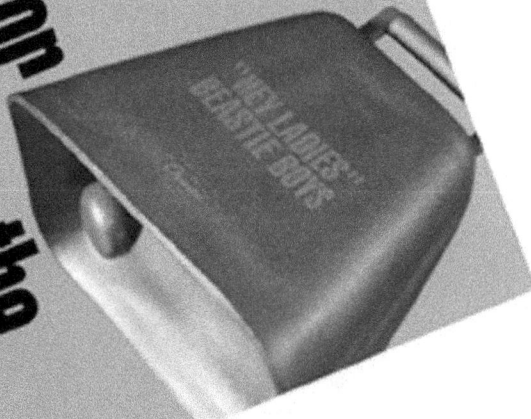

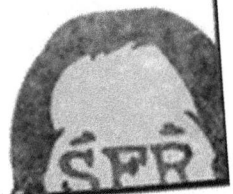

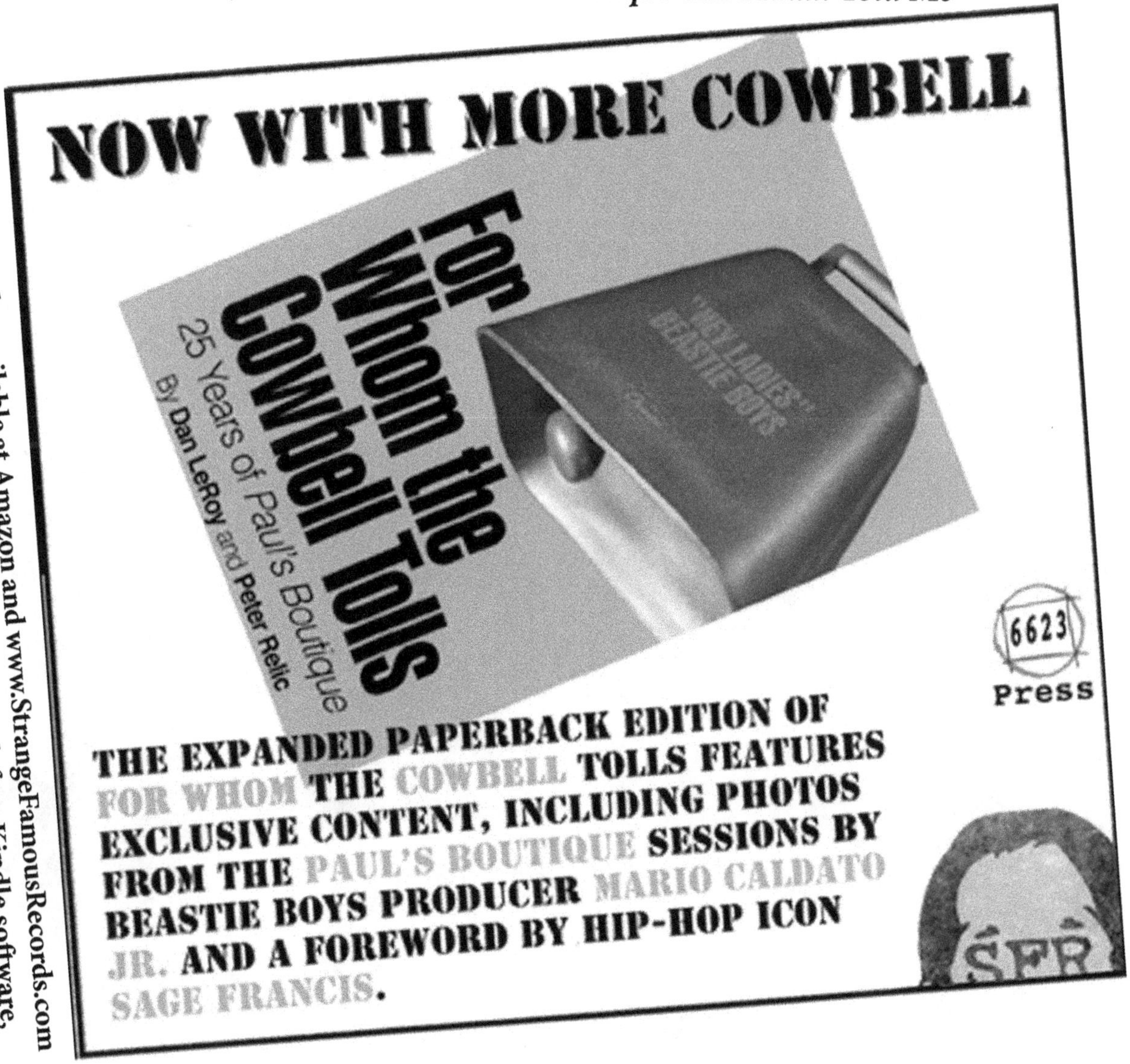

www.ingramcontent.com/pod-product-compliance
Lightning Source LLC
Chambersburg PA
CBHW081249040426
42452CB00015B/2763